Three Religious Rebels

The Forefathers of the Trappists

M. Raymond, OCSO

St. Paul Books & Media

De Licentia Superiorum Ordinis

NIHIL OBSTAT:
  M. Alberic Wulf, O.C.S.O
  M. Maurice Molloy, O.C.S.O

IMPRIMI POTEST:
  +Frederick M. Dunne, O.C.S.O

NIHIL OBSTAT:
  Arthur J. Scanlan, S.T.D.

IMPRIMATUR:
  +Francis Joseph Spellman, D.D.

Library of Congress Cataloging-in-Publication Data

M. Raymond, Father, O.C.S.C., 1903—
    Three religious rebels / by M. Raymond.
        p.   cm.
    "The saga of Citeaux. First epoch."
    ISBN 0-8198-7340-3   (pbk.)
    1. Robert, of Molesme, Saint, ca. 1027-1110. 2. Alberic, Saint, d. 1109. 3. Stephen Harding, Saint, d. 1134. 4. Christian saints—France—Biography. 5. Trappists—France—Biography. 6. Trappists.
BX4659.F8M23   1988
271'.12'022—dc19
[B]   88-6992
                                                             CIP

Previously published by P.J. Kenedy & Sons, N.Y.

Printed and published in the U.S.A. by St. Paul Books & Media, 50 St. Paul's Avenue, Boston, MA 02130

St. Paul Books & Media is the publishing house of the Daughters of St. Paul, an international congregation of women religious serving the Church with the communications media.

1 2 3 4 5 6 7 8 9   99 98 97 96 95 94 93 92 91

To the distinguished memory
of the Most Reverend Hermann-Joseph Smets
Abbot General
of the Cistercian Order
of the Strict Observance
1930–1942

Contents

Part III
St. Stephen Harding the Rationalist

Foreword
to the First Edition

Frederic M. Dunne, O.C.S.O., present Abbot of Our Lady of Gethsemani, entered this monastery fifty years ago. One of his first moves was to seek information about his Trappist forefathers. Imagine his surprise to learn that they were not Trappists at all; they were Cistercians. Imagine his chagrin to find next to nothing written in English about these strong, silent, saintly men. Whatever information he gathered he had to dig from books in French, German or Italian. He found the digging hard work, so he resolved that if he were ever in a position of authority one of his first moves would be to prevent future American aspirants to this life from going through the same agony.

An early appointment as Guest-Master

brought him into contact with many interested visitors. Their innocent questions showed him how little was known about his Order, and their naive remarks proved to him that much error was commingled with the little truth that was known. Some people asked if it were true that most Trappists became such because they were disappointed in love or with life; whether they had to dig a foot of their own grave every day that they lived; whether many lost the use of their voice because of their vow of perpetual silence. Such naivete provoked his smile but it also deepened his resolve to give America the truth about the Trappists whenever he could.

In 1935 he was elected abbot. Before 1936 was very old his forty-two-year-old resolve was being executed—the Saga of Citeaux was taking shape. That name calls for explanation. It is a saga, for it is a history of a very heroic family; but it is the Saga of Citeaux only because it is a history of Cistercians. Many a person has read a history of Ireland without learning much about the Irish people who made that history. Likewise many a person can learn much about America, but little about Americans, in books that bear the proud title of "American History." That mistake must not be repeated here. So the history of this family will be told by telling the histories of this family's members.

I frankly admit that my purpose is pragmatic. I want no modern juvenile to say: "Virtus laudatur et alget"(Virtue is praised and neglected). I want some moderns to say what Augustine said: "Si isti et istae, cur non ego?"(If these men and women could do it, why not I?) In other words, it is not admiration for Citeaux that I want to stir up; it is imitation of Cistercians. Hence, because we more quickly catch the American fever and fervor for freedom from a Patrick Henry crying, "Give me liberty or give me death!" rather than from any erudite analysis of the Constitution, the simplicity, humility, fidelity and flaming love for God that was Citeaux will be wrapped in the warm flesh and blood of a faithful St. Robert, a humble St. Alberic and an unshakably loyal St. Stephen Harding. Americans want tangibility. Before virtue will ever attract them, it must be incarnated, so these men and women will speak.

Pardon my sudden pause but allow me a sincere protest. I say these men and women will speak. I mean that literally. Dramatic dialogue will characterize this Saga from beginning to end. It is not because I am fond of dialogue, but because I have always found life dramatic and many conventional "lives of saints" unlifelike. These men and women of Citeaux *lived*. They will be presented that way.

This treatment may mislead some readers into classifying this book erroneously as a "novel" and as "fiction." Actually, when an author dramatizes fact, he does not write fiction;

nor does one who dramatizes history write a novel. The latter is a fictitious tale. History is never that. So call this, if you must label it, "novel-hagiography," or even "novel-history" but do not accuse me of writing fiction when I dramatize fact.

This is beyond question: they are facts which I dramatize. Father Amedeus, O.C.S.O., who helped me gather them, has rightly been called "the human ferret." He burrowed into more manuscripts than I care to name; read careful studies, enthusiastic briefs, full-length biographies and clever monographs. He then made available to me the results of his years of burrowing. As well as I could, I separated legend from actuality before casting the real facts into this presentation. Were I to give the complete list of our sources, I might dazzle; I would not greatly aid. Elsewhere in this edition appears a partial list. Its only practicality is that it may dissolve the doubts of a few skeptics. For myself, it permits opportunity to pay some of my debt of gratitude. I do owe these authors much. They furnished the substance; I merely supplied the form.

There are others, too, who merit my thanks. There are the two censors of the Order: Father Maurice, O.C.S.O., of Our Lady of the Valley, Lonsdale, R.I., and Father Alberic, O.C.S.O, of our own Gethsemani. But my deepest gratitude goes to one who sacrificed most for the good of this book. I speak of my ever generous and always helpful brother, Reverend John P. Flanagan, S.J., of Boston, MA.

Before closing this Foreword, I want to say that I accept full responsibility for every blemish in this book. That there are many, I know only too well. It has been many years in the making and more perfection may be rightly expected after such a lapse of time. But Trappists are adorers, not authors. Whatever time is given to composition is usually snatched from the real employment of their life—the Sacrifice of Praise, the Sacrifice of the Mass and the Sacrifice of Manual Labor.

Now let me state a fact even though it may sound facetious. I say, "Let us give the devil his due." I mean it, for if these "lives" are lively, he put life into them. He complicated the romance between these men and their Maker. It was the solution of that complication that gives interest to this Saga just as it gave sanctity to these saints. There is always the "devil to pay" before a person can get to God. Read and see.

—*Fr. M. Raymond, O.C.S.O.*
1944

Introduction

Robert the rebel, Alberic the radical, and Stephen Harding the rationalist were the precursors of the Trappists. Their biographies are interwoven like the links in a chain. With lively narration, dialogue, anecdotes and personalized reflections, the late Fr. M. Raymond has brought to life the genius of these three men, dedicated body and soul to observing the rule of St. Benedict without compromise or mitigation. The events occurred between 1033 and 1133. The reference to "33" is deliberate—recalling the traditional date when Jesus showed the height of his love for the Father and for all people by dying on the cross. The three monks responded to this love in their pledge to love God with all their hearts.

Robert was the first of the three; he was seeking the highest nobility. At age sixteen he discovered it and declared himself a "rebel." He did not want to be elevated as a knight because he had decided to become a monk. His father opposed him. His mother instead, supported Robert's choice. After a long dispute, the father too gave his consent, but he urged his son to be truly a knight of God, without second thoughts or regrets! Robert carried out his father's recommendation with incredible generosity. He dreamed of restoring the observance of the Benedictine Rule to the original fervor. But for years he struggled in vain. Failures followed him from Tonnere to Saint-Pierre, Colan, Molesme and finally, Citeaux. Yet ultimately he was a success: the Abbey of Citeaux was the first foundation of the Cistercian Order. In 1221, Robert was proclaimed a saint, a knight of the highest nobility— that of the love of God.

Alberic continued the work of Robert. He was a "radical," that is, he wanted to get to the root of things. He experienced failures and made mistakes, but he realized his ideal. Robert had the crucifix as his symbol, Stephen had the devotion to the Blessed Mother; Alberic chose the Heart of Christ and considered himself the "Lance of Christ." He was a mystic and a poet, he had intuitions, and he coined joyful slogans. Above all he became holy, heroic in love, to the point of meriting the title: "Alberic, the loving hero of Jesus Christ."

Stephen Harding, "the rationalist," completes the triad and continued the work begun by his two friends, Robert and Alberic. He walked heroically in faith, surviving almost total failure with his imperturbable smile. He was immovable in his efforts to restore observance to the original spirit: self-sufficiency, solitude, prayer in common and work in the fields. When the Order was dangerously close to extinction and it seemed that all of Stephen's efforts had failed, Bernard of Fontaines arrived with thirty-two companions. And from then on the Abbey of Citeaux was "taken by assault," so much so that branch foundations multiplied.

The lives of these three religious rebels perfectly completed one another: the rebellion of Robert against mediocrity, the radical search of Alberic, the rationality of the total love of Stephen Harding. And the efforts and holiness of each one paved the way for St. Bernard and the marvelous growth of the Cistercian Order.

—*The Editors*

Part I

St. Robert the Rebel

Chapter One

"I Know a Higher Chivalry"

"Oh, what a dolt I am!" growled young Robert to himself. "I'm forever blurting out my inmost thoughts. I do it at school, at play, and now I've done it before my father. When will I learn to keep my mouth shut!" He groaned as he laid his head against the window and gazed into a November sky.

High above him the evening star began to sparkle. In the deeper west, night stood like a black-cowled monk waiting the compline bell of what had been a beautiful day. But Robert saw no star, no cowled night, nor dying day. He saw nothing but the amazed look his father had flashed at him when he had overheard him say to his cousin, "I will never be knighted. I know a higher chivalry."

Behind him an aged serf was quietly removing the last traces of the banquet that had been spread for the newly knighted Jacques, Robert's cousin from across the Seine. The old man now lit a torch, placed it above the table, and left the hall. As he opened the heavy oaken door, the booming voice and laugh of Theodoric, lord of the castle, carried into the quiet of the room. Robert stirred uneasily. He stood in awe of this giant father of his. He knew that his remark at table had been displeasing, and that he would be called to answer for it before the night was out. For a moment longer he pressed his forehead moodily against the window pane. Suddenly he straightened. "All right," he said, "I will answer for it. The truth must come out sometime. To-night is as good a time as any." And his hands tightened into fists above his leather belt.

It was thus his mother found him when she returned to the hall after bidding her guests adieu. For a moment she stood watching him. His head was lifted to the skies. The firm, straight lines of his jaw and chin were bas-reliefed against the blue-black of the twilight. Ermengarde thrilled at the sight. Her boy was fast becoming a man, she thought. Then as a half sigh escaped she softly chided herself, "Ermengarde, babies become boys; and boys fast become young men." Then she proudly murmured, "He's becoming quite like his father. He will be a big man."

As Robert had not stirred, she quietly came up behind him, laid her hands on his shoulders and asked, "Is my boy becoming a star-gazer?" The lad started at her touch, but at the sound of her voice his hands shot up and drew her arms around his shoulders.

"Look!" he said and pointed to the white radiance of the solitary star that shone in the broad blue bosom of the twilight. "It's beautiful, but so awfully, awfully alone. It looks lost, doesn't it?"

Ermengarde laid her cheek on his shoulder. "Star-gazer! Dreamer! Poet! Just what is to become of you, my boy?"

Robert's arm stole around his mother's waist. A mischievous twinkle came into his eyes as he said, "Your words are right, Mother, but their order is wrong. You should have asked what father will ask the moment he returns. You should have said: 'Just what are you going to become, my boy?' And wait until you hear the way he says it."

The last word had hardly been spoken when Theodoric burst into the hall. "Ermengarde," he cried in his heavy, booming voice, "my brother Léon tells me his harvest was just like ours— three times normal size. Indeed, we will make up for the past three years of...." But then his gaze fell upon Robert. The lights in his large black eyes changed. A frown clouded his forehead and his chin drew in towards his chest. This was what Ermengarde always called "swallowing himself in his bushy, black beard." She smiled to herself as her husband noisily cleared his throat, strode to the fireplace, and threw on a heavy log. She recognized these as his usual prelude to broaching an important subject. What a transparent person was this giant knight!

Sure enough, as he stood dusting his hands, Theodoric said, "Son, you made a remark to your cousin tonight that I did not understand." Ermengarde felt Robert grow tense. "I want to understand it, son—fully! Just what did you mean by saying that you will never be knighted?"

Robert's hands gripped the table. His father was a giant of a man in any setting, but outlined as he was now by the leaping blaze in the fireplace, he loomed larger than ever. The room grew very still. Robert's throat felt terribly dry. He knew that his father had his heart set on the day when he would be dubbed knight of Champagne; that he had dreamed fondly of the time he would ride with him to tournament or to battle, armed as he was armed, strong as he was strong, and brave with his own undaunted bravery. Robert did not question his father's love, nor did he fear his flashes of anger; but he did dread the hurt he would give this huge kindly man when he told him the truth. As his father broke in on his thoughts with an impatient "Well?" the latest log on the fire snapped and crackled fiercely, sending fountains of sparks leaping up the chimney and arching down upon the stony apron of the floor.

The two sharp reports in the otherwise still room made young Robert start visibly; but, paradoxically, this uncontrolled action gave him the control he had longed for. His arms relaxed. Although his nails were still digging into the palms of his hands, his voice and gaze were steady as he answered, "I meant what I said, Sire, I will never be knighted for I know a higher chivalry."

"And what is that?" asked Theodoric as his black eyes bored into the brown ones before him.

"The highest chivalry this side of heaven, Sire. The chivalry of being gallant to God!" Robert's head lifted with the last word and his shoulders squared. He was staring at his father with a look that was almost defiant.

Ermengarde caught her breath as she gazed from the challenging tilt of her son's young head to the sunken chin of her lord. Theodoric heard her and deliberately turned his back on the boy. He carefully brushed a few of the cinders back into the base of the fire with his boot. Then with a forced calmness he strolled to the back of his wife's chair.

"Won't you sit down, son," he asked as he gestured toward a chair, "and explain yourself more fully? I know of only one chivalry for the knights of Champagne. What is this higher chivalry of yours?" His tone was deeper and his voice softer; but Robert, looking into those boring black eyes, found their light unchanged.

"I'll stand, Sire, if I may," answered the lad as he stepped away from the table and moved toward the fireplace. He turned and faced his parents. The dancing flames sent strange shadows flickering across his set features.

Theodoric, studying those features, suddenly realized he was talking to a man, not to a boy. His son seemed to have aged before his eyes. He looked down at Ermengarde and found her with her hands folded in her lap. Calmness marked her whole posture. He was glad he had shifted his glance, for her composure steadied him. Looking up a moment later he was not surprised to see the shadow of a smile flit across his son's face.

"Well?" said Theodoric as Robert stood there seemingly waiting for an invitation.

"Sire, I am as stout and as strong as cousin Jacques, am I not?" His father nodded. "I can ride as well as cousin Jacques, can I not?" Again his father nodded. There was vibrancy in the lad's tone. "I can tilt as well as cousin Jacques, can I not? I have unhorsed him twice while jousting in our own yard." Theodoric wondered where his son's questions were leading. He simply nodded a third time. "Cousin Jacques was knighted in Troyes last week. We banqueted him this afternoon to do him honor and to show our joy. Sire, I am not jealous of my cousin. I am not afraid of knighthood and all that it entails. But there were two reasons I was not dubbed last week. Age was one. The other lies here." One hand clenched over his heart. Then his whole countenance became alive with light as he blurted out, "Sire, I want to be gallant to God. I want to become a monk."

"A what?" barked Theodoric, and the thunder of his tone filled the hall.

Robert's color mounted, but his eyes held their unwavering gaze. He had expected this. Only last week he had begged his mother not to say anything to his father before the end of the year. Well, now he knew in early November. The boy felt relieved in spite of his anxiety. Before his father had fully recovered he pushed on, "Sire, I have been schooled by the monks. But from them I learned more than my trivium. From them I learned the higher chivalry. You gave much to the poor and the starving during the past three years of famine, Sire. Uncle Leon across the Seine gave much also. I am justly proud of the blood from which I am sprung." Again that vehemence came into his voice as he cried, "But, Sire, the monks gave more!" Theodoric waited. Never before had he heard his son speak thus. The boy was aflame. "For the past three years the gate of St. Pierre de la Celle has been thronged with the starving," said Robert.

"No single serf ever left that gate empty-handed. To do that the monks starved themselves! Do you hear, Sire? They starved *themselves!* "

After a pause Robert added, "It was then that I began to see that one did not have to wear mail, or wield a battle-axe, in order to be brave. It was then I saw that there was a higher chivalry than chivalry itself!"

Robert's tone deepened. "Since then I have prayed and consulted. The priests will receive me. Mother is willing that I go. I confess my cowardice in not telling you sooner, Sire, but now I beg your pardon, your blessing, and your permission."

The last words had tumbled out. It was the longest speech Robert had ever made to his father. He knew that he had been headlong in his confession. He now felt self-conscious and somewhat abashed. There was a strong temptation to enlist the aid of his mother, but he resolved to hold his ground and stand on his own feet. His father's boring black eyes never wavered. The boy thought he saw the lips draw in beneath the bushy beard, but he was not sure. His own fists tightened. He waited.

"Who put this idea into your head?" asked Theodoric coldly. "Your mother or the monks?"

"Neither," said Robert as he felt his anger surge.

"Then who?" questioned Theodoric, and there was a noticeable edge to his tone.

"God!" answered his son, and the word rang through the room with all the sharpness of sword clashing on shield. More. It had the effect of a thunderbolt bursting. There was no rumble or reverberation after that word, but the silence that held the hall seemed to shake it.

Theodoric shifted his position to the side of his wife's chair. He had been startled by the answer his son had given, but more so by the fires he found in the depths of those two brown eyes that gazed at him so steadily. Silence still held the hall. The only sound heard was the gentle murmur of the fire and the soft fall of the ashes as the log crumpled within the flames.

Theodoric was stunned by this announcement. Robert had been the sun of his life. He doted on him. To other nobles he had often boasted what a knight his boy would be. The ceremonies of last week and the banquet of this afternoon had filled him with one vision—that of his son at the feet of the Count of Champagne, surrounded by the knights of the realm, with the flat of the Count's sword on his back. The picture called up by the night's announcement—that of his boy with shaven head and flowing cowl—did not strike his fancy at all. He grew angry. But two things held that anger in check—the presence of his gentle wife and the ring of the last word his son had spoken.

Walking away from Ermengarde's chair, Theodoric motioned his son to the cushion at his wife's feet. He himself took his stand before the fireplace.

"Sit down by your mother, Robert," he commanded. "This calls for more explanation than you have given." The boy marveled at the quietness of his father's voice and manner. "You say God put this idea into your head. May I ask when?"

"That would be very difficult to say, Sire, I really think the tendency has always been there."

"Oh," said Theodoric. "So it is no more than a tendency. God made no direct, personal manifestation of any sort, eh? Well, that, of course, changes matters." Robert started to his feet, but his mother's hand falling on his shoulder restrained him.

"Be calm, son," she cautioned. "Your father is right. He should inquire."

"Don't you know, my boy," began Theodoric, "that practically everyone is struck by such a fancy sometime or other in his youth?" The lord lifted himself several times on his toes before adding, "Why, even I was struck by it," and Theodoric gave vent to a deep, throaty chuckle. "I don't think your mother will deny that that was pure fancy. Can you imagine me as a monk?" Again Theodoric's laugh filled the room.

Ermengarde smiled, but Robert only shifted uneasily on his cushion. Theodoric eyed him carefully. He had hoped to see a smile light the face of his son. He grew restless. Theodoric had no patience with opposition, for he had experienced very little. His serfs were always subservient, and his fellow lords respectful. The present attitude of his boy made his blood boil.

Since there had been no special manifestation from God, he felt sure that his son's attraction to the cloister was but a passing phase of youth. He would end this interview before it became painful. Robert would outgrow this fancy and one day as a staunch knight of Champagne would make him proud. Maintaining his former light tone, he said, "Your shoulders are too broad and your thighs too thick to be hidden by a cowl, my boy. God blessed you with the body of a warrior. You belong astride a swift horse with a mace or a battle-axe in your hand."

"Is the cloister only for weaklings?" challenged Robert.

"No, no," answered Theodoric quickly, "but real warriors are for the world." He tried to stir the boy's pride in arms. "And you are going to be a real warrior, my boy. Your eyes have told me so. You have more than a magnificent physique, son. You have fire!" The remoteness of Robert's expression disappointed Theodoric, but it showed him that nothing was to be gained by further argument. So, with an air of confident command, he said, "But come, it's growing late. It's time for young men to be in bed. This fancy will pass."

"Sire," blurted Robert, jumping to his feet despite his mother's restraining hand, "it is *not* fancy. It will not pass! I am no longer a baby!" The boy was trembling. His face was more flushed than ever. He stood before his father with brown eyes ablaze and fists clenched at his sides.

Theodoric had never before seen his son aroused. The sight startled him. He noted the quivering lips and the tremor in the arms and hands. He saw that he had stung the boy to near fury. At the moment he knew not what to say or do. A wrong word would unleash the pent-up anger; a false gesture, wound the strong, young heart. He simply met the burning gaze of his boy with a steady, level glance.

Ermengarde, who had risen from her chair as Robert had sprung from his cushion, now stepped to the boy's side, circled his shoulders with her arm, smiled slowly, and said, "Father may forget that time flies, son; but if you keep springing up like that he'll never forget you're no longer a baby."

But not even Ermengarde could bridge the gap between them.

"Father," said Robert in fiercely earnest tone, "I'm sorry if I have shown anything bordering on disrespect. But, Sire," and the old ring of deadly determination came back into the boy's voice, "I wish you would remember that I am three years older than Theophylactus, who Uncle Léon said is going to be elected Pope."

Robert could have said nothing worse. Had he drawn sword and openly attacked his father he would not have wounded him so deeply as by this reference to the papacy. Theodoric was a vibrantly Catholic soul. Nothing caused him so much concern as did the condition of the Church. When he had seen the house of Tusculum dominating the papal throne, he had grown uneasy. When Benedict VIII had died in 1024 and his brother, Romanus, though still a layman, had been elected to succeed him, Theodoric had become angry. But Romanus, as John XIX, while not a saintly pontiff, had been morally clean. He had died only last week. Then the report had come that Romanus was to be succeeded by Theophylactus, his twelve-year-old nephew. Theodoric was near to rage. To have his own son point to this immoral boy as an argument, made the blood in the lord's veins run deadly cold. His black eyes became two tiny pin-points of fire. He pointed to the door. One word only would he allow himself. He said, "Go!"

Robert had watched the transformation with wonder. He was keen enough to realize that this cold sternness was more dangerous than any noisy anger. The boy found his way to his room in a stupor. He did not know what had struck his father; but he never wanted to look again into those two black pin-points of fire that were his eyes.

When Robert had gone, Ermengarde crossed the room quickly, took her husband's arm and said, "Sit down, my lord, we have much to talk about." He was still in the grip of the cold fury that had seized him at the mention of Theophylactus. "Theodoric," she said softly, "that was a most unfortunate reference. Robert loves you, my lord. He all but adores you. He wouldn't hurt you for the world. That is why he has kept me from mentioning this matter to you before. He knows your hopes for him. He feared to disappoint you."

Theodoric sat with forearms on his knees and unseeing gaze bent on the gold-blue flames that leaped in the fireplace. He looked as if he had not heard his wife. Ermengarde waited for a reaction.

When she got none, she decided to use an old stratagem. She would trick him into argument. "But," she resumed, "if you ask me, I would say that the boy had much the better of the debate tonight." Theodoric sat back. "Yes," went on Ermengarde, "much the better. He had sound arguments. You made mere statements."

"What do you mean?" snapped her husband. "Do you mean to tell me that I was wrong when I said he's only a boy?"

"He didn't look much like a boy to me as he stood glaring at you a little while ago." Ermengarde smiled at the memory of that picture. "He looked more like a warrior. And he sounded like a conqueror!"

"Oh, physically he's big for his age," granted Theodoric grumblingly. "But let us not forget his age. He's fifteen years old, and that's all."

"That's only one of your mistakes my noble lord. Fifteen is not all that Robert is."

"This is 1033," said Theodoric who was now equal to attempting irony. "He was born in 1018. According to my poor scholarship that makes him just fifteen, and that's all."

Ermengarde drew her chair nearer. "Mathematically you are correct, my dear. But there are other ways of reckoning the years. What is the age of Robert's soul?"

"The same as his body—fifteen and that's all."

"Still making mistakes, Theodoric." With sudden change of tone and countenance she went on, "You're forgetting the rain, my lord. Sun matures fruit. Rain matures men. Three sunless years of almost uninterrupted rain brought famine; famine brought death; death opened the eyes of men to life. Men matured faster in the last three years, Theodoric, than they normally do in thirty. They have learned what life is for. They have become God-oriented!"

The restless flames in the fireplace threw shadows that leaped and fell with strange, weird life on the blackened rafters of the ceiling. Theodoric lifted his head, stared at them a moment, then murmured, "God-oriented—what a word! Yet, how perfectly expressive! Rain *did* turn men to God. But," he added slowly, "Robert is not a man. He is too young to have been deeply affected by the awful scourge God just lifted from our backs. Youth takes tragedy the way it takes pleasure—merely as a passing phase."

"You don't know your son, Theodoric," said Ermengarde earnestly. "Robert has nothing shallow about him. His soul is deep; his mind, mature. After that debate tonight you shouldn't doubt it. At least twice he had you speechless."

Theodoric nodded assent. "Yes," he said slowly, "he did have me speechless at least twice. He had me frightened. When he told me that God put the idea in his head I grew most uneasy. I thought he was talking about some sort of private revelation...."

"Oh, tush!" broke in Ermengarde impatiently, "What did you expect? Did you think he had been knocked from his horse like St. Paul? Now look here, Theodoric, the boy is a physical giant, isn't he?"

"Yes, he is big for his age. He promises to grow into a stalwart man."

"All right. Then he has the physical qualifications demanded by the cloister—he's healthy. As for his moral qualifications there is no question. The boy is as good as gold. Have you seen a vicious trait in him?"

"He's stubborn and he grows vehement. Why, the way he blurted out some of his statements tonight took my breath away. But it is the stubbornness that is serious."

"Stubborn!" said Ermengarde. "Would he be his father's son if he weren't stubborn? But that's a blessing, my lord. No man ever amounted to anything unless he had a stubborn streak in him. But you give it the wrong name. It's not a vice; it's a virtue. Its proper name is will-power, persistency. And let me tell you, Robert has that! Come now, admit that the lad has the moral qualifications."

Theodoric's teeth gleamed between parted lips. "For the sake of argument," he smiled, "I'll admit it."

Ermengarde was glad to see that smile. She pushed on, "As for his mental ability, you've seen a specimen of it tonight. His record at school is high. He is not a genius; but he is a bit above ordinary. So, my lord, God, by giving him the necessary mental, moral and physical qualifications plus the burning desire to dedicate himself to life in the cloister, has really manifested his divine plans as definitely, if not expressly, as if he had thrown him from his horse and spoken to him from heaven. Any priest will tell you that those are the signs of a genuine vocation."

"But he's too young!" snapped Theodoric testily. "What does he know about life? About the cloister? About himself? Fifteen is no age at which to fling away life. Why, he hasn't even tasted it!"

"Shame!" cried Ermengarde. "Shame on Theodoric. Shame on the giant noble of Champagne. First, Robert is more than fifteen mentally. Secondly, one who goes to the cloister does not 'fling away' life. Finally, what most of you men mean by 'tasting' life is drinking it to its dregs. Oh, you make me tired. A boy is never too young to learn the ways of a warrior. No lad is ever too young to be taught how to ride, to tilt, to kill. No. But there is one profession for which he may be too young. Yes, just one. Never too young to enter the service of his temporal sovereign, but to enter the service of his eternal King...."

"To enter the service of his eternal King he must be a man!" broke in Theodoric.

"St. Benedict took babies," countered his wife.

"Oh, St. Benedict is dead a long, long time," growled the lord of the land, who was now thoroughly aroused. "And the world has changed much since he died. Why, when Benedict was a boy the world was in barbarism. The Roman Empire had collapsed. Honeycombed by rottenness within, overrun by savage tribes from without, ruin was inevitable. And the Church was in as good a condition as the Empire. Rent by schism, beset by heresy, she too seemed on the brink of ruin. No wonder Benedict fled to Subiaco! No wonder he allowed nobles to offer their newborn babes to the Lord! Why, the cloister seemed the only place a man could save his soul. But that was five long centuries ago." Theodoric shifted in his chair before adding, "Today is different. Look at our 'Truce of God.' Look at our chivalry. Look at what you yourself called our 'God-orientedness!' "

Ermengarde sat back, put her head a little on one side, and with the tiniest trace of a frown on her forehead said, "You puzzle me, Theodoric. I don't believe there is another noble in the realm so devoted to the Church as you, and yet you object to your son becoming a churchman."

Theodoric went to the fire and placed another log across the burning embers. He watched the gluttonous tongues of yellow and gold lick at its sides for a moment, then turned full on his wife. "Ermengarde, my dear, it is just because I am so devoted to my Church and so devoted to my son that I object. I don't want our boy to make a mistake."

"Humph! If he doesn't make mistakes, he'll never make anything! He's human. It's no crime to make a mistake. Tragedy lies in failing to unmake them."

"And that's my point precisely," interjected Theodoric sharply. "I'm not afraid of Robert's making a mistake. I'm mortally afraid of his *being* a mistake. You know something of our world, my dear. You know there are those in the ranks of the clergy who should never have seen the inside of a cloister. Now, now," he went on quickly as his wife started to protest, "I know what you're going to say. It is utterly and shamefully true that many have been made bishops and pastors by the will of greedy nobles rather than by the will of God. Lay investiture is a curse. Many, if not most, of the scandals of the Church are traceable to the kings, counts, emperors and dukes who look upon croziers and rings as means to power rather than as emblems of ecclesiastical authority. They don't want pastors of the people in those offices—they want robbers who will fill their greedy purses. I grant all that. In spite of what I said about improvement, the Church is not lily-white. But the point I make is that there is no more sorry sight in all our land than that of a mistake in clerical garb."

"But Robert would not..."

"Oh, I know Robert would not be such a mistake. But frankly I do fear his age. I don't want him to go through life with the scar of a tremendous failure on his soul to remind him always of the folly of his youth."

"He won't fail."

"What makes you positive, my dear?" asked Theodoric with a very noticeable touch of incredulity in his tone. "Do you realize all that the cloister demands?" He paused before saying, "It calls for the noblest of men and the noblest in man. It demands great physical endurance and a startling single-mindedness of purpose. Success can be achieved there only by those who have the inflexible vision of invincible faith. One must stare fixedly and uninterruptedly at God, my dear. Yes, uninterruptedly at God. And I'm afraid that most men have only the eyes of the bat for that strong sun. The eyes of the eagle are required by those who would go to the cloister."

"And do you think our son is blind?"

"Not at all. I only question whether his eyes are fully open at fifteen."

"That is about the fifth time that you have referred to Robert as fifteen. For the last time I tell you that he is more than fifteen! It's not age that you want in the cloister; it is maturity. And Robert is mature. A person is really mature," said Ermengarde, "when he realizes that he belongs to God. And that lesson was forcibly taught by rain. France *has* become God-oriented, Theodoric, for the lack of sun opened our eyes to the Light of the World. Come, face the facts."

With that Ermengarde rose out of her chair, approached her husband, reached up, and with pleading eyes said, "My lord, take my word for it, our boy was *born* for the cloister. He will make no mistake. He will be no mistake. God gave him to us. Let us give him back to God." When Theodoric made no reply she added, "Chivalry is growing in the world. Let our boy bring it to the cloister. Let him go and be gallant to God."

Theodoric was startled by her earnestness. Slowly he clasped her to his breast. He bent his head to her ear and said, "My dear, you have never told me whether there is any truth or not in the tale that has oft been spoken in hushed tones by our serfs. They say that some months before our boy was born, the Blessed Virgin came to you and spoke of espousing the child of your womb." Ermengarde held him closer. "The bent wife of Ulric, the oldest of our vassals, says the Virgin placed a ring on your finger as a sign of the sacred espousal. Is that why you say Robert was born for the cloister?... Is it?... Or is this pious legend only serfs' simplicity?"

The fire had died to glowing coals. No single flame flickered on the hearth. No shadow waved upon the wall. It seemed a long time before Ermengarde answered, "When is a dream not a dream, my love?"

Theodoric drew back to look at her. "Tell me," he pleaded.

"When it's a vision," said Ermengarde. Theodoric's eyes were of a softness that his son had never seen. He could not speak—but kneeling he kissed his wife's hands. Ermengarde bent down to him with a smile, "But I haven't really answered your question. Perhaps it *was* only a dream, but if so wasn't it a beautiful one? Could you fancy anything more heavenly for an expectant mother? If it was more than a dream," she added, "wouldn't one be obliged to keep the se-

cret of the Queen? Come, my lord, let us retire.
Our boy will go to St. Pierre's. He will be gallant
to God."

And she led her husband from the room
where the red glow soon died and the November
moon threw pale shadows across the floor.

As they passed Robert's room, they never
guessed that he was still awake and at the window. At first he only wanted to feel the cool night
air; but soon the jingle of a bridle and the clop-
clop of horses' hooves had him thinking of his
cousin Jacques with his knighthood so newly
upon him. Then he strained his eyes to the north
as if he would see the spires of St. Pierre. Knighthood of a higher kind awaited him there, he
thought. He must convince his father that this
was the year for him to enter. He *must!* Gradually, under the spell of the night, calmness came.
As his parents passed his door, he was marveling
at the multitude of stars that followed in the wake
of vesper's shining. Their footsteps turned him
from the splendor of the skies. He pulled his
robe over his head and wondered what his
mother might have told his father. As he threw
it across the chair he muttered determinedly,
"Well, I *won't* be knighted and, whether he ad-
mits it or not, there *is* a higher chivalry!" Then
kicking off his boots, he turned his back to the
stars and knelt by the side of his bed.

Chapter Two
"Never Sheathe This Sword!"

Ermengarde usually got her way in the castle at Troyes. That is why just three weeks later, as the first snow of 1033 was falling, Theodoric summoned Robert to his study. For a few minutes the two men stood silently together by the window to watch the hushed fall of the flakes.

Finally Theodoric turned and put his hand on his son's shoulder. "My boy," he said gently, "your mother has convinced me. So have you. At last I yield. You may go to St. Pierre's. You may go this year." Robert started to interrupt. "But, son," went on the father, and there was a new ring to his tone, "if you do go—stay! If you become a monk—be a real one! Be steady. Be true. Be ever reliable. You say that you want to be gallant to God—then be so!"

His other hand went to Robert's opposite shoulder. He turned the boy fully toward him. "My son, look upon your entrance into the religious life as the drawing of your sword in the cause of God." There came a pause. Then more solemnly and more fiercely: "Robert of Troyes, son of my heart, I command you: Never sheathe that sword! Do you hear? *Never sheathe that sword.*" And Theodoric emphasized each word with a vigorous shake of his son's shoulders. After a moment of burning and intent gaze he asked more quietly, "Do you understand, my boy?"

"I do, Sire!" answered Robert, and wondered why he found speech so difficult.

Theodoric then took his hands from the boy's shoulders and stepped to the window. With face turned away and eyes on the falling flakes he said, "The Church needs fighters nowadays, son. Needs them badly. As you reminded me the other night, there was an election in Rome not so long ago.... We now have a new Pope.... His name is Benedict IX.... It used to be *Theophylactus!*" The giant lord turned. "Think of it!" he exclaimed. "A twelve-year-old boy in the Chair of St. Peter! The Church of God needs saints to balance that monstrosity. Do you hear, son? *Saints!* You have been burning to enlist in what you call 'the higher chivalry.' Well, burn!

But don't be a fire of straw. Burn steadily—as steadily as the stars and the sun. Burn on until you burn out! If you are going to give yourself to God, give all of yourself, or give nothing. Be a saint!"

Then taking the boy by the arm he led him around to the fireplace. "Watch!" he said, and removed the choke from the flue. The full sweep of the draft sent flames leaping up the chimney's jaws. "Do you see that, son? See the wild fury and flight of those flames!" Robert nodded. "Now watch!" Theodoric closed the choke over half way. Very shortly the flames dropped and the logs burned on with a steady quiet intensity. "See what control does, son? Some call that 'banking the fire.' What I want you to remember is that banked fires burn longer and give more heat. You have tremendous fires in your make-up, son. You grow violent at times, just as that fire did when the choke was out. That means lack of control. That means your flames are leap-ing up the flue, doing good to no one. That also means that your fire will soon burn out! Learn to bank your fires, son, and you will burn on." Then very tenderly he laid his hands on Robert's shoulders, and said, "Son, do burn on for God. He needs some warmth to dispel the chill that must settle round his heart as he sees what men are doing to his Church."

That was the martial music and earnest plea to which Robert set off for his novitiate. Nor did that martial air cease to surround him after he had arrived at St. Pierre de la Celle. For Abbot Bernard saw more than eager youth in the eyes of the fifteen-year-old boy who asked admittance; he saw soul fires of chivalry, and secretly resolved, with the help of God, to blow them to brighter flame.

He led him to the novitiate with a smile and said, "Here is your tilting ground. Don't be unhorsed." The lad smiled back self-consciously and even blushed, but inwardly he was saying, "I won't be unhorsed without a struggle." When he turned from the abbot he found twelve pairs of eyes fixed upon him. Instinctively he knew these were his fellow novices. He felt awkward and most uneasy until one of the oldest in the group stepped forward and said, "My name is Maurus." Robert looked into his laughing eyes and knew that he had found a friend. The abbot left then and Robert got his first taste of religious life. It was a taste of loneliness.

Sleep did not come quickly to the lad that night despite the excitement of the day. As he lay on his couch watching the shadows that moved on the rafters, thrown there by the rise and fall of the fitful light that burned in the dormitory, Robert wondered if everyone, on entering the novitiate, felt the fright he had known that day. He was not afraid, he told himself, but he had been, and still was, timid. As he turned on his side he suddenly remembered having heard his father say that every warrior knows a moment of tenseness just before plunging into battle. The memory cheered him. It made him feel bigger and helped him grow more calm. He looked across the room to where Maurus was sleeping and recalled the smile with which the elder novice had greeted him. Maybe it won't be so lonely, he thought, as he settled down in his pillow and finally closed his eyes.

For the next few weeks Robert did not have time to feel lonely. He was up long before the stars had gone to rest, and was kept busy until long after they had come out again to lend their silver to the sapphire of the night. From church to scriptorium to chapter room, to church again the lad was hurried in a series of duties that had him wondering how he had ever managed to while away a whole day when he was at home.

Had there been no Maurus, Robert would have felt lost. The older novice came up behind him one morning and whispered, "Sit your saddle more loosely and you'll ride better." When Robert's face lit up with a grateful smile, Maurus said, "This is not a balky horse nor a battle horse that we're astride, Brother. He's just a good old plodder. Sway with him and you'll enjoy the ride."

Robert laughed then. How well he knew what his companion meant. His father had used identical language when teaching him how to sit his mount long years ago. As the days went by,

Robert found himself growing fonder and fonder of this older novice with his keen, clever, cheerful ways. It was not long before a friendship was formed that admitted of debate as well as of banter. And the recurrence of these friendly arguments kept both novices serious while preventing them from becoming over-serious.

Robert had just rid himself of all feeling of strangeness and had begun to study his surroundings more carefully when he was summoned by the abbot. The novice felt his pulse quicken, but he had not been with the kindly Bernard two minutes before he was placed at ease. He leaned forward eagerly to listen to his abbot talk about the proper way to seek God. Of course, the lad was being introduced into an entirely new world and was straining to understand all the abbot had to say. Bernard noted it and smiled. He had always found novices eager, but he thought he discerned something deeper in this boy. To give the youngster something tangible and something familiar he finally said, "Son, take the Rule as your sword, your shield, your suit of mail." Robert brightened. He understood such terms. "It will be all that to you, my boy, if you will only live it. Believe me when I say it is not only a buckler for defense, but a broadsword for attack. Live your Rule, son, and you will not only be safe, you'll be saintly. You will be a knight of God."

Such concepts set Robert's soul singing and

had him marching around the monastery with his head held high. Maurus noted the change and allowed it to pass for a few days. Then when they were out in the courtyard one afternoon he said, "Did you ever hear about the twelfth degree of humility?"

"Twelfth?" laughed Robert. "I didn't know there were ten."

"I thought so," said Maurus with a knowing nod. "How far have you read in the Rule?"

"Far enough," answered Robert. "I've found the one word I want. It's in the prologue. St. Benedict says we are to be soldiers of Christ. That's all I want to know. '*Militaturus*' is my rule."

"Hmmm," said Maurus with a twinkle. "That explains much. You've been going around here with your head held as high as a war horse sniffing battle. St. Benedict wrote seventy-two chapters after that prologue; and his twelfth degree of humility says that we are to have our heads inclined and our eyes on the ground...."

"What?... Always?" There was incredulity in Robert's high tones.

"Always," said Maurus with a smile.

"Ugh!" grunted Robert. The concept did not appeal to him. "I'm beginning to think I prefer St. Paul to St. Benedict," he said slowly. "He was a fighter. Only this morning I had to transcribe a passage in which he talked about the helmet, the breast-plate, the shield, and the sword. I like that language. He was a warrior for God. I want to be the same. My father...."

"Your father is not your abbot," interrupted Maurus with a laugh.

"I know it; but the abbot told me the same as my father. He said, 'Be a knight.'"

"All right. All right. Be a knight if you want; but remember that St. Benedict wants humble knights. If you don't believe me, ask Father Master."

Robert took that advice seriously. He went to the master of novices. Father William liked the youngster but thought he had too much confidence for his tender years. He could not reconcile the mature mind and the stately manners of the boy with his age. He thought Robert was posing, and had determined to rid him of his conceit before the year was out. Of course, he did not know all the lad had seen during those years of famine, nor had he as yet come to appreciate the expert touch that was Ermengarde's in the molding of a character. So Robert received a very clear but a very curt answer to his question. He was told that Jesus Christ had been a knight—the most chivalrous of all knights—but that he had been meek and humble. The master's closing words were, "Monks must model on him."

Robert took that answer with him to church, to work, to chapter, and even to bed. He understood the words clearly enough, but he did not understand the sting those words had left in his heart. It was not what Father William had said that hurt; it was the way he had said it. Robert felt as if he had been accused of some shameful crime. And while he felt guiltless, he also felt disgraced. It was the youth's first encounter with a subtle humiliation. He smarted under it.

Two days later he was still pondering over his puzzle when Maurus approached, smiling as usual. Robert stopped the pleasant remark that was on his friend's lips with the question, "Maurus, can a man mean more than he says or say less than he means, and yet want you to grasp his full message?"

"You've been talking with Father Master," said Maurus with a broad smile. "And you're talking about Father Master. He always means more than he says, and he wants you to understand not only what he says but also what he means. What's the trouble?"

"Just that," answered Robert seriously. "I know what he said, but I don't know what he meant."

"Well, there's one way of finding out," said Maurus pointedly and gave his young friend a very knowing look.

Robert understood that look, so before the afternoon was old, Father William was faced by a nervous but very serious young novice. Robert spoke most directly that day and was answered the same way; for Father William had to admire the manliness that had prompted such brave action. The result was that Robert heard much about pride and humility. In truth, he heard much more than he could grasp; but one point he could not fail to hold was that he was proud and had to learn humility. The lad was stunned by the charge; but he accepted it with a humility that left Father William wondering if he had made a mistake.

He had, but it would be months before he would be convinced of it. And during those months the young heart of the novice would be pierced often. Fifteen, even an exceptionally mature fifteen, is deeply wounded when charged by one he regards as practically infallible with things of which his conscience does not reprove him. Robert was called haughty, independent, assertive and proud when actually he was only noble in bearing and honest in speech. But this misconception on the master's part brought forth the choicest fruit possible when the lad made a fierce determination to follow every injunction blindly. Six months had not passed before Robert was summing up the religious life in a word; but it was not his favorite *"militaturus,"* it was the shorter, sharper, more incisive word: *"Obey."*

Of course, the lad was too young to realize what was happening to his soul, but the truth was that the Divine Armorer gripped it between the strong tongs of his all-wise providence. He placed it in the fires of adversity to temper it, on the anvil of misunderstanding to mold it, and was now beating it with the heavy hammer of ungrounded accusations to fashion it so that it would never bend or break.

But there was a cooling process, too! God not only plunged this soul into the fires of his forge, he also cooled it in the welcome air of kindness, beneath the refreshing breeze of friendship; for the abbot had seen deeper than the master, and Maurus had been attracted from the start. God tries souls with fire but he never destroys them in the flames.

Thus it was that Robert learned many things as the months of the novitiate mounted; and suffering was not his only nor his best teacher. Maurus with his irrepressible mirth and the abbot with his fatherly encouragement and advice did more for the lad than did the master with his earnest reproofs and some of the novices with their critical looks.

Robert made all the mistakes commonly made by sincere and energetic novices. He was extreme in many things. But the abbot with his kindly advice did much more to curb the youth's impetuosity than did the curt commands of the master. "It took you almost sixteen years to attain your present height and weight, my boy. Why not give supernature a chance? She is founded on nature you know and follows many of her laws. Don't be impatient about your seeming lack of growth," said the abbot one day. "That's nature's way."

When Maurus said with a laugh, "Some

people think they are humble because they think only in diminutives," he greatly cheered a lad who had nothing but big thoughts, big desires and big dreams. More, it helped him to true humility much faster than did the caustic: "You're too ambitious." And when Maurus said, "You know, Robert, great talents stir large souls to emulation, but small souls to envy," the youngster understood better some glances a few of his fellow novices had cast at him.

And so the days of his noviceship went by, some gray, some blue, some black, but the vast majority gold with glad sunshine. All contributed to the boy's growth.

But since the growing Robert was still Theodoric's son, Maurus was not wrong when he called him "exasperatingly stubborn." The two novices argued often, and not infrequently more heat was generated than light. There was nothing they debated more fiercely than their respective concepts of the Rule. Under the abbot's careful counsel Robert had developed a regard for the Rule that caused Maurus to call him a fanatic.

The development was natural enough, for the abbot explained some portion of the text every morning in the chapter room. This daily insistence only sharpened the original concept he had given the lad on the occasion of their early meeting. The Rule became everything to Robert. But this absorption developed a difficulty the abbot never suspected and one that upset the boy. Between the letter of the Rule and its daily observances he found discrepancies! He grew disturbed. With the weeks his disturbance mounted.

The first snowfall of 1034 came in late November and found Robert looking out through the soft downpour of flakes to the gray tower of the new church that was being erected at St. Pierre. The snow and the tower soon started two different sets of memories ringing in his soul. One was of the words Theodoric had spoken just a year before, as the first snow was falling; the other was of the words Abbot Bernard had spoken just the week previous. But the words from his natural father and those from his spiritual father did not harmonize. This discord was something new. Under it Robert grew restless. And though he told himself that his abbot, not his father, was his spiritual guide, nevertheless, the advice his father had given appealed as the deeper, truer, better.

Suddenly Robert realized that this struggle stirred up by the snow and the tower was not exactly new! No. It was the very thing he had faced and fought several times in the past three months under various guises. Each time he thought he had finally settled it; but it always came back with greater fierceness. The falling snow seemed to bring his father nearer, while the thrust of the gray tower stood to him as a symbol for his strong abbot. For once the youngster, who had come to be regarded as the incarnation of energy, stood dejected and idle. Suddenly he heard his name called. He wheeled to find the master beckoning to him.

"Come," said Father William, and Robert obeyed. As he walked behind the master the young novice began to wonder what this summons could mean. Could it be that his latest argument with Brother Maurus had not ended with themselves? Well, if so, Robert would speak out! Father William had changed toward him lately. He seemed much more kind and was noticeably more gentle. Robert determined to be most open. The master was looked upon as learned. Robert knew he was saintly. He should be able to solve this tantalizing difficulty for him.

When the two were seated in the small, bare room, the novice master said, "Well, my boy, it won't be long now until you take your vows. Do you think you are ready?"

"Most unready," came the quick and uncompromising reply.

The master's habitual calm was the only thing that checked his start of surprise. He had intended his question as a mere formality—something to start the conversation. For Robert was being called "the model novice"—and with reason! Many of the older monks had told the abbot that it did them good just to see the youngster around, and Father William now admitted that this was acknowledgement of worth and not paternalism. Robert's energy in everything from singing a psalm to sweeping a floor *did* lift one's heart. The boy was impressive. His physique and bearing made him stand out; but what inspired all—even the master himself—was the manner in which the lad had literally plunged into the life. No hesitancy or half-measures for this boy. He gave his all. And now he was saying he was unprepared to take his vows! Gravely the master of novices asked, "What's the trouble, child?"

"Conflict of ideals, I think you'd call it," answered Robert hastily and his cheeks began to glow. "Look, Father Master, the first week I was here the abbot gave a talk that burned its way right into my bones. Perhaps you remember it. It was the one in which, after almost every sentence, he would ask: 'What would Benedict say?'" The Master nodded. "Well, that has served me as guide most of my days here. At work, in choir, during Mass, in the dormitory, everywhere I would ask myself: 'What would Benedict say?' It helped me very much." The master was watching the novice closely. "It made me study the Rule harder than I would have ordinarily."

Robert stopped. His eyes had been on the master's during this recital. They now fell to his own hands in his lap. He swallowed audibly and shifted in his chair very nervously.

The master waited another moment, then said, "So far, so good, Robert. In fact, I should say, 'So far, excellent.' What comes next?" and he smiled kindly.

Robert saw that smile. It was just what he needed. He answered it with a grin that was noticeably tinged with sheepishness. "Father," he blurted, "I'm not seventeen yet. I haven't finished my novitiate. So I know it's absurd for me to say it, but I must tell you that often to my question, 'What would Benedict say?' I got the answer: 'This is not right!'"

The master's smile remained as kind as before, but a more serious light stole into his eyes. Robert might say that he was only sixteen, but Father William knew him to be keener than some men who were sixty. Further, the master had devoted years to the study of Benedictinism. He knew that there were good grounds for argument. He wondered how far young Robert had seen. He leaned back in his chair as he said, "I'm glad you've spoken, my son. It is not absurd at all. That you haven't finished your novitiate is the very reason you should speak out. Where is the conflict you mentioned?"

"My father told me to give all or nothing." Robert's face was flushed, his eyes flashing. "He said, 'Draw your sword for God and keep that sword unsheathed!' He said, 'Be a real monk—a saint!' To me that means, be like Benedict! At least, that is what I thought it meant after the abbot's talk that day. But, Father Master," and here he shifted to the outer edge of his chair, "we're not like St. Benedict! Only last week I was working around the new church. Father Abbot was telling me about the changes in architecture. He said that the new style, the Romanesque, showed more vertical lines than horizontal, directing us to the heights rather than keeping us on the level. He pointed out the differences from the old style and showed their advantages. It was most interesting. But when he had finished I looked at him and asked, 'What would Benedict say?' I meant it as a joke. He didn't take it that way. He looked at me and asked, 'Do you think we should remain forever in the cave at Subiaco? Nothing is too good for God.' He sounded most serious; even a little perturbed. But, Father Master, just what *would* Benedict say?"

"Do you think he would find it too magnificent?"

Robert squeezed his folded hands, drew a deep breath, and answered, "Maybe not the church itself, but certainly our monastery and our manner of life would strike him as strange. Father, do you really think St. Benedict would feel at home here at St. Pierre de la Celle?"

"Why not, son?" Father William was being wary. He thought of a dozen things that might make St. Benedict very uneasy; but he wasn't going to tell a novice about them.

"We don't do much work in the fields, Father. Our serfs till our land. St. Benedict wouldn't like that, would he?"

"We've got to be free for choir, son. We can't be in two places at once, you know. God hasn't given us the gift of bilocation as yet. He has done that to some of his saints, it is true; but I don't think all of us are saints yet, do you?" and Father William smiled broadly.

"But manual labor seems so important a part of Benedictine life," urged Robert most earnestly.

"Haven't you had enough manual labor? I've seen much of your copying. Some of it good, some of it not so good."

"Oh, Father, do you call copying manuscripts manual labor?" There was indignation on young Robert's face. "St. Benedict didn't mean that, did he? I thought he meant real hard work in the fields; toil such as the serfs perform."

"I think he did, too, my son; for that was about all the work St. Benedict had to do. You must remember that the saint led an extremely simple life. The monks under him were simple men. They were not priests; not even clerics. They weren't destined for the priesthood, you know. St. Benedict himself never became a priest. They had Mass on Sunday and on some of the bigger feasts. That was all. Their life, for the most part, was spent between the oratory and the fields. It was a very simple life for very simple men. But, you see, our community is not of the same simplicity. You are from the nobility.

So are most of the others. You are destined for the priesthood. So are most of the others. It is fast becoming the custom all over the continent. That makes a difference, son. Anointed hands are anointed hands."

Robert blinked rapidly and nodded his head. He was thinking hard. The priesthood did make a big difference, he saw.

"You have the privilege of serving a private Mass every day and of taking part in the community Mass. On Sundays you are blessed with three Masses. That's not like St. Benedict's day. But you wouldn't say it was wrong, would you?"

"Oh, no," answered Robert quickly, "I love the Mass. But how about manual labor, Father? St. Benedict writes about priests in his Rule. He says they can be received into the community. But the only distinction he grants them is that of a higher place in choir than would naturally be theirs. He doesn't free them from manual labor." The boy paused. He was embarrassed by his own intensity. He remembered what his father had said about "banked fires." Yet he could not refrain from blurting, "I'm troubled, Father Master. I want to be the best monk possible. Now, to me that means St. Benedict. But I see so many departures from his Rule that I don't see how I can be like him and like the rest of the community. Do you see my difficulty?"

Father William placed his forearms on his desk, leaned forward and said, "Indeed, I see your difficulty, my boy. But now let me ask you one question. I think it will solve your difficulty. If St. Peter came back to Rome today, this twentieth of November, ten hundred and thirty-four, do you think he would be at home in the Eternal City?" Robert frowned. "Do you think," resumed the master, "that he would recognize the Catholic Church as the same Church he had governed back in thirty-four?"

"I...don't...know," answered Robert slowly.

The master chuckled. "I think the good St. Peter would feel quite lost amidst the pageantry and pomp, say, of the coronation ceremony of an emperor, or even at a solemn pontifical Mass in his own church. I think he would feel most uneasy surrounded by cardinals, archbishops and bishops; by dukes, counts, emperors and kings. I think he would be glad to go back to heaven. But the point is, Robert, that it is the same Catholic Church! The externals have changed tremendously, but it is the same Lord, the same faith, the same baptism. Do you grasp my point?"

"Yes," said the novice eagerly. "You mean that we are essentially the same as the monks of St. Benedict's day."

"Exactly! We are cenobites. We live in community, under an abbot, and according to Rule. The external differences you note do not touch the heart. Benedict would find his spirit here just as it was at Monte Cassino. I think you can keep your sword unsheathed, son, and stop worrying about manual labor. What do you think?"

The look of relief on Robert's face was answer enough for anyone. "What do I think?" he said. "I think I owe you a gigantic 'thank you.' I also think I had better learn how to think." Then after a light laugh he went on, "St. Peter would be very angry to find a thirteen-year old boy on his throne, I'm sure. He would also be angry with many of the bishops and archbishops of the day, I'm equally sure. But he would find the same Catholic Church, as you say. These things do not touch the heart. I see my error."

"I think if you remember that a development is not a departure you will find peace. Look, son. Do you see that tree out there?" Robert glanced through the large window and saw the specter-like arms of the giant oak. "That has changed even since you came here," went on the master. "It is bigger this year than it was last. It is much different from what it was when I first came here some thirty years ago. But it is still the same oak that came from the same acorn. Development is not departure. We have developed since Benedict was at Subiaco."

He stood up now and looked out at the storm. "Growth," he said with his face turned to the falling flakes, "is a sign of life, Brother Robert. But growth means change. So if you want St. Benedict's Rule to live, you've got to expect change."

Robert was silent. At last he said, "Brother Maurus said much the same thing the other day. He asked me if my mother would recognize me with my big head, my big mouth, my big hands and my big feet, as the same baby she had nursed at her breast. We were arguing on this very point."

"So I heard," said the master with a smile. "In fact, it was about that that I wanted to question you. How do you feel about the matter now?"

"Oh, Brother Maurus is older than I and has more intelligence. He was right. No hard feelings. We had a fine debate. But he certainly has a sharp tongue."

"I know it," said Father William. "He doesn't realize just how sharp. He has a very keen mind which seems to give edge to his words. You don't feel antagonistic?"

"Not at all," laughed Robert. "We can have discussion without discord, Father. I like to argue. So does Brother Maurus. Who spoke of hard feelings?"

"I wonder who?" said Father William with a chuckle, and then went on, "You are right, my son, discussion is the mother of discovery. But sharp tongues often wound warm hearts. And now let me caution you. Son, you are full of fire. You blazed away at Brother Maurus the other day, they tell me. And listening to you today I can see that 'blazed away' is an apt term." The master smiled. Robert blushed. "Try the Christ-way, son. Be mild. Hereafter whenever I give you and Brother Maurus permission to speak with each other, remember it is to speak, not to fight. You may go to vespers now. Pray that we may always keep the spirit of St. Benedict."

Robert took himself off, his doubts for the moment dissolved; but the master remained behind staring at the snow which still fell. Finally he muttered aloud, "Was that parallel of mine specious? Has the boy struck the real heart of the difficulty? Are we monks of St. Pierre Benedictines after the mind of St. Benedict? I wonder." This was not a new subject for questioning to Father William. He had spent years among manuscripts, tracing the Benedictines from Subiaco to Monte Cassino, through Augustine in England, over into the monasteries of the Frankish kingdoms; traveling with Boniface among the Germans; watching the Rule take grip in Spain, Scandinavia and the Slavonic countries; seeing it supplant all other Rules so completely that Charles the Great could ask if there had ever been any other monastic legislation. Father William had seen developments *and* departures.

He knew much about Benedict of Aniane and his reform in the early ninth century; he knew even more about Cluny and its reform of the early tenth century. In fact, he himself was now living the Cluniac observances. But he had often wondered if everything that had been called development was really such. He was now wondering if young Robert had not plumbed the very depths of the difficulty with his question about manual labor. The bell for vespers ended his musings, but it gave him no definite answer. Could Robert have been right?

Chapter Three

"I Looked for One to Stand in the Gap"

That first snow of the year lay buried beneath three heavier falls before December was half over. Champagne seemed destined for a white winter and a very cold Christmas. Father William had been watching the weather closely, for he thought he had detected unrest among his novices. If he could get them out of doors for a while, he thought their spirits would lift. He was particularly observant of Robert, for the day of his profession was fast approaching, and he was certain that the lad's soul was not at rest. He wondered if he were being tempted.

Passing through the scriptorium one morning he found Robert with pen idle, eyes away from the manuscript he was copying, and a tense frown knotting his brows. He walked up behind him softly and whispered "Cold in here, isn't it, son? Go down to the heated room for a few moments and warm yourself. I have a special task for you and Brother Maurus."

The lad laid his stylus aside. He had not transcribed a single letter. He arose mechanically and left the large scriptorium where bent heads directed busy fingers in the transcription of ancient scrolls. He made his way along the wide, cold cloisters to the room where some monks were warming themselves before the open fire. Robert walked close to the hearth and abstractedly extended his hands to the flames. His mind was filled with the words the abbot had spoken in the chapter room that morning: "I sought... for a man...that might...stand in the gap before me in favor of the land, that I might not destroy it; and I found none" (Ezk 22:30).

Those words had haunted Robert. They had been with him all morning. They had summoned up the picture of a town besieged with a wide breach in its wall. He saw a lone knight standing in the gap as solitary defense for the whole people. The imagery stirred his martial blood. But what had wrung his heart in the chapter room and was still wringing it was the plaintive wail in the last phrase "...and I found none." He wondered if God would be any more successful in his quest were he to seek for one today. He could not free himself from the idea that there was something personal in the passage, something meant for him. That thought had been with him since dawn. He was now looking into the high leaping flames, but instead of seeing transparent yellow and gold with bases of beautiful blue he was seeing a yawning gap in an encircling wall, and beyond the opening a wrath-filled God ready to execute justice. "I sought for a man...*and found none*," murmured Robert.

"*Benedicite....* Talking to yourself, eh? That's a bad sign."

Robert turned with a start and met the dancing eyes of Brother Maurus. "Say '*Dominus*,' you sleep-walker. Father Master has given us permission to speak and a commission to fulfill."

"*Dominus*," answered Robert.

"That's a little better," said the cheerful Maurus. "Now listen. We've got to go out. We've got to clear the snow from the platforms the builders use in the new church. That's good news in itself. I haven't been out for a week, have you?"

"No."

"Well, here's better news. We are to stay out until midafternoon, and we can argue all we want. Father Master's orders. Come on, let's get our mittens; the heavy brooms and sweeps are over in the church."

Robert's immediate reaction disappointed Maurus, who had enthusiastically started for the door. Wheeling on the still abstracted Robert, he demanded, "What's gnawing at that brain of yours? You act as if you had been bitten by some sleep-producing bug. What's the matter?"

"That gap." answered Robert.

"What gap?"

"Weren't you in chapter this morning?"

"Of course I was, but I was observing my Rule."

"What Rule?"

"The Rule that says you are to follow the example of your seniors. I followed it. I was half asleep!"

"Oh, be serious, Maurus."

"Oh, be sensible, Robert," laughed the elder novice. "Don't take this life too hard; they won't let you take it too easy. Come on," he cried and turned toward the door. "You can tell me all about the gap over in the church. Plenty of gaps there." And he led the way out of the room.

Robert followed, and soon the rapid pace set by Maurus robbed him of some of his abstraction. The keen, cold December air knifed at his nostrils and pierced his lungs.

"Better than the scriptorium, isn't it?" said Maurus.

They made their way out across the spacious courtyard, while the sun's glare on the snow made their eyeballs ache. Robert put his hand across his eyes and exclaimed, "Whew, that's blinding!"

"Better to go blind out here than in the scriptorium copying meaningless manuscripts," laughed Maurus. "How many letters did you illumine this morning?"

"None," grunted Robert as he pushed through a heavy drift.

Maurus turned in surprise. "None? What's happened to our model novice? Were your fingers frozen?" Robert did not answer. Soon they were across the courtyard and Maurus was fumbling with the latch on the door that would let them out of the enclosure. "Well," he asked, "how about it? Were your fingers frozen?"

The elder novice turned and was just about to add to his bantering remarks when his eye was caught by a motion in one of the upper windows of the monastery. "Oh! ho!" he whispered softly. "The walls not only have ears, they have eyes as well. Don't turn, but know that in the middle window of the top floor stands our good Father Abbot looking down on his two best novices and wondering what in the world they are up to. Out we go!" he cried as the latch lifted, "and leave His Lordship to his wondering."

Robert held the door ajar a moment and looked around at the three sides of the gray monastery. On each side three rows of windows threw back the glare of the sun which was well up the eastern wall of the sky. He did not catch sight of his abbot, but the utter silence of the enclosure, the two sets of tracks across the virginal snows, and the fixed stare of the windows gave him a sense of desolation. This was his monastery—the buildings in which he had elected to serve God, for the rest of his life perhaps. St. Pierre's was large and prosperous; her community was numerous; always there throbbed under her silence that stirring energy and subdued bustle inseparable from an alert, industrious body of men. This momentary stillness was more barren than silence. To Robert, made perceptive by inner suffering, it bespoke emptiness. Maurus' chiding tones came as a relief, "That's no gap you're standing in, brave one. It's the monastery door. Close it and come on."

A footpath had been trodden in the snow close to the monastery wall. Maurus took it to the corner of the building. Then he turned sharply and made his way among the mounds of snow that hid the lumber and stone that lay scattered in the area about the new building. The church was roofed, but no windows had been fitted in. The two novices entered the structure, picked their way across the piles of rubble, around the drifts of snow that had blown in through the open window spaces, and found snow sweeps under a rough platform. Climbing the platform, they set to work with a will.

They swept one section clear in silence. Robert was enjoying his work. The snow flew from each side of the platform as with mighty strokes he plied his large wooden sweep left and right. Action was a relief. The pent-up energies of the past two weeks were released. Even his thoughts seemed to flow faster. He smiled.

"That's better," said Maurus who had been watching him closely. "Do you know that this is the first crease I've seen in that face of yours all day? You're more handsome when you smile. You should do it more often. We haven't got the world on our shoulders, man, cheer up! And now tell me what is all this about a gap?" Maurus swung his sweep slowly from side to side.

Robert rested a moment. He was breathing hard. "I don't know whether I had better tell you," he said and began to laugh. "It's a gap that will show a bigger gap in that brain of yours if you really meant that remark you just made about not having the world on our shoulders. What's your concept of a monk, Maurus?"

"A wise man who, instead of carrying the world on his shoulders, flees that world."

"A selfish soul, then?"

"Oh, selfish with a healthy selfishness. He knows he's got a soul to save, and he knows one place where he can save it."

"Did you ever think of saving other souls?"

"Leave that to the pastors. We're only monks."

"Well, that's where your gap is and my gap comes in," said Robert as he bent to swinging his sweep again. "The abbot talked about God this morning."

"He does almost every morning," grunted Maurus. "That's why I can hear without listening. I never knew another man who could say the same thing in so many different ways. He didn't say anything new this morning, did he?"

Robert could not repress his smile. Abbot Bernard with all his sincerity *did* repeat himself often.

"Yes," chuckled Robert. "He not only talked about God this morning; he also talked about the missing man."

Maurus' sweep came to a stop. "What missing man?"

"The missing man who lost the lives of the whole city. The man who didn't fill the gap."

"Who was he?"

"Tell me, too," broke in a third voice from behind them. The two novices turned quickly to meet the kindly gaze of the abbot himself. He smiled at the surprise and embarrassment on the two young faces. "I needed some air," he said. "And I was anxious about these platforms. But now I am curious about Brother Robert's missing man. Who is he, Brother?"

Robert became a trifle self-conscious, but soon he recovered and bowing low, said: *"Benedicite."*

"Dominus," replied the abbot and he pulled

his cowl more closely around his partially bald head.

"I was talking about the man God sought and could not find. The man you spoke of in chapter this morning. I was wondering if we could be he."

The abbot smiled. Then turning to Maurus with a meaningful twinkle in his eyes, he said, "That's a queer combination of singular and plural, isn't it? What do you think, Brother—could we be he?"

"Put me down for a sinner, Reverend Father," replied Maurus. "I dozed this morning. But I'd hate to be among the missing if he were looking for me."

The abbot laughed. Robert envied the older novice—his ease in the presence of the abbot. He could never have made such an admission so calmly.

"Well, Brother Robert, what do you think? Did God ever find a man to stand in the gap?" And the abbot's blue eyes studied the face of the young novice.

Robert looked down at the dust of snow on his boot for a moment. "Yes, Reverend Father, I think St. Benedict stood in the gap back in the sixth century."

"Good for you," cheered the abbot. Then as he stroked his gray beard he asked, "And could he find one today?"

Robert's face sobered. He stamped the snow

off his boots before he said, "He could if he could find someone like St. Benedict."

The abbot's breath was showing white in the cold air. He shook his head a moment in silence. It was not the answer he had expected. He wanted to learn more of what was in this youngster's soul. However, he himself was chilled, and he feared that the novices might catch cold, so he said, "Come to my room after you have finished what Father Master assigned you, Brother Robert. And you, Brother Maurus, see to it that neither of you freeze."

"We won't if we keep moving, Reverend Father," said the elder novice as he again sent the snow flying from the platform. "Father Master told us to stay out until midafternoon. Will it be all right for Brother Robert to see you then?"

"Perfectly," said the abbot as he turned and stamped away.

When he had rounded the corner of the main building and was lost to sight, Maurus murmured, "Whew! That was close. We almost lost our outing. I saw some tracks down by the fish pond I want to investigate. We can do it if you hurry with that snow."

"If *we* hurry, you mean," retorted Robert as he gave a wider swing to his wooden sweep. Snow was cascading from each side of the elevated platform under his steady plying. For a little while they worked in silence. Then Maurus rested, and while puffing exclaimed, "Boy, you're strong! You're going to be as big as your father. You'll make a regular mountain of a monk by the time you're forty."

Robert's sweep went back and forth tirelessly. He was nearing the end of the platform when he said, "I wonder what the abbot wants with me?"

"Perhaps he wants to find out why you didn't say God could have found the man he was looking for in this monastery. That would have been the diplomatic thing to say. But you don't believe in being diplomatic, do you?"

"I don't believe in being dishonest," said Robert. He removed his mittens and bent to tie up the end of his robe. From his crouched position he went on, "I fear God would have as much success here at St. Pierre as he had back in the Old Testament. He couldn't find anyone like St. Benedict here simply because we do not live St. Benedict's Rule."

Maurus calmly leaned on the long wooden handle of his sweep. "Robert," he said, and there was a ripple of laughter in his tone, "you remind me of an ox in more ways than one. You're not only as big and as strong as one, you're also as dull and as stubborn."

When Robert made no rejoinder Maurus asked, "Did you ever see oxen treading out corn?"

"No."

"Well, they go round and round and round;

tirelessly round and round and round. That's the way your brain is working now. You're simply going round and round and round, and getting nowhere fast. We *are* Benedictines."

"But we're not like St. Benedict," said Robert hotly as he finished the platform and stood his sweep up in the corner. "Come here," he commanded impatiently as he caught hold of Maurus' scapular. "Count those buildings with me. Guest house, one. School, two. Monastery quadrangle, three stories high, a hundred and fifty feet long, three. New church with tower thrusting itself one hundred and twenty-seven feet into the sky, four. Four massive buildings surrounded by I don't know how many barns, shops, sheds, and serfs' dwellings. This is a little city in itself, and the abbot is a feudal lord."

"What do you want? We're not solitaries."

"But where is the Benedictine simplicity?" argued Robert fiercely. "It's like the man for the gap, I guess. It, too, is missing."

The elder novice squinted at him for a moment. "Come on down to the pond," he said in a disgusted tone. "You're obsessed. You not only need exercise, you need to be exorcised. Come on. I'll exercise you. Let the abbot do the rest." Then just as he was about to climb through one of the window spaces he turned on Robert with the question, "What time did you get up this morning?"

"About two o'clock," replied his friend, puzzled.

"And it's not twelve yet. Here you've been up for something under ten hours, over five of which have been spent in a chilly church chanting the praises of God, and yet you say we're not Benedictines. Could anything be more Benedictine? He wanted men to sing the psalter, didn't he?" Robert nodded. "Well, we do it. So forget your obsession. Don't be such a glutton for penance." Then he glanced at his companion's face. "Whoa!" he cried. "Don't take me too seriously. Just now you look like old Father Deusdedit. Did you ever see a more God-help-us expression on any man's face?" Then as he led the way up to a clump of trees that topped a knoll and led into the woods, he continued, "That man must have vinegar in his veins. What a face! Every time I look at him I think of the vials of God's wrath."

The smile on Robert's face widened. Then, seeking to say something good for the man whose character often caused him to wonder, he remarked, "Well, you must admit that the old frozen-face observes the Rule. He's most regular."

"So are the cows," replied Maurus abstractedly. He had just found the tracks between the trees. He now looked up and said, "There's regularity and regularity, Robert. Old Deusdedit is inhuman. God doesn't want that. He's worse than the novice Father Master was talking to me about the other day. 'He never gives any trouble,' he said. 'No,' I answered, 'neither does he give anything else.' The master didn't like it for a moment but he saw the point." Maurus turned and led the way into the woods saying, "That's, the way it is with many of them up there. They don't give any trouble because they don't give anything. If instructors and cantors and superiors would spend more time waking these people up and less keeping the energetic ones down, maybe God could find the missing man you've been talking about."

"Oh, so you haven't forgotten."

"I don't forget many things you say, Brother; but I'm glad to see that the sun, snow and air have made you forget for a little. You're too serious. Here, do something like this, and you'll live longer." With that Maurus turned a handspring in the snow, but just as he completed the turn his foot slipped and he went sprawling.

"The 'old man' isn't dead yet, is he?" laughed Robert as he helped him up and began to brush him off.

"Dead?" asked Maurus indignantly. "Dead? He must be buried! I never missed a handspring before in my life. But come on, these tracks go deeper into this wood."

When they were back again at the monastery gate after the long tramp through the woods Robert said, "I hope I don't sound wierd, Maurus. But I don't feel as though I am giving enough to God. I expected a hard life. I haven't found it. I love to sing. The work is too easy. I feel as though I am giving too little."

"Too little?" exclaimed Maurus incredulously. "You're giving as much as the founders of Cluny gave. And they were saints! Why can't you be satisfied with what the others do?"

"Because," said Robert earnestly, "because I've learned a little of the generosity of Calvary." Robert started. "Because I believe that God is looking for a man to fill the gap."

The older novice slowly turned and fumbled for the latch, but before going in, he said, "Robert, you're going to see the abbot. I think you ought to tell him every single thought you've had on this matter since the first day you came here. You owe it to him and to yourself." As he opened the door he whispered, "In we go. Silence now."

When Robert entered the abbot's room he found him with a yellowed, wrinkled manuscript before him. He looked up from the scroll and smiled at the young novice. Robert had always marveled at that smile. It suffused his countenance with a light seldom seen in the face of man.

"Primarium officium nostrum est in terra praestare quod angeli in coelo," the abbot said. "Can you translate that, son?"

"Our primary duty is to carry out on earth what the angels do in heaven," said Robert with a trace of timidity.

"Good!" exclaimed the abbot. "This man is talking about us, Brother Robert. Do you think he is right?"

"I suppose he means our choir chant. That is a beautiful concept of our life, isn't it?"

"Beautiful," said the abbot as he sat back from his desk and waved the novice to a chair, "but inadequate. I did something this morning no angel has ever done, and no angel shall ever do. And, please God, one day you, too, will do this greater thing."

"Greater than the angels?" Robert could not conceal his surprise.

"Indeed," said the abbot with a nod of his head. "You were not brought here to be an angel, my son. You were brought here to give God something no one in the nine choirs of the angels, none of the nine choirs, no, nor all the nine choirs together can give him." Robert was lost in wonderment. The abbot went on, "You were brought here not to do angelic work, not to do human work, but to do a divine work. You are not here to be another Michael, another Gabriel or another Raphael, my son. You are here to be another Christ!"

The abbot paused. Robert's eyes brightened. He had caught the concept. The abbot, seeing the light of recognition in the novice's eyes, went on, "The sacrifice of praise is great, my boy. In very truth, it *is* an echo of heaven. But the sacrifice of the Mass is greater. For that is not an echo of Calvary; that *is* Calvary! And Calvary, you know, was the one sacrifice that adequately satisfied God and saved human beings. So you see why I say that this line about our life is beautiful but only half true," and he gestured toward the scroll on his desk.

Awed, Robert nodded. The abbot pushed the scroll aside saying, "Yesterday, I read a line about us saying *'propter Chorum fundati'*—we were brought into being for choir work. That is another half-truth, my boy. Or at least a truth that calls for fuller explanation. We are not here to be psalm singers only. It is not David we are to imitate; though his psalm singing praised and pleased God. We are here to be crucified men; for it is Christ we are to reproduce. He not only praised and pleased God; he saved men. He was the man who stood in the gap, wasn't he?"

"Oh," exclaimed Robert, "indeed he was! I had never thought of him in that light, Reverend Father, but I had told Brother Maurus that we were to save men as well as serve God. I told him, as I told you, that St. Benedict appealed to me as a man who had stood in the gap and I said that the world needed another Benedict."

The novice paused. The abbot smiled and prompted, "And now?"

"Now I see that I have a higher vocation than to be like St. Benedict. I have to be like Jesus Christ. We monks must stand in the gap the way he did."

"Excellent!" encouraged the abbot. "For we are Christians—other Christs. But we must never forget that we are Benedictine Christians. Therefore, we are to follow Christ St. Benedict's way."

That was the remark that precipitated Robert's full confession. He told the abbot everything that had attracted him to St. Pierre's. How he had admired the monks and their charity during those three awful years of famine, plague and death; how he envied their opportunity of giving glory to God; and how he had finally resolved to bring chivalry to the cloister. He then recounted what it was that led him to his concept of the Rule, lived as Benedict lived it, as perfect gallantry. When the novice told him, in a voice that was vibrant with passion, of his eagerness to rival the generosity of Calvary, Dom Bernard put his hand to his head to hide the tears that welled up from his heart. Then Robert hesitated. He feared to hurt this kind man by pointing out the discrepancies he found between the Rule and its observance. The abbot encouraged him with: "Speak out, son, I want to know your mind."

Robert looked at him a moment, then in a voice that was almost beseeching, he asked: "Reverend Father, wouldn't the original observance be a more generous gift to God? Wouldn't it be the nobler thing to live the simplicity of Monte Cassino, with its solitude, its hard manual labor, and its complete separation from the world, than to live the life we are leading at St. Pierre?"

The abbot saw that the lad was deadly in earnest. He reflected a moment. He thought of the comparative ease in which he and his community lived. He had once called it "leisure to love God"; he saw now that it *was* leisure, and that one could love God without so much of it. It was a big decision for him to make. He shook his head slowly, but said, "Yes, son. I think you're right. I think it would be the nobler thing."

That was the sentence that settled Robert's life.

When talking to Brother Maurus the next day he said, "It's decided. I take my vows. But the abbot agrees with me. There is a nobler way of living; and I'm going to live it as far as possible."

That same afternoon the abbot sent for the master of novices and told him of his talk with Robert. The master smiled and said, "An enthusiast, that boy."

"Enthusiasm is a precious gift today," replied the abbot. "You, Father, do not see as much as I must of the simony and immorality among the clergy in the world. As I tried to show this morning—not too successfully, I fear—*there is a gap*, and God must be looking for 'a man to stand before him in favor of the land, that he may not destroy it.' Keep your eye on young Robert. He may be the man."

"Oh, Father Abbot," objected the master, "the boy is uncontrolled. He's not only vehement, he's actually violent at times. I've advised him to study meekness and the mildness of Christ. After all, the Lamb of God *is* our Model."

"Yes, Father, that's very true," said the abbot with a smile. "The Lamb of God is our model. But never forget, and never let your novices forget, that the Lamb of God was also the Lion of Judah!"

Chapter Four

Silver-White on Flaming-Red

It was in the newly erected church that Robert sang his profession. Abbot Bernard had invited the boy's parents to the ceremony. Theodoric's dark eyes followed every movement his son made. The giant lord was surprised to find a striking similarity between the dubbing of a knight and the profession of a monk. He saw his boy place his hands within those of his abbot, just as he had seen many a fledgling knight place his within those of his liege lord; then he heard him pledge a vow very much like that offered by a vassal—it was a pledge of service unto death. But it was not until Robert had prostrated himself face downward at the feet of his abbot that

Theodoric said within himself, "The lad was right. There *is* a higher chivalry!" Then bending over to Ermengarde whose eyes were filled with tears of joy he whispered, "Our boy is being dubbed knight by Jesus Christ. The abbot is Christ's proxy. I'm proud of our son."

At the moment, Robert, too, was proud; for he looked upon his profession more as a gift *from* God than a gift *to* God. He knew he was being dubbed knight; so he mounted the altar steps with a pounding heart. He had to place his profession, which he had written on parchment, on that stone of sacred sacrifice as an outward expression of the inward surrender he so gladly made. Just as he reached the last step, the sun broke through the clouds that had veiled it all morning and through the stained-glass windows sent streams of red, gold, yellow, green, brown and blue light upon the floor of the church. As Robert placed his parchment on the altar he noted that its silver-whiteness floated in a pool of flaming-red that had poured down from the nearest window. He was too excited to reflect but the color combination impressed him, and vaguely he sensed that it had some special message for him. As he walked back to the abbot he quietly murmured, "Silver-white on flaming-red."

When the ceremony ended he hurried to greet his parents. He was surprised to find his mother in tears. As she hugged him, she whispered, "You've done the noblest thing possible to man, my boy. You've been gallant to your God."

Robert was very happy that day. But, as is often the case, ten full years had to intervene before he realized that it had only been his *profession day.* His real *vow day* came in May, 1045. On this day the abbot summoned him and appointed him prior of the monastery, but in the same breath informed him that there would be no innovation, no renovation. The customary observance of the Rule would be followed. That was the day Robert learned what it cost to vow obedience. As he made his way to the same high altar on which he had placed his silver-white parchment ten years earlier, his heart was not pounding with the same glad joy. But it was the same heart, and it was a truer chivalry that pulsed from it as the young monk knelt and again pledged his service unto death. That was Robert's real vow day.

During that swift decade much had happened to the soul of the young noble. In it, love for the Rule had deepened; for Father William, who had become his fast friend, introduced him to manuscripts that enabled him to follow the life of the Rule from Monte Cassino to St. Pierre. Robert was young enough to be surprised at what six centuries of time had done to that Rule, and just old enough to wish to undo it. He discussed the matter often with his former novice master, but never succeeded in winning him to the conclusion that the Rule could be observed to the letter and thus a greater glory given to God. Maurus, of course, only laughed at the concept, told Robert to take his head out of the clouds, and advised him to be human even as he strove to be divine. Abbot Bernard was the only one who would listen.

But an older and more important history had gripped Robert's soul during that decade— it was the one told in the Gospels. Again and again St. Benedict had said in his Rule, "Let them prefer absolutely nothing to Christ." That injunction Robert took literally. Every known detail of Christ's life from the annunciation to the ascension was pondered long and lovingly by the young man. The borrowed cave hewn in Bethlehem's hillside held Robert's imagination and mind. That God should become man astounded him. But the borrowed tomb hewn from the rock near Golgotha all but stupefied him. That God should die for us, then rise again, a promise of our own future resurrection, left the young monk's imagination stunned and his mind groping in bewilderment. The inevitable followed. Robert fell in love with Jesus Christ.

The manliness of the God-man was what especially gripped the soul of this youngster who was himself so virile. He saw Jesus as the bravest of the brave, and long before his twenty-first birthday had dubbed him, "The Red Cross Knight of Calvary."

When Maurus found him with a drawing of the cross on which, in place of the corpus, he had superimposed an open Rule book, he asked lightly, "What proud title are you going to give this bit of wild fancy?" Robert looked up with eyes that held flame, and solemnly said, *"Quis non redamaret?* Who would not return such love?" Then placing his finger first on the Rule book, then on the cross, he said, "That's my return for this!"

And so the concept grew. Love could only be repaid by love, chivalry by chivalry, and the cross by the Rule. But it won scant sympathy from anyone save the abbot. Dom Bernard loved to listen to the young monk tell of Christ and his knighthood. That is why Robert's hopes for a trial of his idea soared on the morning the abbot told him he was to be prior. They fell, however, before the abbot had completed his sentence. So when Maurus met the newly appointed one, the warm congratulations that were trembling on his lips remained unspoken and in their place came the question, "What's the bad news that has set your face in stone?"

The sharp lines of Robert's countenance did not alter as he replied, "The worst news of my twenty-seven years of life. I'm to be prior, but there's to be no reform."

"Conform! Conform!" cried Maurus with a

laugh. "Or the first thing you know you'll be deformed."

Robert only shook his head. "Maurus," he sighed, "let me tell you it costs to obey. Believe me when I say that the abbot gave me the saddest news of my life this morning."

At that precise moment, in the great hall of the castle, Theodoric was saying just the opposite. Only the moment before he had charged in through the castle gates on a mount that was lathered with sweat and whose large eyes were bulging from their sockets, so furiously had he been ridden. The excited lord had flung himself from the saddle, tossed the reins to a groom, slapped his horse on the buttock, and made for the house with giant strides. Bursting into the main hall he shouted, "Ermengarde, Ermengarde!" When his wife appeared at the far end of the hall, the jubilant Theodoric hurried toward her with arms widespread. "My dearest," he cried as he clasped her in his arms, "I've got the best news of the decade!" As he now held her off at arm's length he exclaimed, "We have a new Pope! Benedict IX has resigned! Oh, I'm happy, happy, happy! We must visit Robert this afternoon. Let us be the bearers of this glorious news."

The thought of visiting her son thrilled the mother as much as the news of the new Pope thrilled her husband. She cried an enthusiastic

"Let's!" and immediately began to prepare for the journey.

They found the monastery grounds delightful that afternoon. They seemed alive with bees and blossoms and nest-building birds. All nature was in fellowship with the exuberant Theodoric who paced the paths impatient for the appearance of his son. Robert had not finished greeting his mother before the glad news came tumbling from the lips of the lord between smiling nods of the head and hearty slaps on the shoulder. Then, in the full flush of his enthusiasm, Theodoric sketched the world for his son with a few bold strokes and told of his high hopes for a rebirth of fervor. The young monk's eyes grew brilliant as his father talked, and Ermengarde, who was watching the kindling of those flames, suddenly realized that she was looking into a mirror that held the image of her husband's soul.

When the crest of their high emotion broke, the mother plied her boy with the usual questions about his health, happiness, and life at the monastery. Under this rush of what he termed "useless questions," Theodoric was just beginning to grow restless when Dom Bernard approached. After cordial greetings he invited the lord to visit the stables and to pass judgment on some horses that had just arrived. It was a fortunate interruption for everyone.

Almost two full hours had elapsed before the abbot and Theodoric returned, but neither

Robert nor his mother noticed the flight of time. While still ten paces away, Theodoric called out, "Son, why didn't you tell us you had been made prior?"

Robert flashed an accusing glance at his abbot, then as his mother breathed a joyous, "Oh!" he said, "It seems to me that I wasn't given much of a chance to tell you anything. Then again, Father, there wasn't so much to tell; for, you see, a prior in a Benedictine monastery is little more than a messenger boy for the abbot. Nothing to boast of in that, is there, Reverend Father?

Dom Bernard chuckled. Before he could reply, however, Robert went on, "St. Benedict says in his Rule that the prior is not to consider himself 'second abbot'; and when he appointed me, Reverend Father was good enough to tell me I was only 'first monk.' In fact, he was honest enough to say that he had placed me in the middle. I am between the community and its ruler. I suppose I'll be pressed from both sides and quite completely squeezed out. So offer me condolences, not congratulations."

The abbot's laugh was warm. He was delighted with the little speech, and told himself that Robert would be a good prior. Then bowing to Ermengarde he asked her if she would like to go over to the church to see some of the new vestments. While they were gone, Robert and his father strolled in the orchard, and there, amid the snows of Mary's white blossoms, Robert opened

his heart. He told his father of the ambition that
burned within him; he pictured for him the gap
he was always seeing, and behind that gap
showed him the face of a justly angered God.
The young prior grew flushed as he spoke. His
father listened closely and watched even more
closely. His son was a man now, and yet, in him,
he found much of the boy. This walk was a revelation in more ways than one. It set Theodoric
pondering deeply.

The parents stayed for vespers that afternoon and saw their son take the stall across from
the abbot—the highest dignity possible to a
monk. They felt proud and grateful. As they
rode home, they found the waters of the Seine
flushed to a burnished gold by the declining sun.
Impulsively Ermengarde turned to her husband
and begged, "Let's send the carriage home, Theodoric, and spend an hour by the river. It's many
years since you and I sat by those waters."

Theodoric smiled, and the carriage was sent
home. After they had strolled along the bank for
a good stretch, Theodoric pointed to a stately
chestnut tree and said, "Let us sit here awhile.
This is a lover's nook."

When Ermengarde had settled herself com-
fortably against the smooth trunk, she smiled
contentedly and said, "Well, more than ten years
have passed since that night you feared your boy
would make a mistake or would be a mistake.
What do you think now?"

Theodoric looked out across the water, and a serious light stole into his eyes. Then shaking his head he slowly said, "The boy is no mistake. The boy has made no mistake. But let me tell you he has all the makings of a rebel. I don't know how much he told you about his one great burning ambition, but if it ever flames forth—and I'm sure that it will one day—there will be a monastic bonfire. Robert, my dear, is different from most monks and most men. Different men are dangerous."

"I don't know just what you are hinting at," said Ermengarde indignantly, "but I can tell you that no man ever made his mark in the world, and no man ever left his mark in the world, unless he was different. Fishes run in schools, sheep in flocks, and cows in herds. I don't want my boy to be a poor fish, a silly sheep, or a stupid ox. I'm glad he's different. And as prior I think he will be dangerous to the lazy, the self-centered, and the too easily satisfied. That will be a blessing. I'm proud of our boy."

"So am I. So am I," said Theodoric soothingly. "But you asked a question. I gave an honest answer. Robert has a firmly fixed ideal, my dear. It dominates him." Then as if in afterthought he said, "But I wish he weren't so mystical. Did he tell you about his silver-white on flaming-red?"

"Indeed he did," came the enthusiastic reply as Ermengarde sat up away from the tree. "While

you were strolling with the abbot he told me
about that ideal of his. He longs for the Rule to
be kept to the letter. He said this longing is set in
his soul as resplendently as the evening star in an
empty sky. He said that he sees it as clearly as a
disc of silver-white centered on a background of
flaming-red. As he went on with his confession,
I noticed that he used these colors to describe
things more than once. When I called his attention to the fact he simply said, 'They are symbolic.' That set me thinking. At vespers I think I
found my solution. Do you know what those
colors symbolize?" Theodoric shook his head.
"Picture to yourself a snow-white host," said Ermengarde slowly, "centered in a heart that is
blood-red." Theodoric's gasp was audible. "Yes,"
continued the mother more quickly, "that is my
explanation of Robert's silver-white on flaming-
red. I am convinced, my lord, that our boy is
more than God-oriented; he is thoroughly God-
absorbed. I feel sure that Jesus throbs in the heart
of our son."

The parents sat in silence then as the shadows crept toward the east and the red-gold on
the waters slowly turned to purple, silver and
black. When they at last arose and faced home-
ward Ermengarde lifted a hand to the sky and
softly exclaimed, "Look! It is Robert's symbol—
the lone evening star."

At that very moment the son was pointing to
the same sky and the same symbol. At his side

was a belligerent Father Maurus. They had been discussing the visit. "Yes," Robert was now saying, "I told him about that. I also told him about the agony I know because of the ache in my heart to give God more. I even told him about the anger I sometimes feel because of the mitigations that have crept into the observance of the Rule."

"And what did he say?" demanded Maurus hotly. "Didn't he tell you what I've so often told you? Didn't he tell you that you're dreaming?"

Robert, who had started for the window, stopped in his stride, flashed around on his friend and said, "You're forgetting that it was my father who told me to keep my sword unsheathed. No, he didn't tell me that I was dreaming. But he did tell me to remember that parallel lines never meet. He said that I was on one level; the monastic world on another."

"Well, that's as good as saying you're dreaming."

"Is it? Well then it is a strange command he gave me immediately after. For he told me never to descend! He told me a day will come when some will climb up to where I stand if I will only burn on."

"Did your father really say that?"

"His final words were, 'Burn on, my boy, burn on, until you burn out!' And that," said Robert grimly, "I'm going to do."

Maurus turned from the prior and walked to the window. With his face lifted to a blue that was gradually showing more and more sparkles of silver, he softly exclaimed, "What a father! What a father!"

The sound of the compline bell precluded further discussion. Maurus followed Robert from the room, puzzled. He had admired Theodoric from the first day he had seen him. The lord's size, noble bearing and direct speech were just what Maurus demanded in a real man. During the past ten years of acquaintanceship he had found in the giant lord a staunch ally for his battle against what he called Robert's "excessive idealism." This latest development disconcerted Maurus. He wondered why the prudent, practical and ever penetrating Theodoric had told his son to "burn on."

Compline was not well sung by Maurus that night. Memories of Robert and his ideal kept breaking through. He recalled their novitiate days. He had tried to dissuade him then. During the past ten years he had never ceased from that effort. But instead of fading, that ideal was brightening until it seemed to be a steady glow. Now had come this confirmation from his father. Maurus groaned inwardly. "Robert should not have been told to 'burn on,' he said to himself as compline ended, "he should have been told to 'burn it out.' And I'll do the telling! This argument is not over yet. Others can do some burning on."

Chapter Five
Life's Only Mistake

More than one among the elders of the community secretly resented the appointment of this "twenty-seven year old boy" to the priorship of the abbey. Six months had not elapsed, however, before even these few were congratulating Dom Bernard on his excellent choice. A new Robert had been revealed to them. The same energy was there and the same enthusiasm, but closer contact with him showed most what they had never seen before—a crystal clear sincerity and a simplicity that was transparent. All appreciated his kindness, but the more deeply discerning admired his majestic calm and marvelled at his control. But not even Maurus knew the price the young prior was paying for his mastery. With each new dawn he had to take his heart into his own hard hands and say, "Obey!" It was the only way he could crush down the surge of his soul for a more literal observance of the Rule.

Toward the end of his third year in office, when abbot Bernard talked about the generosity of the community and the grand return they were making to God for all that he had given them, Robert thought an opportune time had arrived for a hint at the possibility of making a greater return through real manual labor. Dom Bernard smiled.

"Father Prior," he said with a kindly grin, "you will never make a diplomat. God has given you a soul as open as the air. You are more transparent than stainless glass. No, my son, the suitable time for the introduction of reform has not yet come."

Maurus found Robert at the window that afternoon with his eyes in a fixed, unseeing stare. When he laughingly accused the prior of idleness, Robert gave a disdainful grunt and said, "It takes a gigantic faith to believe that our whole life is anything else but idleness."

"Whe-e-e-ew!" whistled Maurus. "It seems ages since I heard you use that tone of voice." Then sagely shaking his head he added, "But I thought you were up on the heights too long."

"Heights?" snorted Robert without turning. "It seems to me that I've been in the depths ever since I was made prior." He felt the critical eyes of his friend studying him closely. "See that haze on the hills?" he asked. When Maurus gave an "Uh-huh" as answer, Robert went on, "Well, I've been living in just such an atmosphere for years. I've been walking through fogs toward hills that ever remain purple on the distant horizon. I plod along but I never get any nearer my goal. What a life!"

"What's wrong, Robert?"

Maurus put so much sympathy and genuine concern into these three words that the prior was won to a full confession. He told his friend of the latest disappointment received from the abbot, then proceeded to lay bare his heart. Maurus saw that Robert needed an outlet, so he wisely determined to let him talk. And Robert did talk! Convictions that had been elaborated in hours of deep reflection poured out of him with such rapidity and lucidity that even Maurus was surprised.

The prior did not argue his case; he simply presented convictions that had been won through hard and consistent reasoning. He was giving vent to the accumulated thought of years. He presented his ideal and his reasons for striving for its fulfillment with a forcefulness that shook the stubborn Maurus. He climaxed his confession with, "And yet, the community quietly laughs at me, the abbot humors and patronizes me, while even you and the rest of my friends think I'm deluded. Can it be that I'm the only one who is wrong?"

Maurus was dumbfounded. Of late years he had secretly envied Robert the air of solid assurance that seemed to mark his every step. He thought him devoid of doubt, free from all harassing questions, and living a life that was utterly simplified because his goal was clear and the way to it as open as the skies. He honestly believed that Robert was walking a highway as broad as a Roman road and as bright as a cloudless noonday heaven. To hear him now claim that he was groping in a fog disconcerted Maurus. He did not know what to say.

Robert turned from him and walked to the window. "Yes," he murmured, "this life seems terrifyingly empty at times."

"Did Christ's seem any fuller?" The question came hesitatingly. Maurus knew that it was the only answer, but he was not sure that Robert should be faced with the only answer at the moment. "You need a rest," he added quickly.

"I need a chance..." retorted Robert, then checked himself. Slowly a smile softened the hard lines of his face. Turning to his friend he chuckled very self-consciously and said, "Didn't I tell you I was walking in a haze? Here I am seeking a chance to do something for Christ while I am actually stumbling over an opportunity to suffer for him. Thanks for clearing the atmosphere, Maurus. But between ourselves I must admit that I'd love to try that primitive observance."

"Forget it!" was Maurus' only reply.

And for years Robert did seem to forget it. But on the day Theodoric was buried, Maurus learned that Robert had not forgotten. He found the prior that afternoon seated at his desk staring fixedly at the crucifix he held in his hands. Maurus entered quietly. "Thinking of death?" he asked softly.

"Of life, Maurus, of life!" came the unexpected, firm reply from the man who had not lifted his eyes. "It is not death that matters. It is what goes before death." Then turning to his friend he said, "Think of it! My father's eternity was settled by what he did in time. Actions that we call 'passing,' deeds, that we say are 'things of the moment,' have an everlastingness to them. Our lives are lived under the white glare of eternity, if we only had the eyes to see it. Maurus, our days are flung against a background of finality that frightens one. Did you hear my father's last words?"

"No."

"There is only one mistake in life—*not to be a saint.*"

"Wh-a-a-t?"

"Yes, Maurus, those were the dying words of my father, and he never uttered a truer syllable all his days. That's why people are born, Maurus. That's why you and I are here at St. Pierre de la Celle—*not to make life's only mistake!*"

The prior laid the crucifix on his desk. "My mother is lonely today, Maurus, but she is happy in her loneliness. She wept as she spoke to me. But the light that shimmered in the midst of those tears told me of the glow of happiness in her heart. She looked at me and said, 'Your father did not make life's only mistake.' I believe her. I believe that I could have answered, 'And neither is my mother making it.' But, Maurus, I'm wondering about their son."

"About their son?"

"Yes. Am I making life's only mistake?"

"Of course not!" came the indignant reply.

"I wish I were so sure as that," said Robert as he slowly turned and looked into a twilight sky. "God has given us such opportunities, Maurus...."

"And you have made the most of them. You have ever walked the narrow way...."

"Ah, but there is a nobler way. And you know it."

"Nobler?"

"Yes. There it is in symbol," said the prior and pointed to the evening star.

Maurus looked up, then musingly asked, "Oh, you mean the Rule to the letter?"

"Exactly!" said Robert. "The Rule to the letter. What wouldn't I give to try it!" Then sighing deeply he added, "But it seems as though my dream must die with me. I shall never have a chance."

"Who knows?" said Maurus. "Who knows?" He meant the remark merely as comfort for his friend, for he did not sympathize with the ideal, though he did with the holder of that ideal.

But Maurus had good reason to recall that last remark a few years later when the abbot summoned him and said, "You lose a friend tomorrow, and I lose the staff of my old age." When Maurus asked what this meant, old Bernard replied, "Father Prior has been elected abbot of St. Michael of Tonnerre. We shall both miss him much, but...."

"*Dominus est*," finished Maurus, not too enthusiastically, "I suppose it is selfish of me not to rejoice, but this is all a bit sudden, Reverend Father. What do you know of Tonnerre? Will Robert like it?"

"I don't know," answered the abbot a trifle dubiously. "Hunault, its last abbot, dubbed the community 'cold.' He said they were posers, always talking about 'crosses' but thinking little of the Crucified. He said that the shadow of a real cross would break most of their backs. But Hunault had that kind of a tongue. He said the same thing was true of many religious. But what I am wondering is whether Robert will attempt his reform. The time seems ripe."

Maurus looked at his abbot quizzically, then asked a question that had bothered him for years. "Why didn't you allow him to do it here?" he asked.

"Do I have to answer that?" asked the abbot as he lifted his eyes to Maurus' face. "You know the temper of my monks and the tempo of this monastery. I've sympathized with Robert for decades, but..."

"But you didn't think it practical," urged Maurus. "Now tell me Reverend Father, do you think it possible anywhere?"

"All things are possible to God, my son."

"Which is not an answer to my question."

The abbot turned slowly, rested his weight on his left forearm, and faced Maurus fully. "Father Maurus, I don't know whether it can be done or not. But I do know this, if any man can do it, Robert is the man! I am an old monk. I am a very old man. I have seen many monks and many men in my almost eighty years of life, but I have never yet seen a man or a monk with as much tenacity as Father Robert."

"Oh, I admit that," Maurus said with impatience. "But the question that has always baffled me is whether he is holding on to the right thing or not. Father Abbot, why is it that I have not been convinced? I see everything else with him eye to eye, but I cannot see this ideal of his."

"Have you tried?"

"With all my might. When his father was won over I made a supreme effort. But, as usual, I came back to my old illustration: the oak is not the acorn. No, it is the living, growing, everspreading tree. So, too, with Benedictinism today. It is the logical, living development of the seed that Benedict buried in the furrow at Subiaco and Monte Cassino. We should no more go back to that than the oak should go back to the acorn from which it sprang. Our Lord said, 'Unless the grain of wheat die...' "

The abbot's head shook in slow negation. "Father," he said kindly, "that is a perfect example of an utterly unanswerable speculative argument. But now look at the practical. Listen to me. I have seen over half a century of attempted reforms, Father. They did not take. They are still attempting them. Every new Pope calls a council. They gather. They face the facts. They draw up decrees. Read those decrees, Father. Read them for the last sixty or seventy years. They are all the *same!* Simony and incontinency. Incontinency and simony. But the traffic still goes on. Bishoprics are bought and sold, and the clergy is not clean."

"But the monks..."

"Father, you have lived all your life here at St. Pierre's. Thank God we have had a very regular community. But there are not many St. Pierre's on the continent. Cluny was a reform. It effected marvels. But today Cluny..." And the old man stopped.

"What about Cluny?" prompted Father Maurus.

"Never mind," said the abbot quietly, "but know this, that the monastic world needs something drastic, something radical, something that will shake and shatter its complacency. Robert has an idea. Maybe it's the thing. He has made me ashamed of my too ready acceptance of things as they were. We don't live the Rule to the letter, Maurus."

"Of course we don't. The letter kills...."

"Yes," said the abbot quietly as he sat back in his chair. "The letter kills—it kills the slothful, grudging, ungenerous 'old man' who lives deep in all of us. Robert believed in killing that 'old man,' Father Maurus. He has succeeded in his own case, I'm quite sure. I think he may be able to succeed in the case of others. He will have his chance at Tonnerre."

For a moment the two men sat in silence. Then the abbot looked up, squinted at Maurus quizzically and said, "You, too, are to have your chance, my son."

"What chance?" asked Maurus.

"I wish to inform you that I need a prior, and that you are the man I need."

"I?" It was a shout of incredulity.

The abbot chuckled. "Yes, you."

"But my sharp tongue..."

"It can be curbed."

"Thirty years of vigorous effort haven't done it."

"Keep on trying," smiled the abbot. "Go now and see Father Robert. He will have some matters to explain to you."

Father Maurus left the abbot's room in dismay. He passed several monks in the cloister without so much as a nod: He had not seen them. He found Robert seated at his desk with his hands idle. The two men looked at one another. Then Robert smiled. "Hello, Father Prior. Won't you come in and sit down?"

"So you know?"

"Yes, I know. And now you know. Yours is a responsible position, Maurus. Dom Bernard is old. You will have to be abbot in everything but name."

"Never mind me; think of yourself," said Maurus as he rapidly crossed the room and drew a chair close to the prior's desk. "Tell me, are you going to attempt the reform?"

Robert sobered. His eyes were fixed on the crucifix before him. After what seemed a very long time he asked, "Do you think conscience would allow of anything else?"

"Oh, bother conscience," snapped Maurus with an impatient flick of the hand. "What does common sense say?"

Robert drummed on the desk a moment, then turning to his friend he said, "Is it that you simply refuse to understand, Maurus? For over thirty years you have known what has burned in my soul. Now is my chance. I will have my own monastery, my own men. What can I do but try to make them burn as I have burned and am still burning? Would I be loyal to Christ, would I be true to myself, if I did anything else? I have told you of the Host in my heart...."

"Yes, yes, I know," interrupted Maurus. "But you have conformed for thirty years. It has sanctified you. Why now attempt a reform that is liable to upset the whole tenor of your life, to say nothing of the lives of those around you? It's too great a gamble, Robert. Don't do it."

Robert lifted the crucifix in his hands, looked at his friend, and asked, "Hasn't it ever struck you, Maurus, that the soldiers were not the only gamblers on Golgotha? They shook dice beneath the cross. They gambled for the robe of the God Man. But the greatest gambler hung on the cross! Jesus flung his life away, had his heart pierced, on the long chance that he might win the hearts of men. Don't say that he has lost."

Silence again held the two friends. As he laid the crucifix back on the desk, Robert said, "There is a gap to be filled, Maurus. I am convinced that God's wrath must be greatly kindled against the people. Look at the papacy. The Chair of Peter has been the pawn of politicians ever since you and I came here. First it was the Count of Tusculum who shifted it to whomsoever he would. Now it is the Emperor of Germany. That should not be. That gives us anti-popes. That sets the people wandering like lost sheep."

"I know. But look at the cloisters. Think of the saints at Cluny and among the Camaldolese.

"Yes, think of them. In your new office,

Maurus, you will come in closer contact with the men of this monastery and the men of other monasteries. You'll soon see that there is a gap. I'm going to try to fill it."

When Maurus made no further comment Robert said, "I wish you were coming with me. I'm going to need a staunch friend; and that you certainly have been."

"And still am," asserted Maurus vigorously.

"Then, since you can't come physically, accompany me with your prayers. I'm not closing my eyes to what lies ahead, Maurus. It is not going to be easy. But my hopes are high, for it's God's work, after all. He'll have to see it through. Pray that I don't make life's only mistake."

Chapter Six

Parallel Lines Never Meet

Robert sat struggling to capture a very tantalizing but very elusive memory. He was trying to recall what the look in his prior's eyes reminded him of. For four months now he had passed through this same teasing experience daily. Every time Father Antoine left his room Robert would strain after that memory which ever remained just out of reach. He was striving hard to like this middle-aged, broad-shouldered man with the short neck and the head that jutted out from his shoulders like the head of a duck.

He had found him acting as prior when he came to Tonnerre. He had left him at the post. The man was capable enough. But Robert did not like his too easy acquiescence, his smiling obsequiousness, and his over-facile tongue. He had often studied those wide-set, small eyes that looked at him from above a veritable beak of a nose and from below a narrow forehead that was split in the center by an arrowhead of thin, black hair. It was the look in those eyes that puzzled him. It stirred something in his memory that simply would not come out beyond the veils and be seen in the clear light of the intellect. Four months of effort had yielded nothing. The look was still there. The stirring of the memory was still there. And the elusiveness was still there. Robert shrugged his shoulders, snorted derisively at himself, and put the prior out of his mind.

Four full months had elapsed since the morning he left St. Pierre's with tears in his heart. He felt as if he were uprooting his life that morning. The first wrench had come as he embraced Father Maurus. Robert was surprised at the depth of his love for his monastery.

But Tonnerre did much to make him forget, for it welcomed him warmly. The sincerity of that welcome had thrilled the young abbot and set his secret hopes soaring. With men as cordial as this, he thought, he could do much. Of his hopes he said nothing as yet. He wanted to know his men, and he wanted his men to know him before he told them what had been the rapture and the anguish of his soul since the day he said, "I vow...."

He found St. Michael's little different from St. Pierre's. The community was of the same size, and there was much about the ground plan of the monastic buildings to make him feel at home. He had spent a few weeks examining the property. He found the granges in excellent order, the buildings in good repair, and the serfs contented and industrious. He was very well pleased with the condition of the cattle and the appearance of the soil. Everything bespoke the diligence and the ability of the cellarer. He smiled to himself as he said that it would not take a great amount of talent or intelligence to be abbatial feudal lord of this domain. The cellarer would allow him to be the figurehead.

The community, of course, absorbed him. His years as prior had been excellent preparation for his present position. He had little trouble roughly classifying his community. As usual, he found the very fervent, the fairly fervent, and the not so fervent. But he had not been a month at Tonnerre before he resolutely faced the fact that, while his monks were regular, their regularity was mechanical. They answered bells promptly. Every stall was occupied at the Night Office. But while there was good volume to the chant that rose and re-echoed in the dark silence, Robert detected little fervor. Soon he accepted the truth that the community of Tonnerre was rutted. It was easy-going. It was ordinary.

But Robert was not discouraged. He found

most of the monks good-natured. On that he could build. As he now sat at his desk he determined to make his first attempt at stirring them to greater generosity on the next day—the Feast of Sts. Peter and Paul. Under the patronage of these men who had given all, he would place his appeal.

After Mass, the community assembled in the chapter room. Robert was surprised to find his pulse rapid. He was hoping, by his effectiveness as a speaker, to startle them out of their apathy. That must be the first step in his program. He took as his text the words, "Let us make God forget." "Let us make God forget the world that is forgetting him," he said, and then painted for them a vivid panorama of the world in 1065.

He told them of the gluttony that had gripped men and made them mad with a lust for power, for wealth, for personal pleasure. He used only broad, bold strokes without any shading. He omitted nothing from the indulgence of the hierarchy to the petty greed of the serfs. He called it a "God-oblivious" world, and begged his monks to make God forget its forgetfulness.

When he had their full attention, he changed his tone and told them of the light that had flooded his mind ever since he was a novice, showing him the discrepancy between the written Rule and the Rule that was observed. He told them of the fire that flamed in his soul to live the monastic life a more generous way, the way of being gallant to God by living a stricter observance. Then he proposed his practices. There was to be stricter silence just to make God forget. There was to be greater solitude just to make God forget. There was to be closer adherence to the text of the Rule governing food, and all was to be done just to make God forget.

The ardor and enthusiasm of the moment did not distract Robert from his audience. He was watching their reactions to his every word. He saw Father Jean-Marie, the very talkative guest-master, look uncomfortable when he spoke of silence. He noted that Father George, the procurator, did not like the appeal for greater solitude. There were quite a few who shifted about uneasily when he mentioned food. But on the whole he thought they were taking his talk very well.

As soon as Robert had left the room, one of the oldest of the fathers turned to his companion and said, "When God wants a big man he makes him big. We've got an abbot at last! Big physically. Big mentally. Big spiritually. That man's heart is as big as himself; and you must admit he's no pygmy. As for his soul...! Yes, we've got an abbot."

The other shook his head and said, "We've got a volcano; and it's far from extinct!"

That same day Father Antoine came after midafternoon and was actually effusive. He told

his abbot how moved all had been by the address. But as he went on, Robert noted that all
the enthusiasm and admiration was for the rhet-
oric. Nothing was said of the reform.

He began to doubt. Within a week that
doubt had changed to opinion. Before the month
was out that opinion gave way to certainty. There
was no improvement in silence. The solitude was
violated as often as ever. And there were noisy
murmurs about the quantity and quality of the
wine at table. Robert was disappointed, but he
refused to become discouraged.

Six months later he made another appeal. It
was New Year's Day. He took as his text, "Let us
make God remember." Fundamentally it was the
same address that he had given last June. He
merely twisted the concept of making God forget
the world to making God remember his mercies.
The same panorama was presented, but the
highlights this time were on the need the world
had of grace. He then insisted that the two shafts
certain to pierce the clouds and bring down a rain
of grace were the shafts of prayer and penance.
He pleaded for more heart and head in choir,
even if it meant less voice. "That will make God
remember," he said. He asked them to be satisfied with the clothing that became poor men,
and rest content with the food St. Benedict prescribed. He ended each appeal with the refrain,
"That will make God remember."

When a number shifted their feet in evident

opposition, Robert paused. "Men of God," he thundered, "I am introducing nothing new. I am only asking you to do away with what should never have been introduced." This change of attack won instant silence. "Mitigations are not for men. At least," went on the abbot, "not for men who are anxious to be gallant to God, so anxious that they have voluntarily vowed their lives away that they might live to him alone. Let me tell you that mitigations in food, in clothing, in manual labor ill become those who have shaved their heads so that the whole world may recognize them as slaves of Jesus Christ."

Despite the flush on his face the abbot left the room chilled that New Year's morning. He never believed men could be so cold. Father Antoine came as usual, full of compliments. Robert watched him closely, and it was on this day that he captured his elusive memory. He tried to dismiss it, but it remained. When the prior left Robert said, "So that was it all the time, eh? The rat I saw at the famine time back in 1033. He had the same shy, nervous, sinister look in his tiny, greedy eyes."

Late that afternoon he sent for Father Charles, a short, stocky, gray-haired monk, whose large, wide-set eyes were windows to a deep, generous soul. Robert felt he could trust this man's judgment and his tongue—a thing he was beginning to doubt about his prior.

Father Charles assured him that there were

many in the community who were anxious to follow his lead; that the complaints he heard were nothing but human nature's instinctive reactions. He then reminded Robert that he had to undermine the citadel of long-established custom, and that such undermining would take both time and labor. The abbot went to bed that night hopeful again.

Before the winds of March had blown, however, those hopes had been rudely shaken. Robert suspected that someone was talking openly. There was too much uniformity to the objections raised for them to be the products of different individuals. From his prior he could learn nothing definite. The man was cleverly evasive. The abbot could only wait and watch. As the weeks mounted he noted that more and more often men were saying, "Father Antoine says this," and "Father Antoine thinks that," and "Father Prior is of the opinion...."

His heart lifted when he found Father Charles and a few of similar sincerity becoming more and more observant. But it soon fell when it became all too evident that they were the few, and that there was no change among the vast majority. Complaints continued about the food and drink, and demands were even made for the usual high quality of clothing.

He prayed earnestly those days and held long consultations with his crucifix. He began to believe that he had been too fiery, too precipitate.

He had pleaded too soon, and pleaded too vehe-mently. Perhaps he had asked too much at one time. Maybe he could achieve his end by more gradual steps. He would concentrate on one thing. Ask that, and let the others go for a time.

His plan seemed practical. So on March twenty-first, the Feast of St. Benedict, he stole a page from old Abbot Bernard, and gave his monks a talk in which "What would Benedict say?" echoed and re-echoed. But Robert differed from Bernard inasmuch as he gave Benedict's answers by reading different chapters of the Rule. It was a talk that was logically irrefutable, but psychologically unpalatable. When Robert came to the matter of manual labor, the one point he intended to stress, and asked, "What would Benedict say?" there was a restless stirring all over the chapter room. When he went on with "This is what Benedict said," and began to read the Rule, a distinct hiss was heard followed by the clearly audible whispers, "Not today! That's out of date!"

His old impetuosity flared. "Let us truly seek God," he cried, only to hear, "We do!" an-grily whispered from both sides of the room. Robert looked down the two lengthy rows of men. A few were as shocked as himself, but most had hard, set faces, and many were openly mur-muring. Robert found himself struggling with a temptation to lash these men mercilessly for their cowardice. To hold himself in check he cried out in the words of the Rule, "Then they are truly monks when they live by the labor of their hands as did our fathers and the apostles."

It was at this point that Father Henri, an irritable individual, stood up and called, "Read the next sentence! Read the next sentence!" When Robert stared at him, he continued, "It runs: 'Let all things be done with *moderation.*'"

Robert's eyes fell to the text of the Rule. The man was right. That was the next sentence. But he had omitted the last few words: "*propter pusillanimes*—for the sake of the weak." Robert's whole being craved to cry that phrase aloud, to shout it more vehemently and more scornfully than had his objector. That was the answer to the whole situation! These men were weak. But they were strong in their weakness; they were stubborn. This morning they were openly antagonistic. Robert arose. He knew that if he stayed another moment he would deliver a diatribe. The murmurs gradually died away; but the hostile looks remained. Raising his right hand in blessing the young abbot said, "*Pax!* Peace be to you!" and walked from the room with all the majesty and dignity of a king. At that moment externally he was the most self-contained and controlled man in the assembly, but inwardly he was seething with passion and his heart was sick and very, very sore.

It lacked an hour to Mass time when Father Antoine knocked on the abbot's door. In his hands was the text of the Rule. He bowed and smiled to Robert, his eyes cunning and sinister. "If you have a few moments, Reverend Father, I would like to propose a few questions."

Robert gestured toward a chair, but the prior said, "I'll stand, Reverend Father." He waited. "Was St. Benedict ironical or rhetorical when he wrote his Rule, Reverend Father? Or did he write his mind sincerely?"

Robert glanced down at his desk. His eyes met the crucifix. The sight steadied him. "I think that question answers itself, Father," he said quietly.

"I think so, too," said the prior, and his lips parted in a shallow smile. Holding out the text of the Rule he went on, "Then when he writes in the prologue that he is 'about to establish a school of the service of God, in which we hope we will ordain nothing rigorous or burdensome' he really meant it? His words are to be taken literally, are they not? Surely, the boy who fled from the schools of Rome *'scienter nescius,'* as his biographer quaintly phrases it, was not being rhetorical."

Robert gripped himself inwardly, for he felt his anger rising. "He is to be taken literally, Father."

The prior laid the text of the Rule down on the desk. "In fact, that is the keynote of his whole Rule, isn't it, Reverend Father? 'Nothing harsh. Nothing burdensome.' You know when we compare Benedict's Rule with the records of the monks of Egypt, or even with the Rules practiced in Europe in his day, we find that Benedict's is the easiest of all Rules."

"I think that is historically true, Father," said Robert, digging his nails into his palms to hold his calm. "What follows?"

Antoine's lips were still smiling, but the film lifted from his eyes for a second as he said, "Doesn't it follow that St. Benedict's Rule is not a penitential Rule? That his spirit is one of moderation?" Robert said nothing. The prior went on, "Doesn't it seem significant that nowhere in his Rule does the saint use the word 'mortification'?"

"Does he use the word 'mitigation'?" burst Robert. He felt it was a mistake the moment he had spoken it. He should not enter into argument with this man. His heart was too sore, too aflame. The very sight of Antoine stirred the deepest resentment within him. He had his eyes on the crucifix, but he did not miss the confident way the prior's hands went out toward the text of the Rule.

"Chapter forty," said Antoine silkily, "runs: 'Though we read that wine is not for monks at all, yet as monks in our day cannot be persuaded of this, let us at least use it sparingly.' That, I think, most men would call a mitigation, Reverend Father."

"Mitigation?" Robert exclaimed. "Why that's a condemnation."

But Antoine paid no heed; he laid the text before the abbot, placed his finger on chapter forty-nine and said, "Now, Reverend Father, here is another appeal to monastic tradition regarding austerity of life. It runs: 'Though we read that the monk's life should at all times have the lenten observance...' That's the appeal, isn't it, Father?" Robert noted the omission of "Reverend" but simply nodded. "Well, here is the deliberate setting aside of that tradition by mitigation. The saint goes on: '...yet as few have this courage, we urge them in these days of Lent to wash away the negligences of other times.' Now, that's explicit and implicit enough for anyone. Why, even in the matter of the Office, Benedict was moderate. Benedict was a very human saint, Reverend Father," said the confident prior as he turned the text back to chapter eighteen.

"I really think that will do, Father," said Robert pointedly.

"I only wanted to show that, while Benedict recognized the fact that the old Fathers of the Desert recited the *entire* psalter every day, he deliberately set that practice aside, and would have his monks say it only once a *week*. Clearly a mitigation. Clearly a moderation. Clearly a human bit of legislation. You see, Father Abbot, we here at Tonnerre are quite convinced that Benedict of Nursia was not a developer. He was a revolutionizer. He didn't take Eastern asceticism and adapt it to the West. He struck out for himself on entirely different lines. He eliminated great austerity; introduced moderation; and made his asceticism consist in the submerging of individuality, the sinking of the individual in the common life."

Robert moved the text to one side and fastened his eyes on the crucifix. This man was trying his patience more than it had been tried since coming to Tonnerre. He hoped the tension did not show on his exterior; inwardly he felt tighter than a bow-string. Antoine's voice seemed to come to him from a distance as he continued, "We here at St. Michael's also know that Benedict of Aniane considered the Rule of the great Patriarch of the West as a Rule fit only for beginners, for babies in the way of God. So, my good abbot, we have been wondering to whom you were referring this morning when you kept asking, 'What would Benedict say?' Many are of the opinion that it must have been to Benedict of Aniane."

Robert arose. He towered over his prior. The latter gathered up the text of the Rule and while closing it looked expectantly at his abbot. Robert thought he detected a flash of defiance in those eyes, but he was so deeply stirred he did not trust his judgment. "I think we had better prepare for Mass, Father," he said very quietly. There was not the slightest tremor in his voice. His look was level. Calm marked his whole bearing. But inwardly he was burning.

Father Antoine looked at him from those shifty, little eyes of his. He was angry to find his giant abbot so composed. "But, Reverend Father," he cried in a voice that had taken on an edge, "you haven't answered any of my questions. We here at Tonnerre..."

"I happen to be one of you *here at Tonnerre*," broke in Robert sharply. "By the grace of God I am abbot at Tonnerre. What means this distinction?" And his voice was as sharp as a sword.

Had Antoine known Robert as Father Maurus did, he would have recognized the danger signal. But he had not Father Maurus' power of perception. Antoine had never studied men to see what was in them, but only to see what he could get out of them. He had been sorely disappointed at Robert's election. He had expected to succeed Hunault. The community's present opposition to Robert was Antoine's opportunity. He had decided to make the most of it. He had fostered discontent by sly innuendoes and subtle asides. He felt his position was now safe enough to allow him to unmask. He became openly defiant. "The distinction means that you are abbot *at* Tonnerre but not *of* Tonnerre. The distinction means that we want no reform, for we need none. The distinction means that what you call 'mitigations,' we call 'Rule.'" Robert's face was as if cut from stone. "You," cried Antoine

furiously, "are not a Benedictine. You are a *rebel!* "
There was a rustle of a robe, the slam of a door,
and the abbot was alone.

With the slam of that door something broke
within Robert. He flung himself back into his
chair, seized paper and stylus, bent over his desk
and muttered, "We'll see who's abbot *at* Tonnerre
and *of* Tonnerre!" Then with rapid hand he
wrote:

Prior—Father Charles
Subprior—Father Pachomius
Guest-Master—Father Corentine
Procurator—Father Lambert

He looked at the list. "These men will obey.
These men are loyal." Then he wrote again.
There was a savage thrust to his stylus every time
he dipped it in ink. He wrote: Excommunicated—Fathers Antoine, Henri, Idesbald. "That
will keep them quiet for a while," he said aloud.
Then he paused as he mentally ran his eyes
down the list of the community. He was seeking
malcontents for punishment. The murmurers he
would silence by a public penance. More names
darkened the paper before him. Again and again
he muttered fiercely, "We'll see who's abbot *at*
Tonnerre and *of* Tonnerre!"

Suddenly three strokes of the large bell
broke in on his writing. "Mass," he said. "I must
go. I'll finish this after dinner."

As he neared the door of the church he

heard a single voice leading the chant. It was clear and confident, almost contemptuously confident. Robert recognized it. It was the voice of his prior. The man was doing his singing as he did everything when he had an audience— magnificently. The abbot's lips pressed one another angrily. "You're efficient, Antoine, but your days of efficiency are over."

At the beginning of Mass Robert's anger was a deadly, cold, seemingly implacable thing, but at the offertory he became more attentive to the sacrifice. Father Joseph, the master of novices, was celebrant. Robert thought of his own master of novices, and from out of nowhere came the whisper of Father William's words: "Study the mildness of Christ, son." Robert started. It was all of thirty-three years since he first heard those words. And all those three and thirty years he had labored to understand and imitate that mildness. And yet, here he was aflame with anger. He secretly struck his breast. Before the Mass was ended, Robert was torn between the urge to righteous indignation and the urge to self-immolation.

That afternoon he spent at his desk. Before him was his crucifix and the sheet of paper he had used that morning. For a long time his eyes traveled from one to the other. Then with a mighty effort he brought himself to a dispassionate review of the fourteen months he had been at Tonnerre. Every effort he had made was examined coldly. He weighed the reactions of the community both as individuals and as a unit. He was painstaking in his review and as objectively honest as it is possible for a person to be. Before the sun set, the results were before him clearly. He pushed the paper aside and said, "My father was a prophet. Parallel lines do not meet. I am on one level, my community on another."

He arose then and began to pace the room. The conclusion was evident but what was he to do? There had been open antagonism in chapter. His prior had been defiant and insulting in private. There was only one thing to do: force the community to come up higher! He stood there staring at the sheet and the names he had written. His hands trembled. "What of it?" he thought. "Fire must be met with fire." Then his eyes fell on the crucifix and the old battle began anew: "Mild as Christ? Mild as Christ? Mild as Christ?"

The question stopped him. Robert crushed the paper in his hands angrily, and began to pace the room again. He could not bring himself to accept this mutiny. He must show himself stronger than the community. Back and forth, back and forth he paced, while his thoughts kept step with his turnings. First the crucifix, then the paper. His emotions swung from anger to mildness and back to anger again.

As the evening wore on, the agony grew. With the dusk it seemed that his mind came to a standstill. He could not think. He could not plan. He could not even pray. Justice and mercy, propriety and mildness, were the only words that would come to him. The very monotony of their rhythm almost drove him mad. In a sort of a frenzy he threw himself on his knees and seized his crucifix in angry hands. "Jesus!" he breathed. Again he said it, "Jesus!" Then for the long hours of the night the only word he said was "Jesus!"

With the bell for the night office his decision came. He told himself that it takes more strength to be mild than to be bold; that it demands more real manhood to dominate self than to domineer over others; that it calls for greater gallantry to be meek and mild like the Christ than to be a blustering commander of men. He resolved to humiliate himself rather than his monks. It was a weary and emotionally exhausted abbot who attended the vigils that morning.

The community grew nervous as day succeeded day and no reference was made to the outbreak in chapter. Robert sensed it and realized that silence was his most potent weapon at the moment. There were no apologies, no reactions, but the uneasiness grew. Robert allowed the Easter season to come on before he acted. Then one morning he opened the text of the Rule to the second chapter and read: "Let the abbot know that any lack of profit which the Master shall find in his flock, will be laid to the fault of the shepherd." After that brief passage he looked at his community for a tense moment before saying, "Since I am preparing my judgment here at Tonnerre, and since you are writing my final sentence, I must *command* a more literal observance of the Holy Rule from this day out. Conscience permits no other course."

It was Robert's final effort to arouse Tonnerre. The command was received in silence, but more than one pair of eyes sought out Father Antoine. Robert noted it and knew that the crisis had come.

Two weeks later Father Charles knocked on his door. When Robert admitted him he found tears brimming in the old monk's eyes. "What is it, Father?" he asked kindly.

"I was wrong, Father Abbot. I was wrong. I told you once that it was only a matter of patience and time, that the community wanted to be more generous; that it really longed for a stricter observance. I was very wrong. I must have judged them from myself. They do not want to reform." The old man's heart was aching.

Robert laid a grateful hand on his arm, smiled and said, "I know it, Father. But we will give them a little more time. You pray for them and for me."

"But, Reverend Father, you're right and they are wrong."

"Not wrong, Father Charles—just rutted in convention. We will continue our effort to lift them out of that rut. Pray for our success."

For six full months Robert continued that effort, exhausting his ingenuity in plans and stratagems. He pleaded with some; he punished others. Some he scolded; others he cajoled. But the end of the time he had set himself found him again pacing the floor in the dark of the night with the only word on his lips: "Jesus!"

The plan that had suggested itself before came back to him. Why not remove the prior? Why not segregate the malcontents? Why not staff the monastery with the few who wanted to obey and drive the others to conformity? It was more appealing than ever. Robert suddenly felt that he had the fire to drive them. But there he stopped. That would be unworthy of himself, of his monks and his God. God did not want snarling obedience. That belonged to brute beasts under the lash, not to men who had vowed their lives to God. But again and again the temptation came back. Finally the crucifix called to him and before morning he had reached the only conclusion.

The next day he resigned! It was the lesson he had learned from the outstretched arms on the cross. And just as Christ had offered his supreme humiliation as a plea for the salvation of humankind, so Robert now offered his humiliation with all its bitterness as a plea for the dawn of a day when men would follow where he was so anxious to lead.

Riding home he reviewed and rationalized

the whole situation. He argued that people cannot be *dragooned* into sanctity. That was the root of the whole difficulty. As a monk in the ranks, he could follow the interpretation of the abbot over him and know peace of soul; but as abbot the responsibility for the correct interpretation of the Rule fell on his shoulders. After two years he saw that he could not shrug those shoulders. So he did the prudent, practical and humble thing for the peace of his soul; the peace of the community under him, and the peace of the immediate monastic world around him. Rather than give up his ideals, he gave up his abbacy. He called it the humble thing; but there were those who called it heroic!

But even the consolation of having done the Christlike thing did not lift his heart. As he neared St. Pierre's, it felt leaden. For it seemed that his beautiful bubble had burst; that his first great opportunity had ended in dismal failure. He drew his cloak around him more tightly as a breeze came off the hill. The early night air was cold; so was his soul. But suddenly he caught sight of a lone star in the wide white sky. With its sparkle there came to him the echo of his father's words "Burn on! Burn on until you burn out!" He straightened in his saddle, put spurs to his horse and lifting a hand in salute to the star cried, "I will!"

Chapter Seven

"Row, Sailor, Row!"

The old abbot gazed with admiration at the garden in front of his room. The sun glistening on the dewy grass and flowers reminded him of a jewelled landscape of the Apocalypse. Father Maurus put an end to his musing by entering after a sharp knock. "Come in," said the abbot. "Your face is not much like the face of nature this morning, Father Prior. You should steal dewdrops from the night to brighten your morning."

"I often wish there was no morning to my night," answered the prior sourly. "What is this I hear about Father Robert? Are you sending him away again?"

"Again?" echoed the abbot. "Did I ever send him away before?"

"Didn't you send him to Tonnerre?"

"Of course not," said the abbot. "He was elected by St. Michael's community, just as he has been elected by the community of St. Ayoul."

"Why couldn't they elect one of their own?" frowned the prior.

"For the same reason St. Michael's couldn't. They think Robert better than anyone they have. And," added the abbot, "I don't think they are greatly mistaken, do you?"

"You know what I think of Robert," Maurus said. "You know what I have thought of him for the last forty years. But," and an anxious look came over the prior's face, "aren't you afraid?"

"Of what?"

"Of Robert's spirit. He's sure to try his reform again," argued the prior, "and of course it will fail. Oh, I know he came back and admitted his defeat like a man. But even though it's seven years since he's returned, I can still see at times that he has not forgotten."

"You have good eyes, Father Maurus," was the only comment that came from the abbot. The prior noted the tremble in the old man's wax-like hands as they lay in his lap. Both men were momentarily lost in reverie. A knock aroused them. "Come in!" called the abbot. "Ah!" he exclaimed as the door opened, "it is you, my good son, Robert. Come in and cheer an old man's heart. And perhaps you can also chase the gloom from the sour face of our very excellent prior."

Maurus snorted as he drew two chairs nearer the abbot's desk. "We were just speaking of the opportunity that is yours at St. Ayoul's," said Dom Bernard.

"Opportunity for heartbreak," growled Father Maurus.

"How cheerful!" said Robert as he studied the face of his friend. "And what were you saying, Reverend Father?"

"Well," said the old man smilingly, "I wasn't allowed to say very much. Our prior here did most of the talking. He accused me of sending you to torture or some such thing. But that doesn't matter. What we want to know is what *you* think of the opportunity."

Robert looked from the abbot to the prior and back again before he said, "I'm very grateful for it. But I must also be honest. I'm fifty-five years old." Then after a slight pause he smiled and said, "I know both of you are wondering if I will repeat my performance at Tonnerre."

"No," said the abbot musingly, "not exactly. I think myself and our grouchy prior were really wondering if St. Ayoul's will repeat the performance of Tonnerre. We both knew you would try...."

"But what's the use?" broke in Maurus. "Didn't Tonnerre teach you anything? Why can't you go on as you've been going these past seven years? You didn't attempt any reform here. You conformed. And you didn't lose any merit by it;

neither did God lose any glory. Ah, you'll never learn," he concluded disgustedly. "Think of it— forty years with one idea!"

Abbot Bernard touched the aroused Maurus gently on the knee, "Forty is a mystical number, Father Prior. Remember your Scripture: forty years, forty days, forty nights. Perhaps our Robert is approaching his Promised Land."

"Who ever promised him any?"

Robert smiled but said nothing. Abbot Bernard fingered his crucifix. Maurus turned and looked out the window angrily. Just before the silence became oppressive, Robert straightened in his chair, ran his tongue across dry lips and said, "Look, my Fathers, don't you think I have seen how much easier it would be to follow the general trend of the times? Don't you realize that Tonnerre showed me clearly just how deeply the monks of the day are rutted?"

No answer came from either of the men facing him. Robert's voice lowered as he went on. "To have a whole community rise up and reject a man's ideal before his very face sobers him. You can be sure that I have prayed and thought. Again and again I have asked myself what I would do were I given another chance. My Fathers, the answer has always been the same. There it is!" and his hand pointed to the crucifix on Dom Bernard's desk.

A new and unaccustomed tenderness crept into Robert's tone as he concluded, "Christ did not come down from his cross. Why should I shrink from shouldering mine?"

"Because it's of your own making," snapped Maurus. "What justification have you for forcing your subjective interpretation of the Rule on any community? Why can't you take the current opinion?"

"Perhaps because it is current, and only an opinion," answered Robert. "If Christ fought one thing in his day, it was current opinion."

"You're right," came the fiery reply from the prior. "And if I mistake not, the current opinion he excoriated was the one of observing the letter of the law while neglecting its spirit."

Robert's head shook from side to side quite wearily. "Maurus, how many times do I have to insist that I am going back to the letter only to recapture the true spirit?"

"But why go hunting for something you already possess? Haven't you been living the true spirit for forty years?"

Robert looked at the old abbot and shrugged his shoulders helplessly. The old man smiled at his evident distress. Maurus caught the interchange. Then bending forward he included both in his address. "Let me ask you two this one question: Is it our duty to do today just exactly what our forefathers did in their day, or to do just exactly what our forefathers would do if they were living in our day?" Both abbots pondered a moment. Maurus went on, "In other words, are

we to be guided by their practices or their principles? That's the point at issue in this whole
affair, and nothing else."

Slowly Dom Bernard nodded affirmatively.
Maurus proceeded, "I admit that we are far from
Benedict's primitive practices, but I stoutly main-
tain that we are following every one of his prin-
ciples. And that," he concluded, "is exactly what
Benedict would do in this year of grace, 1073."

"I'll call it year of disgrace if you keep arguing that way," said Robert. Then lifting the edge
of his scapular toward the prior he said, "Feel
that." Maurus rubbed it between his thumb and
index finger. "Need any knight, lord or duke be
ashamed of such material?" Maurus did not answer. "Do I live by the labor of my own hands or
by that of the hands of others?" Still Maurus did
not answer. "I've heard some people insist that
our Lord beatified poverty of spirit, not actual
poverty," said Robert tersely, "but in all my fifty-
five years of life I have learned no surer, safer,
speedier way of arriving at that poverty of spirit
than by being actually poor. Reverend Father,
isn't the fundamental weakness in the monastic
world today its lack of true poverty?"

"Bah!" snorted Maurus.

"Not so fast, Maurus. Not quite so fast.
You've told me yourself that the present-day
monk hasn't enough to do. Liturgical functions
crowd his day. He has few interests. Mentally he
goes to seed. Physically he gets fat and lazy.

Here's the cure: let the monastery be actually poor, as well as poor in spirit, and your monk will not be mooning away his life."

The aged Bernard had listened most attentively. "There is just one thing that worries me, my good Robert. Father Maurus gave it to me this morning. It is this. Can you, my son, can you sustain another failure?"

Robert reached across the desk and laid his hand on Dom Bernard's crucifix. "May I?" he asked as he lifted it. The abbot bowed. "Tonnerre put me on my knees before this crucified King. It put me there crying as one wounded, pleading as one distraught, begging as one beside himself. And there on my knees I learned the lesson of the cross. Christianity is *not* a cult of success!"

No one spoke for a moment. "Do you now see why I have no fear of failure?" Robert's eyes were still fastened on the crucifix. "For me there can be no such thing."

Dom Bernard arose. "With that spirit, my son," he said, "there can be no failure for you in any sense...."

Not four months later, when autumn was holding high carnival before the long white fast of winter, St. Pierre's prior was hastily summoned to the gate by a breathless porter. Father Maurus did not like the summons at all. He was on the point of scolding the porter for such an intrusion but on hearing the man's message, he hurriedly left the room. Impatience was evident in the very flutter of his scapular as he strode down the avenue of trees that led to the gate. He brushed through the porter's lodge and flung open the outer door. Throwing both arms wide in a gesture of welcome, he cried, "Robert!"

The chestnut mare with the blaze of white on her forehead pranced uneasily. Robert smiled down from the saddle. "I have a mettlesome mount, Maurus, but she isn't half as spirited as her rider. I can't stay long, but you must read this." He drew a scroll from beneath his belt and handed it to the prior.

Maurus unrolled the letter hurriedly. It was from Rome. Then his eyes opened in wonder. Pope Alexander II was commanding Robert of St. Ayoul's to take charge of the hermits at Colan. The message was brief. It ended with a blessing. But it left Maurus bewildered.

"Just a little secret I kept from you for years, Maurus," said Robert as he rerolled the document and tucked it beneath his scapular. "When I was at Tonnerre, these men asked me to guide them. I was willing, but the community at Tonnerre refused to let me go."

"Get off that horse," Maurus commanded. "Get off that horse and spend the day with me."

"Can't," came the short reply as the mare sidestepped impatiently. "I must cover ten more leagues before nightfall. Sorry Abbot Bernard is away. I wanted to see both of you before I rode on."

Seeing that his friend was in earnest, Maurus wheeled about and called to the porter "Have a horse saddled at once. I would ride with the abbot."

Ten minutes later the two monks had left the city of Troyes behind them and were entering a shady stretch of wood. Bit by bit Maurus drew the story from his friend. In 1065, just when the clash between Robert and the men at Tonnerre was at its height, a lone hermit from Colan had come to the monastery begging Robert to lead him and his companions on the way to God. The young abbot had considered him a messenger sent by heaven to end the impasse between himself and his community. But as he had been voted into office, Robert would have to be voted out. So sure was he of the outcome of the balloting that he had the hermit remain at Tonnerre, confident that he would be accompanying him back to Colan. But the next morning he learned much about the contrariness that lies deep in the sons of Adam, for the men who would not receive his reform rejected the opportunity to be rid of him. The vote was almost unanimous against his going to Colan.

When Maurus asked why he had kept this matter secret these past seven years, Robert said he was afraid old Abbot Bernard would get in touch with the hermits and send him on to them.

Then it would look as if he had resigned from Tonnerre only to go to Colan. He had resolved to place the matter entirely in the hands of God. At this point Maurus turned to his companion and said, "Has no one ever told you the advice of the captain to the man in the boat: 'Trust in God, sailor, but *row* for shore'? If you had pulled an oar back in 1065, you would have saved yourself and these hermits seven and a half years."

"Yes, and I would have spent the rest of my life wondering whether I was doing my own will or the will of God," replied Robert. "Now there can be no doubt."

As they neared the edge of the wood and caught sight of the sun-drenched, square stones of the old Roman road, Maurus reined in his steed and told Robert that they could water their horses at a brook that was a little to their left. The abbot dismounted and led his mare after the prior's dappled-gray mount. As the two horses stood with their forefeet in the swirling waters drinking noisily from the stream, Maurus frowned angrily and said, "But the agony of seven years' waiting!"

"I have my scars, Maurus. But don't forget that he was *crucified*."

"But..."

"There are no 'buts,' Maurus," said the abbot as he examined the bit in the mare's dripping mouth. "Even though men do to us all that his enemies did to him, we can only do what he did—we must pray for their forgiveness by the only One who has a right to be offended."

Maurus was silent. He could never get anywhere with Robert once the latter began to talk about Christ. Soon they were on the road again, and the refreshed horses set the stones ringing with their trotting hoofs. Robert had little to say about St. Ayoul's. He had not been there long enough to try his reform. All his thoughts seemed focused on Colan. When Maurus learned that only seven men awaited him there, he showed his distaste. But Robert laughed away his opposition with the merry words, "Better a few good, than a multitude not so good."

By the time they reached another wood the sun was well down toward the west. Robert pulled up his mare and insisted that Maurus turn back. As it was, he pointed out, the prior would not reach Troyes before dark. Maurus resisted for a while. He had a feeling that this parting was final; the feeling had increased with every step of the way. He was loath to leave his friend. But he knew that Robert was right. At last he brought his mount alongside the mare, laid his hand on Robert's shoulder, and said, "God be with you always!"

Robert leaned out of the saddle, gave his friend the kiss of peace, and whispered, "He will abide though all else abandon." They exchanged blessings, turned their horses' heads, and rode away: one into the setting sun, the other into the green shadows of the grove. Neither looked back....

Next day Robert learned why he had not heard from these zealous hermits for so long. When the community of Tonnerre had thwarted their original plan, they had struggled along as they had been doing. But soon their unrest had grown. They needed a leader. They wanted someone to take them along the way to God. They knew such a person and resolved to obtain him. Finally they hit on the one way. One of their number went to Rome. He presented their plea to His Holiness, who listened sympathetically and finally granted them the rescript that brought Robert from St. Ayoul's. The pilgrimage to Rome and back had taken time. But now...

"Yes, now!" thought Robert. He studied the seven men, looked into the tiny cells they had constructed for themselves, inspected their small garden and then made a general survey of the immediate surroundings. He was wasting no time before getting an insight into the lives of these men. And his most thrilling discovery was that their common desire was for the Rule of St. Benedict in its purity.

Before the evening star was shining solitary in the white sky Robert was thanking God from an overflowing heart. The community was small. He considered that an advantage. They had not lived in any of the monasteries of the day. He considered this a greater advantage. They appeared perfectly docile. And that was the greatest advantage. Robert almost wept as he talked to God that night. Here there was nothing to reform; there were no customs to abolish, no mitigations to rescind. All he had to do was fulfill their desire and his own by giving them the Rule of St. Benedict in its simplicity! It seemed that the rebel had co-workers at last. His dream was coming true. He could now live the "nobler way."

Before a month had passed Robert had the community completely organized along the lines of the Rule. He even had his prior—a hermit who had especially impressed him the very first day. He was the most cheerful of the group and one of the most energetic. When the man told him his name was Alberic, Robert said, "It should have been Hilary. I like your smile, Father. Keep it ever shining."

Alberic smiled wider at that, and whispered, "Owls can only hoot; dogs can only bark; and I can only smile. A leopard can't change his spots, Reverend Father."

"No," retorted Robert, "but an abbot can change positions. From now on you're prior."

Alberic broke out into a laugh and said, "I'm here to obey."

"The first command then is to keep smiling." Alberic bowed and immediately fulfilled the first command.

Robert's early moves were significant. He remembered Maurus' charge about forcing his subjective interpretation on others, so every morning, just after their sunrise song, he gathered his little group about him and discussed the Rule. He told them just what had happened to that Rule during the centuries, and what was happening to it today. He was most honest. After his talk he invited discussion and suggestions. The result was that the Cluniac order of the day was adopted, and many of Cluny's more rigorous customs; but, to a man, the hermits begged for poverty, simplicity, solitude, and hard manual labor. It was just what Robert wanted.

He was very happy over their determination and he showed it. When he told them that they must be ready for misunderstanding, misrepresentation and even ridicule, Alberic spoke up and said, "Oh, don't worry, Reverend Father. There will be only three classes of men who will misunderstand us."

"Only three?" asked Robert.

"Only three," repeated Alberic. "The young, the middle-aged and the old!" Robert laughed and admitted that only those three classes would misunderstand.

With the months Robert's happiness mounted. It seemed that after forty years of waiting his dream was coming true. The waiting had been long; and at times he had been very lonely. But now it all seemed eminently worthwhile. He grew younger. He felt bigger, better, braver. He went to rest these nights more tired than ever before, but always less weary. And never did that paradoxical distinction strike him with more force than when he recalled bedtime at Tonnerre.

For a full year nothing troubled the abbot. The community had almost doubled. They were thirteen now. But then one morning he called Alberic. He was worried. The little community was not well. Sicknesses had been recurring and recurring lately. Alberic tried to cheer him by saying, "Nothing serious, Reverend Father. Just little shadows; that's all. But sure, shadows are proof that the sun is shining!" But Robert insisted that the sicknesses were becoming chronic, and that they must make a thorough investigation.

As the weeks went by they probed into many possibilities. The diet was watched. One meal a day, and that of vegetables, taken during Lent at sundown, and outside of Lent at about two in the afternoon, was hardly calculated to produce physical giants, men of strong sinew, hard muscle and brawn. And yet, it was universally admitted as sufficient to keep men in sound health. The two superiors soon concluded that it was not the diet alone that was causing the illnesses in the community. They then looked into the manner of work, the amount of sleep, and even into the mental habits of the ailing brethren. The frown only deepened between Robert's eyes. After more than a month of such investigation Alberic suddenly said, "We've looked behind us. We've looked about us. It's time we looked before us."

"Meaning?" prompted Robert.

"Meaning that it's not the food; it's not the lodging; it's not the labor. Nor is it the combination of fasting, watching and work. It's the *place*."

"You mean Colan?"

"I mean that Colan is unhealthy."

Robert consulted everyone he could on the matter. All agreed with Alberic. Robert wondered what he should do. Then from out of nowhere came an echo. It was Maurus' voice. It was saying, "Trust in God, sailor, but *row* for shore!" The abbot chuckled. "He's right. Presumption is not a virtue; prudence is! Piety does not consist in impracticality. We shall move." And Robert kept his resolve.

Autumn of 1075 saw the little band of thirteen lose itself in the seclusion of the forest of Molesme. Some months before, Robert had gone to Burgundy and there found a place that he considered ideal. It was far from any village; that meant solitude. It was virgin territory; that meant hard manual labor. It was healthy; that meant the Rule in all its rigor could be observed. Poverty in its every aspect, thought Robert, would find fulfillment at Molesme.

Nature was gaudy in her garb of green, gold, russet, red and burnished brown as the little band plunged deep into the wood. But these men gave her no second glance; they had eyes only for the white of winter. They well knew that after the frosts would come the snows. These men were builders.

And such builders! Trees came down. Branches were lopped off. Trunks split open. And an oratory arose. It was not much to look at. Even Alberic had to say it was picturesque rather than Romanesque. But crude as it was, it satisfied this handful of ardent men. It was their house of God. They knew it to be the very heart of their whole establishment and realized that if this did not pulse with warm love and life, the rest of the buildings would be but the tomb for a corpse. All autumn and even some of winter went in the construction of their little oratory. For themselves they constructed tiny cells from the lopped-off branches. This motley collection of small huts clustering around a rude wooden oratory was the original Abbey of Molesme.

In the snows of late December, 1075, the little church was dedicated. To Robert the evening star looked not so lonely. He now had his monastery, his men and his movement. He thanked God and swore to be gallant....

One day when the jonquils were just pushing through the remaining patches of snow, Robert came upon Alberic wrestling with an unwieldy tree stump. Without a word he bent over and helped his prior roll the stubborn thing to the side of the clearing. As they both paused for breath, the abbot smiled and pointed to the long line of shapeless trunks as he said, "That represents a winter of work."

"And this," replied Alberic gesturing toward the clearing, "represents a spring of no leisure and a summer of hard labor. But," he added with a smile, "I hope it also represents an autumn with harvests. We can't eat stumps."

"No," said Robert slowly, "we can't. But tell me, how high are your hopes for a harvest?"

"Virgin soil will not give bumper crops the first year tilled," replied Alberic honestly. "However, we'll trust God." Then with a wide grin he added, "And *row* for shore!"

"It looks to me as if you've been rowing all winter. Come, show me all you've done."

Alberic first took his abbot to a distant spot in the woods and showed him a deep ditch. This was the beginning of an aqueduct, he explained. The mountain stream yonder was to be harnessed so that the monastery and its gardens would never know drought. Then he took Robert to where a cistern was being sunk. Cold water would be welcome after the summer solstice, was Alberic's opinion. The abbot smiled. Then wheeling him around, Alberic took Robert far back in the woods and pointed to a swamp. "This is being drained," he said. "It will provide arable ground when it dries." Then looking up he pointed and said, "Those monks yonder are leveling that hill and filling the gullies round about, for one day that will be a waving field of wheat."

"Optimist!" laughed Robert.

But just then the ring of an axe broke on their ears. Robert looked his question. "That," smiled Alberic, "is my optimism! I sent two of our monks to prepare lumber for the barn we haven't got, to house the stock we do not own."

"You've got faith, Father Prior," said the abbot, "and hope!" Then more seriously and more softly he added, "And charity."

"Just at present I've got plenty of work," said Alberic. "We may not be the chivalrous knights you long for us to be, Reverend Father. We may not be as gallant to God as you think monks ought to be. But at least you must admit that we are the manual laborers you say Benedictines should be. That much of your reform is accomplished."

"I'm glad you call it 'reform,' Alberic. Others are calling it 'rebellion.'"

"Who?"

"Monks of other monasteries," said the abbot. "We are being criticized."

"Good!" cried Alberic. "That will bring us to people's attention. Our critics are doing us a favor. They are stirring up curiosity. You can prepare for postulants, Reverend Father. Two kinds: the merely curious, and the sincerely zealous. And I," he added as he moved off, "must prepare more ground for both kinds."

Alberic proved a prophet. The curious did

come. They found that for once rumor was right. The men at Molesme were living a stricter life than any other men in the land. Most of these were merely curious; so after a week or so they left. But the zealous also came and rejoiced that rumor was so right. They stayed and became grubbers of the soil in order to glorify God.

Chapter Eight

The Bishop Goes Hungry

Troyes was sparkling beneath the early morning sun; but Troyes' bishop was in as sullen a mood as if the world was gray with gloom. "Are you sure there are only twenty in the company?" he asked his vicar testily. The vicar, who could read His Excellency better than a farmer can read the skies, saw that he had no relish for the work that lay ahead of him that day. This surprised the vicar, for he knew that the trip to Burgundy would not be tiring; and he was sure that the visit to these new monks would be full of interest. They had become the talk of the town. His own curiosity to see these men who set so many tongues wagging was at fever pitch. He wondered why His Excellency's was not the same.

When he had told the bishop that only

twenty would accompany them, the latter frowned and said impatiently, "I wish I knew just what to wear." He caught the surprise in the vicar's eyes and laughed. "Don't you realize that I can make a fool of myself today? If these men are what some people say they are, I shall appear like an ecclesiastical bird of paradise or a clerical peacock if I go there with my usual trappings. If they are what most say they are, I will appear like an impostor if I haven't all my brightest regalia." He turned aside irritably. "I don't see why I should be making this investigation anyhow. I'm bishop of Champagne. Molesme is in Burgundy."

"It isn't much of a ride, Your Excellency. We'll be there shortly after noon, and back before nightfall."

"I haven't much use for monks," retorted the bishop. "If these are the pharisees many say they are, I'll suppress them without a regret. Come, I think this attire is modest enough, and yet sufficiently dignified. I'll conceal this jeweled cross," and he tucked it beneath the folds of his robe.

It was a colorful group that cantered toward Burgundy this bright morning. The vicar had told them their destination and had set the entire company chatting as to what they would find there at the much-talked-of Abbey of Molesme. Speculation was especially rife concerning what His Excellency would do. They knew him to be swift of decision and inflexible once the decision was made. Would he suppress the monastery and disperse the monks? Watching him as he rode along on his spirited milk-white mare, and noting the grim line about his eyes and mouth, most prophesied short shrift for the monks in the woods.

By noon they were nearing the stronghold of Molesme. The vicar brought his glossy black mount alongside the bishop's mare. He found the bishop a little more talkative than he had been all morning. Knowing his dislike for monks, the vicar chanced a pleasantry about what an anomaly it would be to find a monastery that was cloistered and monks who worked.

"Anomaly? It would be a blessing," said the bishop. "If monasteries were really cloistered and monks really worked, bishops would have fewer worries and the Church less scandals." After they had ridden along in silence for a stretch, the bishop continued, "No, I wouldn't object to that, Your Reverence, but reports go deeper. They speak of starvation, silence and slavery. They say this man, Robert, is a rebel who has forced his own ideas on a group of innocent men, and has them living as no one else is living. No man has a right to do such a thing. If all they say is true, Robert will come back to Troyes, and Molesme will become a forest again." One glance at his face told the vicar His Excellency meant what he said.

When they had entered the woods, the

bishop informed the vicar that his particular duty would be to look around the monastery while he, the bishop, engaged the abbot in conversation. The vicar was to learn the spirit of the monks: find out if they actually lived on vegetables, truly worked as serfs, and really followed Benedict's Rule in all its rigor.

The vicar said that he had heard that Molesme was following the hourly schedule of Cluny. "Yes, yes," said the bishop impatiently. "I follow Cluny's horarium rather closely myself. But that means nothing. Anyone can recite the Office at stipulated hours. What I want to know is, are these men monks or are they only the masks of monks. In other words, are they fanatics or are they saints of God?"

Soon the winding paths prevented horsemen from riding two abreast. The vicar's black fell behind the milk-white mare. He was grateful to the narrowness of the paths. He had seldom found His Excellency so acrid. He fell to musing on all he had heard of these men. But he soon saw that the reports had been so contrary that they canceled one another. Lost in his perplexity he did not notice that His Excellency had halted. He was brought out of his reverie by, "What's wrong with you?" from an exasperated bishop. "Were you asleep? Ride ahead there and see why those others have stopped."

The vicar hurried on to a clearing that was sown with grain. His Excellency came up, saw the field, and said, "The monastery can't be far off. Find the path that leads from this field." Just as the men wheeled their horses to skirt the field the bishop cried out, "Here comes a monk. He'll show us the way."

Among the trees on the far side of the field the bishop had spied a solitary figure walking with bent head. It was Stephen Harding. At the sound of a whinny, Stephen's head came up. He saw the horsemen and hurried around the field to learn their desire.

"This is the Bishop of Troyes," said the vicar bowing toward His Excellency. "He wishes to visit the monastery of Molesme ruled by one Father Robert. Can you show us the way?"

The monk came forward and kissed the bishop's ring. He said that, as a member of the community, he would deem it a privilege to be allowed to lead His Excellency to the monastery. As Stephen stroked the mare's nose and expertly took hold of her bridle, the bishop marveled at the courtesy and culture of this young monk. Assuredly someone had erred. This was no frenzied fanatic.

The path from the field was well beaten, but very narrow. Suddenly it ended and the bishop found himself looking upon the rough wooden oratory and its cluster of misshapen huts. His antipathy returned with greater vigor. This was worse than he had expected. This was not poverty; it was destitution. Stephen led them to the church. While the party was dismounting, the bishop grudgingly admitted to his vicar that there was an air of silence and solitude about the place that bespoke recollection. In the meantime, Stephen had beckoned to a monk who had been at prayer and sent him to Robert with the news that the Bishop of Troyes with some twenty horsemen was here for a visit.

Just as the last attendant was dismounting a bell rang.

"What's that for?" asked the bishop.

"Time for prayer, Your Excellency," answered Stephen.

"Good. We shall attend."

No, the bishop would not preside. He and his party would remain in the rear. Let the monks file in as usual. He wanted to witness the ceremony. The horsemen crowded into the back of the little oratory as silent figures emerged from the various huts and, with bent heads, hurried towards the church. The vicar was crushed in beside the bishop. Before the last monk took his place in choir, the vicar leaned toward His Excellency and whispered, "Have you noted their modesty? Not one has given us so much as a second glance." The bishop simply nodded, but his eyes were darting from figure to figure.

The last monk was in his place. A hush filled the oratory. The entire party in the rear was gripped by the solemn silence. There came a knock and a little group of monks fell to their knees with the uniformity of a troop of highly trained soldiers. They prayed a few moments in secret. Another knock brought them to their feet, and a single clear voice rang through the stillness, "God come to my assistance," to be answered by the united voices of the little choir in a unison and a volume that was vibrant, "Lord, make haste to help me." Then the monks sang the hymn and the psalms, verse after verse in alternate choirs, first one side, then the other.

When the last response had been given, the monks knelt at their places and the same solemn hush that had so gripped the group of visitors at the beginning of the Office again took possession of the little oratory. Stephen Harding approached and beckoned to the bishop. Outside the door of the church he introduced him to a giant of a man with snow-white hair. "This is our Reverend Father Robert, abbot of the monastery." The bishop extended his right hand. Robert knelt and kissed his ring.

"Your Excellency has afforded us the happiest surprise of the year. Indeed, I might say of our whole five years together. May I extend to you the warmest of welcomes from my own heart and the hearts of all in our little community." The bishop nodded his thanks. "In a few moments we will be having our dinner. Would you honor us by partaking of our humble fare?"

The bishop said, "Gladly." Little did he know how literally Robert was speaking when he said *"humble* fare." The news of the unexpected guests had been brought to Robert while he was talking with Father Alberic, the prior. The latter laughed and called to the cellarer who was just passing.

"Twenty more mouths for dinner," he said. "Can you manage?"

The poor man was a picture of dismay. He held out his hands and said, "My Fathers, you know the condition of our storeroom and cellar."

"Water the soup," commanded Alberic. "And serve wine only to the guests. The community will take what comes from the cistern."

"Shall I water the wine, too?" questioned the cellarer.

"No, no," laughed Alberic. "Wine is good with everything but water; and water is good with everything but wine."

The bell had then rung for prayers, so Robert and Alberic moved off toward the church. The abbot said resignedly, "Not much of a meal for a bishop, but what can we do?"

When His Excellency saw the meal he grew skeptical. "Find out if this is the regular thing, or just a show," he whispered to his vicar. The horsemen were hungry after the morning's ride, so the warm vegetable soup was welcome. But when the second dish of plain, unseasoned lentils was placed before them, even their keen appetites grew dull. The meal was finished before most of them were aware that it had actually begun. In other monasteries of the land such soup, wine and lentils would have hardly been considered a side-dish. Finally convinced that they had been served all that was going to be served, murmurs of dissatisfaction came from the entire retinue, while whispers broke out here and there "Madmen! Hypocrites! Pious frauds!"

The bishop had heard the murmurs of his party. He had studied the demeanor of the monks. There was no question in his mind but that this was their regular meal. They had shown no surprise whatsoever, and had partaken of the two plain dishes with evident relish.

All through the visit the bishop was torn by successive, contrary impressions. The atmosphere of Molesme was one of prayer; he admitted that. He had been moved almost to tears by their Office chant. Often had he heard the psalms recited; today, for the first time, he had heard them *prayed*. The poverty in food, clothing and lodging, however, struck him as excessive. He must also investigate the matter of manual labor.

When the thanksgiving visit to the chapel ended, the bishop arranged to have his vicar go with Stephen Harding to inspect the entire establishment, while he and Robert visited in the latter's cell. For over an hour the two were in closed conference. Troyes' bishop was an expert at extracting information. This day he used all his expertness. The abbot later told Alberic and

Stephen that the bishop had drawn a general confession of his whole life from him.

About four o'clock, as the party was being led out of the woods, they passed a place where the monks were at work grubbing up stumps and preparing a field for fall planting. To the bishop's question as to whether such labor was burdensome, Stephen Harding replied with Augustine's famous line: "When one loves, there is no labor; or if there is labor, it is loved."

The bishop looked at the vicar. "It rings true. That is conviction; not a pious cliché," was His Excellency's comment.

Once on the road and out of earshot of the monks a veritable babel broke forth. Most of the party were giving vent to angry derision. The vicar looked questioningly at the bishop. When the latter maintained silence, the vicar nodded to the grumbling horsemen ahead and behind saying, "I don't think they approve of Molesme."

"Their bellies are empty."

"I'm a bit hungry myself," said the vicar with a smile.

"I'm humiliated," said the bishop.

The vicar looked at him in surprise, "Then there'll be no suppression?"

"Suppression! Suppression! Please God there'll be a diffusion. You were in a city of God this afternoon, my man. Those men are neither fools nor frauds. Would to God we had a few more Roberts in the monastic world! Then God would be getting something from the men he made. That man is the soul of sincerity and simplicity. *Allons!* " he cried, and set spurs to his mare. "We must be home before nightfall." Then the Roman road rang with the clatter of many galloping hooves.

Six weeks later the trees of Troyes stood out in skeletoned ugliness. His Excellency was looking from the window of his study upon a world that had been stripped by the chill winds of November. There was nothing in the vista to cheer one. The sky was gray. A sharp wind moaned. The landscape was cold and bare. Some of that chill had crept into the bishop this morning. His mood was far from pleasant.

The vicar noted the fact the moment he entered and inwardly groaned. The news he had to break would have stirred the bishop in the best of moods; now it most likely would cause an eruption. But duty must be done. He bowed to his superior and informed him that many reports had reached the office about two wild-looking men in the tattered robes of monks, who were begging from door to door in the city.

"What?" snapped the bishop. "Have them brought to me at once! Evangelical poverty is one thing; beggary quite another." The vicar withdrew. Fortunately he had kept the last complainants waiting. He would curb the bishop's impatience by hurrying these off to summon the monks.

Twenty minutes later the two beggars came in. Their faces were gaunt. Their robes thin and worn. Their eyes lit with a strange fire. The vicar hurried them directly in to His Excellency.

"What is this I hear?" thundered the bishop. "You men have been...." But there he stopped, looked more closely, and cried, "Can it be?" Then he came forward with out-stretched arms. "Jean Marie!" he cried, "and Father Louis! Welcome! Welcome! Welcome!" And he embraced the two monks warmly. The vicar stood as one struck dumb. The bishop saw the amazement on his face and laughed aloud. "Ah, my poor vicar, what eyes you have! Do you not recognize your hosts of Molesme?" The vicar looked more closely and memory did the rest.

The bishop made the monks sit down and tell what brought them to Troyes. The story was quickly given. The harvest had been light. The community had increased. The storeroom was empty. Father Robert had sent them to town to buy all that was needed in the line of food and clothing. But he had given them no money! The monks shrugged their shoulders and held out expressive hands saying, "What could we do? 'Buy' means 'beg' when you have no money."

His Excellency chuckled. "Your abbot must have been reading the prophets of late. Isaiah has a line that could have served him as inspiration. He says, 'You who have no money, make haste, buy and eat. Come ye, buy wine and milk without money and without any price.'"

"That may be prophecy, Your Excellency," said Jean-Marie dolefully, "but as yet it has not been fulfilled."

The bishop looked at the disconsolate faces of the monks, recalled the thin soup, the sour wine, and the unseasoned lentils, then smiled. He secretly chided himself for having been so stupidly inconsiderate. He would make amends immediately. He asked a few questions about what was needed, then told the monks to rest.

An hour later he summoned the monks and showed them a wagon piled high with clothes and foodstuffs. "Take that to the abbot with my apologies, and promise him in my name that Molesme will never know want again. You might also tell him this is a matter of self-protection—I don't want to come home hungry again!"

Chapter Nine

Prosperity Brings Disaster

The bishop kept that resolve by making the nobles of the realm conscious of their obligations to contribute to pious causes and he pointed out that Molesme was most pious.

But that was the beginning of the end! The next ten years saw the abbey prosper as very few abbeys have ever prospered. The wooden oratory and the cluster of huts came down, and substantial monastic buildings arose in their place. The barn Alberic had built so optimistically years before "for the cattle they did not own," was replaced by a structure four times the size of the original, and immediately filled. Land was cleared by serfs and donated to the abbey; granges were built and staffed; and the community grew so large that there were as many foundations as there had been original huts.

But Robert was far from happy. In fact, he was worried. He had seen his reform spread through Champagne and Burgundy. Men from his monastery had been asked to introduce the practices of Molesme into many other communities. It was a source of real pleasure to the old man to find others becoming more generous with God. And yet he grew disturbed about his own monastery.

One day he told Alberic that he wished the bishop of Troyes had not gone home hungry that day in 1080, for that hunger had brought too much wealth to Molesme. The spirit of the house was changing. The younger element did not know what it was to suffer! They were too independent in thought and action. They had not caught the spark as had the hermits at Colan. Molesme was deteriorating.

How well Alberic knew that! He had been listening to complaints for months. Many of the younger men wanted more study and less manual labor; more of Cluny and less of Molesme. And some of them were taking what they desired! This was what disturbed Alberic. He could countenance and condone almost anything but he had no patience whatsoever with disobedience.

As he now looked at the worried face of his Abbot, he thought of young Romanus in particular. Alberic had dubbed him "the intellectual"

from the first week he had been in the house.
Romanus was keen, educated, capable and zealous. This last was the element that caused trouble. Had the youngster been lax in any sense, he
would never have won the following that was
his. But far from being lax he was scrupulously
exact in his observance. Unquestionably the man
was sincere. Unquestionably, too, he was the
source of all the unrest in the monastery.

Ambition for exact interpretation had fired
this youngster, just as ambition for exact observance had fired Robert half a century earlier. But
the minds of the superior and the subject split on
the question of manual labor. One citation that
won many to Romanus' way of thinking was
from chapter forty-eight of the Rule which runs:
"If, however, the needs of the place or poverty
require that they gather in the harvest themselves, let them not be saddened."

Romanus took that passage word for word
and used it as proof that it was the *exception* for
monks to help even with the harvest! Poverty or
passing necessity might occasionally demand
such aid, said the Rule, implying of course that
the community did not ordinarily do this work.
He quoted Cassiodorus, a contemporary of
St. Benedict, as saying "Of all the works that can
be accomplished by manual labor, none pleases
me so much as the work of the copyists—if they
will only copy correctly." And he thereby sowed

the seeds of dissatisfaction whose flower would be dissension, and whose fruit, desertion.

Robert knew this as well as Alberic; but while the latter urged a silencing of the youngster, Robert favored the milder course, relying on loyalty and the force of truth. But Robert had miscalculated Romanus' influence. Before he was aware of it, the community was split into two factions, each claiming the same foundation for its starting point, and the identical goal for its strivings. Romanus argued for literal interpretation even as did Robert and Romanus seemed to have the better of the argument! The younger men, who were at once more noisy and more numerous, rallied around their clever and capable leader.

Robert had been so preoccupied with the hundred and one concerns of the monastery that he could not give the attention to Romanus and his movement that this latter deserved. St. Benedict, when legislating for a small community, had placed everything in the hands of the abbot. What Benedict meant to have done with a community of twenty, Robert was attempting to do with a community of two hundred. He was a harassed and hurried man. Frequently he was forced to give decisions on the spur of the moment which should have been given only after hours and even days of reflection. Alberic knew this, and remonstrated with him often. But he was always put off with, "God will provide."

"Yes," thought Alberic, "God will provide a grave for you, if you keep going at this pace."

But one day an aroused prior came and demanded that something be done. Alberic told the abbot that, while Romanus himself would always obey, some of his followers would not. Then he recounted how he had assigned a few of them to the task of clearing away some brambles that were encroaching on a wheatfield, only to be told that they had some work to do in the scriptorium—and they went to that work!

The abbot frowned. Then he remembered that Romanus, who had volunteered to transcribe the *"Gesta Monachorum,"* had lately asked for a few assistants. But Robert did not like the disobedience to the prior even on the grounds of fulfilling a previous command. He would have disliked it more if Alberic had told him that some of the copyists murmured, "Let the serfs do that work. We are monks!" His dislike would have probably changed to consternation if Alberic had gone on to say that the same thing had happened four or five times within the past month.

But Robert did not act on Alberic's advice immediately. He had confidence in Romanus' deep religious spirit. And his confidence was well placed. But where the abbot erred was in having similar confidence in the religious spirit of Romanus' followers. They were not gifted in heart or in mind as was their leader. What he saw as a truth meriting intellectual recognition, they took as a starting point for rebellion. Unwittingly Romanus had robbed many of their confidence in the abbot, and turned them against his idea of the Benedictine life. Gradually all this was brought home to Robert by a series of heated arguments climaxed by some more open acts of disobedience.

Alberic was fuming. He told Stephen Harding that he could not understand how a physical, mental and moral giant like Robert could be so weakly mild. Nor could he understand the blindness that prevented the abbot from seeing Romanus in his true colors. Stephen tried to explain to the prior that a man can be most sincere and yet greatly mistaken; that Romanus could be honest and yet in error. But Alberic would not listen. The youngster's very carriage got on the prior's nerves. He had conceived an antipathy toward Romanus that had him often speaking to his confessor. "Why doesn't the abbot do something about him?" was Alberic's unwearying cry.

Finally Robert acted. One morning he took the words that run through the Rule like a refrain, "Let nothing be preferred to Jesus Christ," and used them as a text for as moving a sermon as Molesme had ever heard. The abbot proved that it was not only St. Benedict's Rule that he knew, but also the Gospel of Jesus Christ. He made the God-Man step from the cold printed page and appear in the warmth of flesh and blood. He showed his monks the many sides of

Christ's character by calling their attention to the various brilliant beams that streamed from his personality. Robert was much like a jeweler turning a diamond to show its many facets and their variegated lights. Finally, he showed them the white heart of that diamond and the source of all that light when he exposed the focal point of Christ's whole character—*humility expressed in obedience.*

He said that true humility was a recognition of God's supremacy and our subjection, with a consequent surrender of our will to the will of God. He showed them how Christ was humble with this humility from birth to burial: for he had surrendered his will to the will of the Father even to death on the cross. Then Robert said, "If you will be Benedictines after the heart of St. Benedict, you must surrender to God as Christ surrendered! Your humility must be complete, expressed in an obedience that is complete. You must be big enough, and brave enough, and bold enough to say to God, 'I surrender!' Thus and thus only will you measure up to the stature of Christ. Thus and thus only will you be Benedictines after the heart of your Father."

It was not often that Robert spoke with fire these later years and not often that he analyzed Christ or the Rule. He had been too busy, and he had taken too much for granted. But in this address the monks were seeing their model as few had ever seen him before. The abbot's final sentence was a sword thrust. It ran: "Humility is expressed in obedience—not to the mere letter of the Rule, but to the living voice of the authority who has the right to interpret that Rule!"

Robert walked out of a hushed chapter room. He had scarcely crossed the threshold when, as if by irresistable impulse, young Romanus hurried after him. He overtook the abbot at the door of his room and, looking at him with eyes burning with sincerity, declared passionately, "Father, I know exactly what you meant. Forgive me for not having been as humble and obedient as was Christ. But believe me when I say I meant to be nothing else. We do not see eye to eye on this matter of the Rule, Reverend Father; but I will always obey. I can't change my intellect, but I can and I do surrender my will."

Robert's eyes filled as he blessed the young priest. He managed to steady his voice as he said, "Romanus, my child, I never doubted it an instant. But not many are able to make the fine distinction between intellect and will that you make, and I'm sure you'll continue doing it. But, child, your personal interpretations of the Rule will have to be kept to yourself. The community is disturbingly divided." Robert went into his room then; Romanus went to chapel.

That afternoon when Robert told Alberic of the apology Romanus had made, the prior only shook his head. "I don't trust him. He's too brainy. He's got too big a following. Why, one of his dupes just told me that he said you were wrong in your interpretation of the Rule, but right in commanding your interpretation to be executed; while they were right in their interpretation, but would be wrong in executing it against your commands. Now, that kind of talk only confuses the majority of them and confirms them in their stand against you. The man's a menace, I tell you," ended Alberic angrily.

Alberic was right. Romanus manifested absolute obedience to Robert; but his followers became more and more assertive. They openly disobeyed and angrily contended with the prior, the subprior, and the other minor officials. Some said that Robert was not commanding according to the Rule, hence, their refusal to execute his commands was not a violation of their vow.

Romanus, seeing the dissension he had created, refused to say anything more about the Rule or the abbot. Had he carefully calculated how to win the unfaltering loyalty of the dissenters, he could not have arrived at a cleverer method of procedure than that of his present silence. They looked upon him as a "martyr," a man who was being "persecuted" by those in authority; and they became more vigorous in their opposition to the heads of the house.

For the greater part of a year Robert gently remonstrated, patiently argued, even pleaded; but it was useless. He punished a few malcontents mildly; but this was only fuel for their fires of resentment. It became so bad that Robert hesitated to command, considering it the lesser of two evils. But after a night of prayer he called Alberic to him and said: "Father Prior, you are to take over. I am leaving."

"You're...you're...leaving?" gasped the bewildered Alberic.

"Yes, action must be taken. I'm taking it."

"But...I can't take over."

"You'll have to. You have Stephen Harding to assist you. He's zealous, prudent and gifted with a talent for handling men. With me out of the way, you two ought to be able to effect something. I mean to startle this community. I'm hoping and praying the departure of their abbot will bring them to their senses. You and Stephen must make the most of the effect produced, and bring this house back to what it once was."

"Where are you going?"

"To Haur. There I'll pray. Maybe my prayer will be more effective than my leadership has been."

"But you're abbot! You can command. Romanus can be expelled...."

"No, Father. We won't discuss the matter. Keep me informed on all that happens."

Alberic argued, pleaded, scolded, begged. But Robert's face lost no shade of its rigidity. That afternoon he left. Next morning Alberic broke the news to the community. The reaction was complete bewilderment. But when Alberic im-

prudently assigned the causes and looked mean-
ingly at Romanus, he fired the youngster's
followers to angry opposition. Alberic saw that
his first step was a misstep, but he was beating
no retreat.

That afternoon he closeted himself with
Stephen Harding and opened his mind and
heart to the Englishman. He said that since Robert had given him the authority of the abbot he
was going to use it. He quoted various chapters
of the Rule which said that murmurers can be
severely punished, malcontents thoroughly dis-
ciplined, refractory monks summarily dis-
missed. Stephen listened attentively. Alberic had
quoted correctly. It was then that Stephen remarked on the oddity of the fact that so literal an
observer of the Rule as was Robert had made
them forget St. Benedict's stringent regulations.

"Well, that was Robert's big mistake,"
snapped Alberic. "He didn't use his authority."
When Stephen quietly said, "Robert's a very
holy man, Father Prior," Alberic actually exploded. "Holy? Holy?" he shouted. "Robert's
not holy, Stephen. He's *saintly.* I know. I've lived
with him night and day for thirteen years. But
saints are not omniscient, infallible, nor all-wise.
No, indeed. They are friends of God; they aren't
God. They can and do make mistakes. Robert
made a big one when he didn't use his authority. I'm going to unmake it."

It was only late in the afternoon that Stephen

won a grudging promise from Alberic to make haste slowly. He admitted the justness of the prior's stand. Robert's reform was being undermined. Molesme was no longer the monastery he, Stephen, had entered ten years ago. But he cautioned prudence. The community was very upset at the moment. Robert's departure had struck deep. Nobody was normal at present. A false move might precipitate disaster. Alberic finally agreed to hold himself in check, but insisted that some small start be made immediately. He cancelled all extra dishes at table. Many knowing smiles greeted the move. But Alberic was not smiling.

Day after day, in his moving chapter talks, he insisted on silence...silence in the cloister...silence at work...silence in the refectory...silence in the scriptorium. When he paused one morning, a hoarse whisper was heard saying, "Yes, and more silence in the chapter room." This time Alberic did smile. He had not lost his sense of humor. But when one of the malcontents laughed derisively, Alberic's smile vanished.

More grumbling ensued on his command that all wear the same garb. Some had received gifts from relatives, others had pleaded ill-health as an excuse, while some others had unabashedly sought the showy, expensive and even slightly ornate, with the result that poverty of dress was not universally observed. Robert had been too lenient in the matter, thought Alberic.

He would right the situation with one sweep of legislation. Many welcomed this command, for they thought effeminacy was creeping in. But some of the most virile resented it because of its utter absoluteness. It seemed as if Alberic could do nothing right. Again and again the saying, "He ought to be locked up!" was heard. Stephen Harding knew that some were using it as a tag. But he also knew there were some who were using it seriously.

Alberic's patience wore thin trying to follow Stephen's plan of one thing at a time and everything slowly. He had effected something in the course of the months, but he was far from satisfied. Silence was kept, and there was more solitude and fewer visitors. The diet was uniform; so, too, the dress. Alberic knew that manual labor was the vital spot. He knew that when he legislated on this, he would be forcing the crisis of the whole situation. And he felt he had to do it.

One morning he directed all to harvest the crop in the hay field. Immediately ten or twelve approached the prior and claimed exemption on the grounds of special work in the scriptorium. In a loud voice Alberic cried, "All will go to the hay field—all!"

Some still made no move and more stood hesitant, watching the conflict of wills.

Alberic called to Romanus who was near him, "You're a scholar. What does 'militaturus' in the Rule mean? Doesn't it mean 'to soldier?'"

Romanus nodded.

"Well, *soldier!* Obey your officer!"

A voice in the rear broke out, "Did you ever hear what soldiers do to officers who lose their heads?"

A low growl of assent encouraged the speaker. "They lock them up!" went on the voice.

Alberic ignored the heckler and singled out Romanus as the key figure.

"You go to *real* work for once!"

Two stalwart admirers of the young monk caught the imperiousness of the prior's gesture, and rushed towards him crying, "Yes, they lock them up."

There was a scuffle. Alberic resisted, and all the pent-up anger of the monks was unleashed Some rushed at the prior, others tried to restrain the attackers, while a third group tried to separate the first two.

Alberic, as the center of the struggle, was battered on every side. His hard frame and muscles were of no use in this melee—it was a matter of sheer weight. He was pinned to the ground in a moment, under friend and foe alike.

Every evil spirit that had opposed Robert's reform showed its force that day. The discontent, evasion, hair-splitting and fault-finding of the past months developed at one stride into ugly mutiny.

But the contest was as brief as it was violent. Alberic, bruised and beaten, lay unconscious on

the ground. One by one, the opponents disen-
tangled themselves from the mass, and formed
silent groups about their fallen prior.

For a moment, pity at the sight of this once
esteemed leader held all motionless and unsure.
Alberic's followers stood tense, with loyal
Stephen Harding at their head, ready to share
their leader's maltreatment, but reluctant to pro-
voke further conflict. Now, even those who had
been most forward in the struggle seemed unable to make use of their victory. In their indeci-
sion, they turned slowly but unmistakably to
Romanus for guidance. The young monk stood
irresolute, shaken by the actuality of bloodshed
and appalled at the realization that all held him
directly responsible for the outbreak.

A loathing for this smug, short-sighted arguing now seized him. He should have foreseen
some such violent outcome. Logical or not logical, he knew that Alberic was his prior, his acting
superior. He, Romanus, should not be standing
here as if in judgment on a man so much older,
so much better, so much more experienced than
himself.

He glanced around at the circle of monks
who stood watching him, waiting for his word.
Was there not one who would step forward—
relieve him of the responsibility of decision? He
felt like Pilate before the Jews. His eyes fell to the
ground. He must say something—and quickly.

He wished he could cry aloud that he had

changed his stand—that, agreeing or not with Alberic, he no longer wished to oppose him. A fear of the scorn, and in some cases the honest scorn, of the monks made him hesitate to do so. And there was another, more honorable deterrent—the knowledge that such an act would not clear the confusion but increase it; that the least capable of his adherents would take the revolt into their own hands; that the morning would only end with Romanus, and perhaps many others, stretched, hurt and helpless like Alberic.

No—the best Romanus could hope for was to save Alberic from further ill-use. If he ordered Alberic to be locked up, it would, he felt, satisfy the resentment of the insurgents, and also enable him to protect Alberic from any future spite. The course appealed to him. He need not yet break definitely with either side.

Romanus' voice held some of its old ring of self-assurance as he cried, "In the interests of peace at Molesme, let the prior be kept under guard until all in council decide what course is fitting to pursue."

General assent was immediate. The assailants wished to avoid further violence—especially if they could attain their purpose without it.

Several of the monks lifted Alberic and began to carry him toward the dungeon. Stephen Harding tried to help, but he was determinedly shouldered off. The prior was too powerful a man to be given any loophole to escape through the aid of his friends.

That night the evening star looked down on a scene of sad contradiction at Molesme—a monastery where the blind led the blind, an abbey without an abbot.

Some days afterwards, the news reached Robert, who had voluntarily retired to exile in the forests of Haur. Here, with three other hermits, he spent his days in penance and prayer.

The messenger, a young monk, travelled as quickly as possible, and at last broke panting into the quiet grove. He found Robert on his knees as usual.

"Reverend Father, Reverend Father," he cried as he came upon the old abbot, "I bring the most terrible news from Molesme."

"What has happened, my son?" asked Robert, drawn abruptly from his other world of prayer.

"The prior! The prior! They have beaten and thrown him into the dungeon!"

"Beaten Alberic? Beaten Alberic?"

"Yes, yes. And locked him in a dungeon at Molesme."

Robert groaned. His eyes filled with tears as he turned to the flushed and heavily breathing monk. "Thank you, son, for coming so far to see your aged father. I will pray. Come back when you have better news."

When the young messenger had left the

grove, Robert turned and fell on his knees. It had all been useless, he thought. He had been wrong from the beginning. Old Abbot Bernard had been right. Maurus had been right. Even young Romanus was right. The Rule could not be kept in its rigor. Men were too selfish, too weak, too unchivalrous toward God.

Had his mother been wrong? His father wrong? Himself foolishly wrong? Was God more satisfied with mitigations than with the naked Rule? "Yes, yes," he sobbed. "It must be that way. I have been deceived. Duped by the devil."

He lifted his face to the sky. Every line spoke of pain. The evening heavens were blocked out by the heavy foliage of the trees that towered above him. Suddenly a wind stirred. The leaves rustled and parted, and Robert was looking through a screen of green and silver at—his evening star. Tonight the mist gave it a new significance—a thin cross of silver streamed from the lone solitary of the sky. "I see! I see!" he cried. "You teach me silently through the star. Forgive me, Lord; I had forgotten. 'If any man come after me...let him take up his cross.' Yes, I had forgotten." The old man struggled to his feet. He swayed as he staggered out of the grove; but once in the open he straightened to his full height, lifted his hand to the heavens and cried, "I'll burn on, Lord; but do, please *do* let my remedy work!" He walked to his hut with head erect. He felt nearer to God than he had felt in weeks.

Chapter Ten

"There Is Only One Way!"

Robert's prayer was heard—but in the strangest of fashions. While the old man gave himself recklessly to penance and prayer at Haur, unusual events took place at Molesme. The serfs near the monastery began to learn that all was not right with the community. Bit by bit they gathered the facts. Soon, from field to stable, from stable to kitchen, from kitchen to the parlor and the lady of the mansion, word of the quarrel reached the nobles. Indignation at the treatment of prior and abbot filled the countryside. From then on, Molesme was avoided like a haunted house, and her monks were shunned as lepers.

Before a year had passed this ostracization showed its effects on the monastery's treasury. All donations stopped and many of the serfs refused to work at the abbey. Soon actual poverty was being felt. As meals grew thinner and isolation more absolute, even the most stubborn showed signs of yielding. Finally, it was unanimously agreed that they must beg their abbot to return.

The delegation appointed to wait on him found the old man at prayer. Very humbly they begged, but Robert met their request curtly. "You don't want my ideals. You want my popularity. You do not beg for my interpretation of the Rule, but only for the donations you once received from the rich."

This reply was more of a blow to the community than Robert's original withdrawal. What were they to do? Romanus gave a solution. If Robert would not listen to petitions from those under him, he would always obey commands from his superiors. They must obtain a mandate from Rome. "But," he warned them, "you will have to pay for that mandate. It may cost complete capitulation to Robert's wishes. It most certainly will cost concessions."

There was no dissent. They preferred strict observance to social disapproval. All were ready to capitulate if there were no other way. Two of their number hastened to the Eternal City. Through influential friends they won an early audience with His Holiness, Urban II. He listened to their story, and when he learned how ready they were to obey, he granted them the desired mandate. Two happy monks hurried from Rome to Molesme; but happier ones hurried from Molesme to Haur.

Robert read the mandate in silence. Without a word to the messengers he turned, closed the door of his little hut, bade farewell to the three solitaries, then said, "Let us go home."

The veterans of Colan and early Molesme welcomed their old abbot with warm affection, some even with tears. The dissenters were very subdued, some sheepish. Life at the abbey soon struck its old tempo. Robert was diplomat enough to make some concessions to the recalcitrants, thus winning them to readier obedience on his more essential reforms. Alberic did not like the concessions, but Stephen Harding reminded him that the breaking of a minor custom was much more bearable than the breaking of a head. With a self-conscious smile and a nod Alberic conceded the point.

But promises are always more easily made than fulfilled. It is true that Molesme flourished as of old. Postulants came in greater numbers; more abbots asked for men to introduce Molesme customs into their communities; serfs once more worked on the granges; the benefactors became even more generous. But...before many years had passed, Alberic was pointing out that it was not the spirit of Colan that fired the community, and Stephen Harding was admitting that it was not the spirit of early Molesme. No individual could be blamed. But the intangible atmosphere was saturated with antagonism to anything that was not in accord with the great Cluny and the almost universal custom of the monastic world. Even old Robert grew discouraged!

One day Alberic asked Stephen Harding what he thought of the peace at Molesme. The Englishman looked at him. "This is not peace, Alberic; this is truce. We will never have perfect peace at Molesme."

"Never?"

Alberic was surprised at the tinge of bitterness that edged Stephen's words. He knew the Englishman for a conservative, far-seeing, mild-spoken man. "Well, what's your solution?" he asked.

"There's only one way out, Alberic."

"Which is…," prompted the prior.

"Which is to quit this place and found a new monastery."

"What!"

"Yes, and in that monastery we must be more radical than Robert has yet been. We must go back to the very letter of the Rule, stripping away everything that smacks of Cluny or contemporary custom. In other words, we must be complete in our rebellion."

"And I thought the English were temperate," exclaimed Alberic.

Stephen smiled. "It is the *only* way. Mark my words. This truce cannot last forever. Either the abbot will have to compromise or the community capitulate; and I don't think either will ever do either. They are asking dispensations again."

"I know," said Alberic slowly. "The abbot feels it keenly."

Indeed, the abbot felt it keenly. Late one afternoon when the day was all red and gold, he sat in his room thinking these same sad thoughts and shaking his aged head in an agony of grief. For sixty-five years the call to a fuller living of the Rule had sounded in his ears incessantly as the "wash of some weariless sea." Why could he not get others to hear the same? Why was it that he could not make heroic monks out of ordinary men? Why? Why? Why?

This was the eightieth year of his life, and the sixty-fifth of his religious service. And what had he to show? He had been unable to revolutionize so much as a single monastery! Ah, indeed he had failed, failed utterly. Men would not catch and hold the spark. The old man shook a sad head and suddenly realized he was tired. All things about him looked barren and black. His white head sank into his aged hands.

Suddenly there came a knock on his door. He was tempted not to answer that knock—so weary, futile, and defeated did he feel. But the discipline of the years won and he gave the signal to enter. Unknowingly he had answered a knock that was to reverberate for centuries. It was a knock that would open the gates of Molesme, and establish a new order of things in all Europe. It was the knock of Alberic and Stephen Harding.

The old man was relieved when he saw them. They would have no complaints. He was grateful on that account. "Why have they come together?" he wondered. He had not long to wonder, for Alberic, in his usual direct fashion, told him that they, too, had seen silver-white on flaming-red; that they, too, had seen the evening star; that they, too, would be gallant to God.

Indeed, Alberic and Stephen had caught the spark. They were ready for real rebellion. They did not want to reform Molesme. That, Stephen pointed out, was not feasible, nor was it compatible with their ideals. They did not want to do away with the dispensations and mitigations that had crept into their present monastery. No. They wanted to do away with *all* mitigations. They wanted the Rule, the whole Rule, and nothing but the Rule. They wanted it as naked as Benedict had written it; as chaste as Monte Cassino had lived it. They wanted to be what Christ had called them to be—penitents for an unrepentant world.

Robert dreamed dreams. He was sixteen years old again. He was back at St. Pierre de la Celle. He was young, eager, brave, and undisillusioned. And yet, he was not dreaming. It was true! His ideal had caught. Men held the spark. His rebellion could be waged. These men would be not only generous but even gallant to God.

"Reverend Father," begged Alberic, "may we have your permission to leave Molesme, and found a new monastery?"

Robert knew he must speak. These two were waiting for an answer. He breathed deeply. "No!" he said. "No! You may not go.... You may not carry out this mad plan of yours.... You may never do this rebellious thing...unless...." Robert stopped. Stephen and Alberic stood amazed at this utterly unexpected reply. "...unless," Robert went on, "...unless I am at your head!"

Robert of Molesme had become Robert of St. Pierre. An old man of eighty had become a boy again. He stretched out two trembling hands toward Alberic and Stephen and said, "Accept an old man's thanks." His voice was rich with emotion as he cried, "Brothers in Christ, let us do this thing together!"

Robert was ready to quit his abbey. He had his men. He had his plans. He had his ideals. He was convinced that only thus could peace be obtained for those who left and those who remained. His heart was singing as he went about his final preparations for departure.

Suddenly the song failed. Stephen Harding found him sitting despondently at his desk.

In response to Stephen's anxious questions, Robert threw out his hands in a gesture of helpless resignation.

"Obedience shackles me," was all the old man could say. He had suddenly remembered that Rome had commanded him to return to Molesme. Rome alone could free him. He could never leave on his own authority.

Stephen was taken aback. He, too, had a passionate loyalty to the Holy See. It seemed that he must either go without his abbot or remain without his reform. Neither alternative appealed to him. As they looked at one another sadly, Alberic entered in boisterous spirits. "Well! Well! Well!" he exclaimed. "Who snuffed out the sun? You two look as glum as Noah must have looked the day his dove didn't come back. What's the matter?"

They told him briefly. Without a moment's hesitation he blurted, "Well, what's wrong with getting the Pope's command? If Romanus and his clique could get a mandate, I judge we can get something as good."

"But the time it will take," objected Stephen.

"No time at all," interrupted Alberic. "The Papal Legate is in Lyons. He can give the release Reverend Father needs, and at the same time we can get papal approbation for our undertaking. Think what that will mean!"

Stephen and Robert exchanged glances. Smiles broke out. Alberic had shown them the way.

Not many days later, seven men stood before Hugh, Archbishop of Lyons and Legate of the Holy See. He listened to them quietly. Soon he had all the facts before him. Contention arising from conflicting ideals. Determined parties on each side. No peace. All the while he had been studying the group of men before him. He marvelled at the light that flamed in their eyes. It told of strong fires in their hearts.

Their reasoning was logical. Since compromise was impossible, contention was inevitable. Their request, then, to be allowed to found a new monastery, was reasonable. Hugh ran his eyes from man to man, recalling each one's name. This was Alberic. Nice smile the man had. Next was Odo. A veritable mountain of a monk. Fasting hadn't hurt him. This was John. Tall, thin, gaunt. With a camel's hair tunic he could pass for the Baptist. Next a quiet man— studious, cultured. Oh, yes, Stephen Harding, the Englishman. The next two were French all right—and fiery French. They had been on edge all during the interview. Letaldus and Peter they were called. And at their head was this old man of eighty, Robert. He had as much youth as the youngest—and more fire.

Hugh cleared his throat. He told the men before him that he sympathized with them.

Peace was an essential in every monastery. He appreciated their predicament. But they must appreciate his. To countermand a papal mandate was no light matter. It called for careful consideration. "However," he added, "it has been done before, and it can be done. Especially when the glory of God and the salvation of souls is at stake." Then he smiled. "My Fathers," he said. "May I offer you my sincerest congratulations on your zeal? You can be sure that I shall weigh the matter, and, if at all possible, will give papal approbation. You may expect final word within a few days."

They left, and on the way home there was much talk. Some said his last speech was just policy to put them off. Others were even less sanguine. They feared that he would not countermand the mandate. Robert was silent for the most part. He simply said, "We must pray that God's will be done."

Two days later the document came. Alberic was in the abbot's room when he unrolled it. The joy in the old man's face prepared him for the excited cry, "Listen to this, Alberic! Listen to this:

> Therefore, consulting the salvation of both parties in the said monastery (Molesme), we have thought it better that you should retire to some place which God in his bounty may point out to you, therein to serve him with greater health and quietness of soul.

And we confirm this our advice to you to
persevere in your holy design by our apostolic authority and seal.

"'Apostolic authority and seal!' We can go,
Alberic! We can go!"

Robert did not wait the day out. He summoned the entire community to a special chapter. "Men of Molesme," he declared, "I am no
longer your abbot. You are no longer my monks.
With papal permission and approbation I leave
your midst tomorrow or the next day. I cease being your leader this moment. Elect my successor
when you will. But...I do not go alone! All who
wish to be gallant to God, to give more than
others give, to empty themselves as Christ emptied himself, to stand in the gap before the wrath
of Omnipotence for the sake of the land; all who
wish to live the Rule they have vowed to live, and
live it to the letter, may come with me. Such is the
will of the Holy See."

He then read them the document from the
Papal Legate. A silence that could almost be
heard filled the room. The men sat as if cut from
stone. Then Robert said, "All who wish to follow,
step forward." Here, there, and further down,
men leaped from their seats and took their stand
in the center of the room. Robert counted those
who were standing. "God!" he cried. "I have
twenty to follow me. Christ had only twelve."

His last action was characteristic of him. He
begged pardon for all the faults he had commit-

ted while abbot, asked the continued prayers of all who remained behind, and gave them his most solemn blessing.

It was 1098, the year all Europe shook to the tread of marching feet as men, women, and even children set off for the first Crusade. "God wills it! God wills it!" was the rallying cry and the marching song that buoyed up and carried on knighthood's most chivalrous members. But "God wills it!" rang in no one's soul more exultingly than in the soul of an old man of eighty as he walked the snow-covered roads of France at the head of a band of twenty monks. Robert felt more knightly than did Godfrey of Bouillon.

They did not make a very impressive group—these men who trudged on the road from Molesme to Chalons. They had vestments for Mass, a large book for the Office, and very little else. And yet this was the group that gave the world a revolution! They stopped at a wood called Citeaux, still in the duchy of Burgundy.

Citeaux. What a place! A more unlikely spot for human habitation could hardly have been found. It was a swampy wood, dark with the growth of overlapping trees, and damp with the ugly damp of many stagnant pools. Twenty-three years before, Robert had left Colan because it was unhealthy. Now he plunged into this swampland with zest! Alberic wondered if his abbot thought there was some proportion between effects and efforts, between sanctity and struggle, between divinizations and difficulties. If so, he told himself, then Robert certainly wanted the highest of high sanctity for his little band of twenty and nothing short of actual divinization for Citeaux spelled difficulty and fiercest struggle.

It was midwinter. Trees were bare. Marshy pools were dirty even in their ice. All was bleak, lonely, desolate, death-like. This was the Citeaux that Robert and his band looked at in the snows of 1098. And into that repulsive woodland they plunged. Work began immediately. Down came trees. Up came briars and brambles. Some fires of waste shone through the trees as twenty-one men bent to the task of clearing a land for habitation.

Hardly two weeks later, Odo, Duke of Burgundy, was riding along the snow-covered road that swept past Citeaux. He was thinking of his earlier days—none too pleasant thoughts. He had been a robber-baron—one of those iron-hearted, iron-handed men who made life miserable for pilgrim, peasant, and even prince. There had been excitement to the life, admitted Odo, a certain zest in every capture. But as he rode along he saw before him the face of his last captive. It was St. Anselm! He smiled at the irony of what had happened. Odo had planned to take everything Anselm had. He was just about to do it, when the saint had turned the tables and took not only everything Odo had, but even Odo himself. He took him from a life of thievery and made him a God-fearing duke.

Odo came out of his reverie with a laugh. He slapped his horse and shouted with joy and relief. But it was not the echo of his shout that came back to him from the wood. No. It was something distinctly different. He turned his horse to the trees. Slowly he picked his way toward that noise. It came to him clearer and clearer. Odo frowned. This woodland had always been deserted. What could such activity mean? He approached more cautiously. Finally he discovered figures moving about through the trees. He watched. They were monks. They were building. He came closer. Calling one of them, he asked who they were and what they were building. When he learned they were from Molesme and that this was a new monastery they were erecting, his hands went up. He cried, "That? That? A monastery?...Where's your abbot?"

Robert came and introduced himself. Odo bowed, then almost barked, "Reverend Father, before nightfall a whole troop of real workmen will be here. Let them put up something fit for man!"

When Robert tried to thank him, Odo laughed, "The shoe goes on the other foot, Reverend Father. You've heard of restitution, haven't you? Well, I have a lot to make. You are helping me make it." He rode away, and before nightfall a whole troop of men came into the woodland and Citeaux teemed with activity.

So rapidly did they work that on March twenty-first, the "new monastery," as it was called, was solemnly inaugurated. Alberic was jubilant. He burst in on his abbot after the ceremony and cried, "Do you know what day this is? I don't want to be superstitious, but think of it, Reverend Father, today is March twenty-first, St. Benedict's feast day, and it falls on Palm Sunday! You've made your triumphal entry into your City of God on the feast day of the man whose Rule you are going to observe to the letter. That's no accident. That's Divine Providence! We have begun well."

"Pray that we continue well," advised the abbot.

"Well begun is more than half done," returned the prior with a smile, and was gone.

Sixteen months later, while Citeaux sweltered under a July sun, another solemn ceremony took place. It was the dedication of the very substantial church of the "new monastery." Odo had helped with men, money and materials. But Robert and his twenty were far from idle. There was too much fire in their souls to allow them simply to supervise. They worked! And Citeaux, birthplace of a new chivalry, came into being.

Chapter Eleven

"Sunset and Evening Star..."

It had been scorchingly hot all morning. And even now in the late afternoon the monks found no breath of air stirring through the woods, nor any relief from the heat in the shade. It had showered during the night and the sun was still drawing up from the earth an oppressive humidity.

Stephen and Alberic were soaked in sweat as they directed the work of drainage. The swamp was wide and fairly deep, but the long channels had been well dug. A few more feet now and they would be into the swamp itself; then that polluting stagnancy would slide down to the boisterous waters of the mountain stream and be carried off first to the river, and then to the sea. It was Odo who made the last cut. As the ooze and slime slowly tumbled over the lip of the channel, he lifted his great round face, which was red as fire, and smiled at Alberic. The prior returned that smile, plunged his tool into the mouth of the channel, deepening its throat and widening its lip. Then he motioned to the puffing Odo to rest. He watched the flow of the squalid stuff a moment, then clapped his hands as a signal for all to cease working.

Stephen came alongside the prior and pointed to a patch of pond lilies well out on the bosom of the swamp. Their beautiful pink and white blooms were resting on broad leaves. "You can have splendor even in a cesspool, can't you?" he said.

Alberic's eyes twinkled as he turned from the flowers. "That sight gives me hope, Stephen," he said. "If God can work such wonders in this swamp, there may be a few white petals on my soul some day!"

"Such presumption!" said a voice behind them.

The two monks turned. "Oh, Reverend Father! I didn't hear you...."

"But I heard you," laughed the abbot. After a swift glance at the swamp and the channels, he said, "That will drain nicely. Now, Father Prior, I hope you are not too tired; for there is work to be done. And Duke Odo tells me he must leave us soon. Will you take all except Father Stephen to that field we cut yesterday and gather in the hay? I'm sure it is dry after this morning's sun, and I'm afraid we are in for another shower very shortly. Leave your spade here. I'll stay with Father Stephen and keep this stuff flowing."

Some time after the prior and duke had gone, Stephen roused himself from a reverie and dreamily asked, "I wonder how long it will be before this wilderness becomes a thriving City of God."

The abbot made no answer for what seemed to Stephen a very long time. When he did speak his tone was that of one in deep meditation. "If I said 'soon,' you might misunderstand me. But the true answer is: soon!" Resting lightly on the long handle of his spade, he turned to Stephen and said in a more lively tone, "It was only this morning at prayer that I saw how quickly time flies. I'm over eighty years of age, Stephen. I've been a monk for all of sixty-six years. Would you believe me were I to tell you that it seems a very short while ago that I left home to enter St. Pierre de la Celle?"

Stephen stepped forward and dug away some mud and some gummy green that threatened to stop up the mouth of the channel. When he had freed the opening he stepped back and said, "I suppose you've bcen so busy the time slipped by unnoticed. Just think of all you've accomplished! Troyes, Tonnerre, Colan, Molesme, Citeaux...."

"How can you speak of accomplishment, my son?" asked the abbot quickly. "All day long I've been continuing my morning's meditation, and all I can see is a series of failures."

"Failures?" asked Stephen.

"Certainly, son," said Robert quietly. "Over sixty-five years ago I was seized with one ambition. I dreamed of bringing men back to the strict observance of the Rule, so that by it they might show gallantry to God. You see how much of that dream has come true. You see how well that ambition has been realized. Here we are beside a swamp; a mere handful is down in the hay field. And you talk of accomplishments! I failed at St. Pierre's. Even as prior I effected nothing. Why, I even failed to convince my greatest friend. To say that I accomplished anything at Tonnerre is pure romancing; I don't want to say 'lying.' The truth is that I had to resign from St. Michael's after two short but very turbulent years. I was a dismal failure."

"Was it you who failed, or the monks?" asked Stephen as the old abbot paused.

"When a commander loses a battle, don't blame the troops. When a leader fails to inspire his followers, don't blame the followers. No, my kind and consoling friend, I failed at St. Michael's and I failed at Molesme. I've failed all my life. It is only now that I have a semblance of what I first ambitioned. It is only today that I see a shadow of what I dreamed." The old man's gaze strayed out across the swamp. "Of course, I can thank God that there has never been a soul failure. I have never lost faith. Mistakes there have been; malice never. But I still think I should have achieved more evident, objective successes for him. There has been no real negligence nor lack of energy. There has been lack of prudence, foresight, tact, and a hundred and one other faults to which his mercy must be extended. But the point I was making," concluded the old man as he turned to Stephen, "is that you cannot speak of triumphs in my long life. And the greater point is that my long life, and every long life, is frighteningly short."

Stephen went across to the lower channel which had become clogged by a tangle of roots and weeds catching on a bit of projecting rock. It took him some time to loosen the mess. When he came back to the abbot he was streaming sweat. Robert made him sit down at the base of a tree and loosen the neck of his robe. He feared that the subprior had become overheated. But Stephen smiled his fears away and pointed through the tops of the trees, saying, "God is going to cool me off in a moment. See that cloud? It's full of nice cool water. It's going to break soon."

He had just finished speaking when a streak of lightning stabbed down from the summer heavens. There was a rumble of thunder, then the woods rattled with the sound of heavy raindrops pelting the leaves. Robert sat down close to Stephen. He watched the dimpling of the surface of the swamp by the rain. Suddenly he swung his old head from side to side and sighed. Stephen looked at him. "Ah, Stephen, wouldn't it be grand if we could be absorbed in God as those raindrops are absorbed in the waters of the swamp. See! You can't tell which was rain and which swamp. They are one. And we...." And again he sighed.

"You want heaven on earth, Reverend Father," laughed Stephen. "It can't be. Paradise lies the *other* side of the mountain, and the road winds uphill *all* the way!"

"What mountain?" asked Robert abruptly.

"Calvary," said Stephen. "Or if you will, the mountain of failure."

"Ah, then I have found my heaven on earth!" exclaimed the abbot as he brushed a few raindrops from his face. "For it seems as though I have climbed my mountain of failures and found—I almost said 'success' but I don't like that word. I'll say Citeaux."

"You *are* happy here, aren't you?"

"Oh, Stephen, happy as a schoolboy on holiday. So happy that the sixty-six years seem like sixty-six yesterdays. This *is* a foretaste of heaven!" Soon the rain stopped, and far down in the west the sun broke through a group of gray and black clouds.

"Look at that for glory!" Robert cried, and pointed to the rich crimson and flaming gold. "That is my life in symbol, Stephen. God is granting me a glorious sunset after many showers. My sunset, too, is rich with rose and gold. I have seen Citeaux. I am now ready to sing my *Nunc dimittis.*"

The subprior made no answer, but as they gathered their tools he looked again to the west, and saw that a cloud had closed in and covered the sun. He hoped this was no sinister foreshadowing of the close of the abbot's life.

On the way home Robert told Stephen more about his joy in Citeaux. The poverty of the place and the fewness of their number did not allow for the perfection of his plans, but the simplicity, solitude, austerity, the spirit of prayer, the zealous seeking after God, the sincerity of the community and its absolute unity delighted him.

As they approached the gate of the monastery, they noticed a stranger. He had evidently just dismounted. Seeing the two monks, he came toward them, bowed reverently, and asked, "Are you Abbot of Molesme?" Robert answered, "Of Citeaux." The messenger presented a small scroll.

Robert unrolled it, read the few lines, and with trembling hands passed it to Stephen. The subprior ran his eye over the message. It was from Hugh, Archbishop of Lyons and Legate of the Holy See. He read on more anxiously. He gasped as he caught the message. It requested Robert to return to Molesme "for the good of all concerned." Stephen noted that it was a request, not a command. He stressed the fact to Robert. The old man said nothing, but eloquently pointed to the words, "Papal Legate."

Stephen understood. He knew that Rome did not have to command Robert; she had merely to request. To him her voice was the voice of God. He watched the old man as he turned to the west with a wan smile. The sun had gone down. Piled on the far horizon were clouds— white, grey, purple, and black. Robert's hand went out in their direction. "Sunset obscured," he said. "My life in symbol."

With a heavy heart the old man turned to the monastery. A battle was going on within him. His will did not waver, but his whole being seemed in revolt. Resignation to this was costing him more than anything had cost him in his long life. Go he certainly would, even though that going broke his heart. Rome had spoken. And go he did!

A fortnight later Alberic got full details. He learned that, as soon as Robert and his twenty men had left Molesme, history repeated itself. A year had not elapsed before the community was again in turmoil and had turned to Robert as the only possible relief. Dispatching two of their number to the Eternal City they waited in great anxiety to learn the outcome of the mission. The two petitioners interrupted a council of Urban II and caused endless commotion by their pleadings. The Pope was a Frenchman. He knew Molesme and had heard much about Robert. He listened to these two with some impatience. To be rid of them more than anything else, he gave them a letter to his Legate at Lyons, instructing the latter to look into the matter and make a final decision.

When Alberic had told Stephen this, the Englishman said, "I should have thought that Hugh would stand by the official approbation he gave Robert less than two years ago."

Alberic shrugged his shoulders. "What could he do? The men of Molesme claimed that spiritual as well as temporal ruin threatened their house. Undoubtedly his sympathies are with Citeaux, but it is terrifying to think of a big monastery like Molesme going to ruin. You notice that he did not command. I think that is significant. It was with reluctance that he even requested."

"Poor Robert!" was all that Stephen said.

But Robert did not need so much sympathy, for when he returned this time he found a community that was thoroughly chastened. True, he could not lead them to his life-long dream—the literal observance of the Rule; but he did manage to have them show some gallantry.

For a little over ten years they so lived that they actually gladdened the heart they had so nearly broken. But they did it just in time; for that giant heart would not beat for them much longer.

In 1111, a light like the silver of the evening star broke over Molesme. It slowly grew to tremendous proportions and threw mighty rays in all directions. "What is this?" asked serfs in awe-filled whispers as they stopped to watch the heavenly rays spread farther and farther. Suddenly they heard the bells of the monastery tolling slowly, mournfully. Soon they learned the truth—the good Abbot Robert, who had burned on so long, had at last burned out! He had gone to God.

A truly heartsick monk brought the news to Citeaux. So evidently exhausted was he from the journey that Ilbode, the guestmaster, insisted on his taking rest and refreshment before proceeding to see Stephen Harding, who was then abbot.

The messenger had not strength enough to refuse, but begged his hospitable brother in religion to deliver immediately his charge—the official letter of announcement –to the abbot. Ilbode complied promptly, surmising the sad contents of the letter from the face of its bearer.

Stephen at once summoned the community to chapel and begged prayers for, and to, Robert. The bell at Citeaux tolled for the old abbot, spreading the news through the country around. Many remembered the great figure of the man who had first brought the monks to Citeaux, and who had so won the loyalty of Odo, their duke.

Later in the day, Stephen requested that the messenger come to his room if he were now strong enough, for the abbot was anxiously waiting word of the last days of his beloved superior. The visitor followed Ilbode willingly enough to the abbot's room, but once there stood hesitantly at the door. Stephen approached to greet him warmly, but paused wondering at the fixed yet somehow pleading gaze with which the other was watching him.

"You—who know men so well—do not remember me, Abbot Stephen?" asked the stranger.

At the sound of his voice, Stephen's usually mild face hardened in spite of himself. He turned and walked back to his desk.

"Yes," he said finally, "I do remember. Come in—Romanus."

Stephen sat in silence a moment, regaining his somewhat shaken composure. As far as personal feeling went, he had long before forgiven Romanus. He had heard that in later years the man had become one of the most exemplary of Robert's followers at Molesme. Many told how he had used his persuasiveness to increase the understanding of his brothers for their abbot. But involuntarily, Stephen's mind still held the two pictures—of Robert praying in tears for his callous monks, of Alberic lying humiliated and beaten on the floor at Molesme. At last he looked up, praying to be neither uncharitable nor hypocritical.

The expression on Romanus' face surprised Stephen—it showed such comprehension of the struggle that had been going on in his mind. The abbot nodded as if admitting that his unspoken thoughts had been heard.

"Reverend Father," said the monk, "I came here, not to trouble you, but from a desire to do a small service for our abbot. I knew from the love he had for you and all at Citeaux, that I could not please him better than by bringing you the news as soon as possible. For this reason, I begged permission to act as messenger."

Stephen softened. This Romanus—who wished to be of service—was another person from the brilliant, somewhat self-centered logician he remembered in other days. He relaxed and sat back in his chair.

"Tell me about our Father Abbot," he asked.

Romanus, who had grown close to the old monk, was able to tell Stephen many of the details he longed to hear—of the more comforting last years, of the peaceful death, of the miraculous star.

"I wonder will the world ever understand him," mused Stephen when Romanus had ended.

"I doubt it," replied the other.

"Why?" Stephen was surprised at the decision in Romanus' tone.

"Most people look only at the surface—as I did once. They see the superficial contradictions—as I did. And to justify themselves before others, they prefer to ignore what they will not try to rival. Surely you know of the sneers that are still being heaped on Robert? For a long time he was accused of stubbornness; now they have changed it to 'fickleness.'"

"I heard of this last charge," said Stephen. "Imagine Archbishop Hugh making even casually such a comment as 'Robert's wonted fickleness.' How could he apply such a word to such a man? He should know beyond all others that every act of Robert's religious life was done in obedience to his superiors. Tonnerre, Troyes, Colan, Molesme, Citeaux—practically every change was made at the will of the Holy See."

"True," said Romanus, "but you must remember that the Archbishop probably did not bother to inquire into the marvel of Robert's obedience. He never understood why our abbot went so meekly from place to place. Then, too, the Archbishop must have known something of Robert's ideal; and when he saw him peacefully agree to leave Citeaux, the one place where the ideal had any chance of being realized, he sneered. He never knew it almost tore Robert's heart out to leave Citeaux."

"He left so quietly that even I did not realize how much it meant to him," said Stephen. "But his first letter back to us made me weep to read it. After all these years, I can remember some of the exact words: 'I would sadden you too much if I could use my tongue as pen, my tears as ink, and my heart as paper.... I am here in body, because obedience demands it; but my soul is with you!'"

Romanus was silent. At last he said, "I was one of the most active in begging for Robert's return. How ashamed I was when I saw what our weakness had cost him! And now to hear him sneered at for his sacrifice—" and his voice trailed off.

"Robert never minded sneers," said Stephen, who did not wish Romanus to blame himself too severely. "And at any rate, we need not worry over Robert now. He is with God, and God is sure to vindicate him. Indeed, Romanus, from what you have said of Robert's death, God has begun his work already. That light over Molesme tells a story."

"Yes," replied Romanus thoughtfully, "it does. Robert is undoubtedly one of God's saints. But, Abbot Stephen, to me and to all of us who doubted, Robert's miracle of miracles is—you, Citeaux. The triumph of his generous love of God is here—in your lives."

Stephen leaned over and clasped the hand of the monk opposite him.

"There are miracles of all kinds," he said, "and I think Robert must be especially happy in the birth of his new brother—Romanus."

"Post Mortem"

You have just met the father of all "Trappists." You must admit that he was not "disappointed in love." You might be tempted to believe that he was in love with disappointments. He had seventy-seven years of them! But that would be a superficial reading. The truer truth is that he was in love with love and his life was not a *failure*.

As proof of that statement you are offered this "post-mortem." A doctor may make a mistake in a diagnosis while a person is living; he never makes one in the autopsy after the person is dead. That is why such examinations satisfy, and that is why you are offered this examination of Robert. At best, a "pre-natal" gives you conjecture; a "post-mortem" gives you absolute fact. Thus, it *may* have been true that our Lady espoused Robert before he was born; it *cannot be doubted* that Robert espoused our Lord before he was dead. For the infallible Roman Catholic Church, through His Holiness, Honorius III, solemnly enrolled Robert of Molesme in the catalogue of her saints in 1221.

For more than seven centuries Office has been sung and Mass has been offered in honor of the boy from Troyes who wanted to be gallant to God—and was! But note that it was "Robert of Molesme" who was enrolled among the saints— and that is the second point of this "postmortem." Robert, the founder of Citeaux was not a "Cistercian." No, he lived and died a "black Benedictine." He founded the Abbey of Citeaux, not the Order. Nevertheless, on the twenty-ninth of April of every year, the entire Cistercian Order celebrates his feast in a very solemn manner. In every house there is a sermon, and invariably the orator argues from the fact of his "post-mortem" to the actualities of his life. They have learned that he died of the saint's disease—"heart trouble." So, they say that he became a saint because he *lived a life of love.*

The final fact of this examination is that the forefather of the "Trappists" was not himself a "Trappist." No, he only *conceived* the rebellion. It took the other two, Alberic and Stephen, to bring it to birth and care for its growth. Robert was the rebel who planted the seed; Alberic the radical who watered it and saw that it took root.

So the rebellion marches on under....

Part II
St. Alberic the Radical

Chapter One

"You're a Radical!"

If anyone should ask: "Where was Alberic born?" the only answer possible is that nobody knows. "When was Alberic born?" Nobody knows. "Who were his parents?" Nobody knows. "What was his family? His early education? His social status?" Nobody knows.

But ignorance of these matters means little. For sanctity is not a question of the cradle or romper days. It is a matter of growth and maturity. In other words, history was kind when she buried all data concerning Alberic prior to his going to the hermits at Colan; for while the boy may be the father to the man, the apple is always a better test of the tree than its blossom! Indeed, the day he joined the hermits was his real birthday, the day he began to live to God in the special way that was to mean his ultimate sanctity.

Of course, you can conjecture on the probable date of his natural birth, for when Stephen Harding met him about 1080, Alberic described himself as a "middlin' man." He said he was "middle-aged, middle-sized, of middlin' brain and middlin' virtue." Stephen told him that he uttered a half-truth, but Alberic would not accept the implied compliment. Therefore, you may conclude that Alberic was born just about the time that Robert had learned that God was looking for someone to stand in the gap, that is, somewhere about 1033.

Concerning his lineage, a plausible guess may be made from the story of the founding of Colan. It was said that two brothers had become the bitterest of rivals for the championship of the various tourneys. They had jousted again and again, but never with any decisive result. First one would win, then the other. Jealousy generated bitterness, and this grew to such an extent that each resolved to get rid of the other.

One day as they were riding home after another unsatisfactory morning of tilting, they passed through the forest of Colan. In the hush of the woods they heard their own hearts beat, and each determined to accomplish his murderous design that day. By common impulse they reined in their mounts, when suddenly both were filled with horror at their contemplated crime. Without a word, they wheeled their horses, dug frightened spurs into their sides, and galloped off together to the hut of a holy priest who was living a hermit's life in the depths of the wood.

After they had confessed to him, they confessed to each other. Shame soon gave way to consternation at Satan's hold on them because of their passion for glory. Kneeling, they clasped hands and vowed to have done with the world. Then, on the very spot of the contemplated fratricide, they built a hermitage, resolving to spend the rest of their lives questing for God's glory rather than their own. Shortly after, four of their former companions, all nobles and warriors, joined them. This was the group of seven who besought Robert to be their father in religion.

On the basis of this account, it is safe to say that Alberic was of noble parentage. That he was not one of the brothers is quite certain; that he was a warrior is absolutely sure. Everything about him, from his ready good nature to his discipline and unquestionable bravery, stamps him as a soldier.

One evening in the August of 1099 Alberic was seated at a rough desk in the abbot's room of little Cîteaux. Beside him stood Stephen Harding, his prior.

The air was filled with the scent of wild roses that came from a thicket beneath the abbot's window. Robert had not been gone a full month. Alberic had been elected to succeed him, and had immediately appointed Stephen as prior. The two were hardly used to their positions but were busy laying plans. Alberic was insisting that "Statutes" be drawn up clearly avoiding all the practices of Molesme and all the Cluniac customs. He wanted Citeaux "to be Cistercian," he said—"pure Benedictine."

Stephen was shaking his head in disagreement. Finally he said, "Reverend Father, it can't be done."

"But I tell you it can be done and will be done. Just look at the spirit of our men!" came the fiery reply.

"Yes," answered Stephen honestly, "the present community can do it, and will do it gladly. But what of the future? You're not forgetting Molesme, are you?"

Alberic eyed him suspiciously. "Am I forgetting Molesme? Is that English humor? If you had been beaten by your own monks, if you had had your head broken and your shoulders beaten black and blue, if you had been thrown into a dungeon and kept there a prisoner, would you be likely to forget it? Am I forgetting Molesme!"

"No, no. You misunderstand me, Reverend Father. I was only thinking of how well we started at that monastery, and how poorly we ended. You must not forget that it was the younger element that failed to measure up."

"And the point of your argument?" asked Alberic.

"You are going to ask for more than Robert ever demanded. You want the utter simplicity of the primitive Rule."

"Right."

"Well, you can do it and I can follow; and the community we have now will be right behind us. But...ten years from now?"

"With God's help," said Alberic, "we'll have a larger monastery, a larger community, and the utter simplicity of the primitive Rule."

Stephen knew what was in his abbot's mind. He had learned a lesson the hard way at Molesme. He wanted no repetition. Stephen liked his ideas, was in favor of his methods, but was very much afraid of the weakness in man.

After some hesitation he finally shook his head, declaring, "Alberic, if Robert was a rebel, you're a radical!"

The abbot's gray eyes held Stephen a moment. "I don't know whether you mean that as a compliment or a condemnation. You English puzzle me. But I can tell you this: if you mean 'radical' in the Roman sense, you have struck me off perfectly. I am and ever intend to remain 'radical.' I mean to go down to the very roots of things. And the present roots that interest me are the roots of the Rule."

"But have you looked far into the future?" insisted Stephen.

"It is the future that has determined me," replied the abbot. "Not my future, nor yours; but

God's future. I know what you're worrying about. You're worrying about the youth of France, aren't you?"

Stephen nodded.

"Stephen, if you were a youngster whose father had taken the cross and gone to battle for God, what would your feelings be? If your older brothers and all your male relatives had battled about Jerusalem's walls and wrested that city from the enemies of the Faith, what would your ambition be?"

"To outdo them," came the unhesitating reply.

"Right," said Alberic. "To be as good as your elders would never satisfy you. But don't you think that the youth of France have as much fire and as lively a fancy as the English?"

Stephen smiled. It seemed that his abbot could never forget his nationality. "To avoid an argument and bring you to your point," he said, "I'll admit that they have."

"Then my point is made!" cried the abbot as his hand struck the desk. "You worry about the community ten years from now. They will be the sons of the Crusaders. Do you hear—*the sons of the Crusaders!* They will have learned how their sires left Europe numbering six hundred thousand; how they took Edessa and Antioch; then marched on, battled on, bled, starved, thirsted and died, until there were only fifty thousand left. Think of it—less than one-tenth of the original army! They will have learned how these fifty thousand camped around the walls of Jerusalem; how it was mid-sumer; how the Brook of Cedron had dried up and the wells all about had been poisoned or destroyed. They will have learned how there, under a brazen sky, in the midst of a blistered plain, these fifty thousand thirsted almost as the God-Man had thirsted outside those same walls the very day he died. They will have learned how this remnant held on, assaulted the city, took it, and then knelt as suppliants and conquerors in the Church of the Resurrection."

The abbot paused. His face was flushed and his eyes held the light of the sun. "Stephen," he said, "with such an inspiration before them, don't you see how the sons of these Crusaders will revel in being gallant to God? Why, they will be aflame with zeal to keep the Rule to its very hilt!"

"If they can see as you have seen," said Stephen slowly.

"They will," replied the abbot. "If I am not here to make them, you will be. The lance that pierced the heart of Christ was found miraculously at Antioch. It became a spur to our crusading knights. It will be the same to the youth of France. Chivalry, Stephen, is not for the battlefields and the secular world alone. It has its place here in the cloister."

As the prior nodded, the abbot went on, "Down deep in the heart of every man, Stephen, is a secret spot, which, if once touched, will make him more than man, will make him hero. I have seen it," said the Abbot with flashing eyes. "So have you. Look at what happened to Europe these past few years! Give men a cause and a commander and they forget that they are men and become lovers! That's the story of Godfrey of Bouillon and the Crusade. And that will be the story of little Citeaux."

"Will you be the commander, and the simplicity of the Rule, the cause?"

"Never!" exclaimed the former warrior. "There is only one commander—Christ. And only one cause—the honor and glory of God."

There was a long pause. Alberic looked off through the trees, but his mind's eye was seeing someone who had never walked those woods.

The abbot arose and went to the window. After looking at the setting sun he turned and said, "I'll be judged, Stephen, according to the Rule of St. Benedict. Not only as to how I kept it, but also as to how I explained it to others, how I interpreted it for others, how I got others to keep it. It's a sobering thought. Another serious thought is that of the centuries yet to come. What you and I do in this little Abbey of Citeaux, Stephen, will affect those centuries. Never forget it. Christ is one. The Church is one. We are all one. Therefore, what we do affects the entire body," Alberic broke off. "And now that Robert has gone from us, how we're going to miss him!"

"Oh, but Alberic, haven't you been doing most of the work for some time?"

"I have. But the responsibility was his. Now it is different."

"You sound afraid."

The abbot sat down and leaned on his desk. "Afraid?" he asked. "Stephen, I'm frightened. Believe me, if it wasn't for the lance the Crusaders found; if it wasn't for the tomb the Crusaders won; if it wasn't for the Christ who lived and died and lives again, I couldn't do it. I'm not brave, Stephen. But, thank God, I've got faith. He put me here. He'll help me here—and help me to keep the Rule to the hilt."

"Robert used to say 'to the letter.'"

"I know it," said Alberic as he straightened. "But I'm going to go further than Robert went. I'm going to go back to the simplicity of the Rule in everything. And that means war. All I can think of is a naked saber plunged to the hilt. Citeaux is going to comfort the Heart of Christ."

"Come," said Stephen, rising to hide his emotion. "It's prayer time. The future rests with God."

As he walked down the chapel corridor behind his resolute looking abbot, the shadow of a smile played around Stephen Harding's lips. It was a smile of admiration and affection. He was thinking how strange it was to call Alberic "abbot." He had known him so long and so intimately. He could remember the first day they had met. It was at Molesme. Alberic was prior. Stephen recalled the torn robe Alberic was wearing. He certainly had been a nondescript monk—except for his smile. He was now thinking of what it must have cost Alberic to smile in those days for this was before Troyes' bishop had gone home hungry. Robert had certainly struck the secret spot in Alberic's soul, thought Stephen. Only a hero or frenzied lover could have smiled so happily during those trying years.

Then came the memory of the wintry night Alberic had taken him aside, pointed to the evening star, and asked what it symbolized for him. Stephen had answered, "Purity—it looks so cold and chaste."

Alberic laughed and said, "Chastity is not cold, my friend. It is white-hot. Try again."

Stephen had looked at the star a moment and said, "Obedience—steadfast obedience. That star has obeyed God, without a single deviation, ever since the moment of its creation."

"Good!" Alberic cried and then asked, "Anything else?"

Stephen studied the star again but finally turned and said, "No. Nothing more at the moment."

Then Alberic asked, "Do you know what it means to our abbot?" Stephen did not know. "It means loneliness, love, leadership," said Alberic. "Robert sees it as the symbol of the Rule—his symbol. He wants the Rule rigidly kept. He knows he'll be alone, and that it will take great love. But he always insists that stars come out after dark. That just as myriads of others stud the skies after vesper's shining, so other monasteries will one day follow Molesme. But, he warns us, before they do we shall have to see the dark."

Stephen prayed for Alberic and himself that night. They were alone now. Robert, who had guided them all their religious lives, had been taken from them by obedience. They would miss him much. But Stephen found great comfort in the discovery he had made that night of the contradictory combination in Alberic's character—timidity linked with intrepidity. He had admitted that he was afraid, and yet went ahead with his plans for a life without compromise. He was going to present the naked simplicity of the Rule, and see that it was observed. There was great comfort for Stephen in the discovery, and yet his prayer was for courage.

Alberic prayed a similar prayer for his thoughts were much the same. He went back over the years. He recalled leaving Colan—the mere handful they were—just thirteen. But they had changed the wilderness of Molesme into a monastic paradise. Then came the change. Compromises crept in. When he tried to curb them there was the revolt. What a nightmare that was! Then came the real revolt—twenty of them with Robert to Citeaux. The work. Success. Then Robert's recall. His own election. What years!

What years! And now..."God, come to my assistance!" What was ahead?..."Lord, make haste to help me!"

Prayers seemed unbelievably short that night. Before he knew it, it was time for bed. He gave the signal, then took his stand at the door of the church in order to sprinkle each monk's head with holy water. It was the custom of the house. As he did it he whispered, "Crusader for Christ, be brave!" It was the real beginning of his abbacy.

Chapter Two

"Shields for the Sacred Heart"

The following morning the community assembled as usual for chapter. Some were still troubled by Robert's recall. Their confidence in the old giant had been implicit; and naturally so, for he had given them birth in the spiritual life and had guided them all their growing years. It was not easy to transfer that confidence to another. Especially when that other had been one of them, was known intimately, and had always been looked upon as inferior to the grand old man. Oh, they admitted that Alberic was good-natured. That cheering smile of his had lifted everyone of them, sometime or other, out of the doldrums. And he was holy enough. Yes, he was a good religious. But to be abbot in place of Robert!...Well, they were uneasy. They had not forgotten the storm he had stirred up at Molesme. A great superior would never have been guilty of such. Perhaps he lacked prudence. And surely, if prudence was ever needed it was now at the beginning of their new monastery. They had elected him because of his experience as prior and his long intimacy with Robert. Unquestionably he was the best fitted to think along the lines of the old rebel. He had been his pupil for over a quarter of a century!

But this morning in August would show them an Alberic they had never known. It was the same middle-sized man who sat a little uncomfortably in the abbot's chair. The same smile seemed ready at the corners of his mouth and the same cheerful good nature. Yet, there was a profound change. He looked more resolute, more of a warrior, more of a commander. A new strength showed in that familiar face. Even the hands seemed to have more power. And the voice!...

"I know many of you are uneasy. I don't blame you. I am uneasy myself." Such was his opening. Its honesty won him confidence. Then in his straightforward fashion he went on to give them better arguments for uneasiness than they had ever thought out for themselves. If Molesme, strong as she was with the strength of twenty-five years of growth, could not survive without Robert, what hope had Citeaux, not yet two years old, with Alberic? Naturally speaking, there was none!

The community was surprised by this forthrightness—the echo of their own doubts. But then Alberic told them that there would be no "natural speaking" at Citeaux; it would all be "supernatural!" It had to be; for since he was so destitute of natural ability, they would have to win for him all that was necessary for the very supernatural living that was to be theirs. He said that he based all his hopes on them; for he was certain that God was ever close to the lips of this handful of heroes, and that they would whisper to God for their poor leader.

He explained that Robert's principles were to be pushed to their logical extreme. He used many of the old abbot's words, but there was a new ring to them. "The Rule was a way of showing gallantry to God," he said, "so was it a way of crusading for Christ—for Christ *was* the Commander and the glory of God the cause."

Throbbing in every sentence and pulsing in every phrase was— *love!* The only reason for this heroic living was—love. And just as they were to live without compromise, so were they to love without measure. The cause was too great for costs to be counted; the Commander was too supremely sovereign for anything less than their chivalrous best. The Rule of St. Benedict must be lived to the hilt just to show Christ the love of their manly hearts!

Even the prior who had heard him the evening before was surprised at the transformation in this middle-sized, affable man. The power, he thought, must be in the Crusader's spear of which Alberic had spoken. Indeed, a lance had opened Alberic's side and shown his heart to be that of a warrior on fire with love. Before he finished, all doubt about the triumph of Robert's rebellion had vanished. It was evident to everyone in that room that it was going to be pushed to a fuller, fiercer fight.

As he closed, Alberic returned to his opening idea of God being close to the lips of a monk. "Whisper to him your love," he said. "Say that you will show it by living the Rule in its naked simplicity. Then beg him to help one who is both naked and simple—your abbot."

Eyes were eloquent as the monks left the chapter that morning. Admiration, enthusiasm, joy, exultation were visible in every face. These men were happy. They knew now that they had a superior. The superior was happy, for he saw that he had men.

The sadness caused by Robert's departure soon passed as the little monastery took on a new tempo and pulsed with greater life. But the abbot was not stopping there. He had plans that went far beyond Citeaux. He spread them before his prior when the latter came to him with frowns and fears.

"Reverend Father," said Stephen earnestly,

"we'll have no trouble from within. Our community is truly zealous. But we'll have plenty of trouble from without. Molesme will never let us alone. Cluny will talk. And the abbeys of Germany will not be silent. We are a condemnation to them."

"A challenge, Stephen, not a condemnation," said the abbot.

"They take it as a condemnation," insisted the prior. "They say we are innovators and Pharisees."

"Pharisees?"

"Yes, Pharisees. They still say that we keep the letter of the law, and they the spirit."

Alberic bridled a bit. He sat up in his chair and spoke more vigorously. "Listen, Stephen. Get this clearly; we are not innovating; we are renovating. This is not Robert's mode of life, nor your mode of life, nor mine; it is Benedict's! It is no new Rule we are erecting; it is the old we are resurrecting."

"And there's the rub," interjected Stephen. "Don't you see that two and two can only make four? If we are right, then they are wrong."

"Not wrong, Stephen. Different."

"My good Father Abbot," said the prior somewhat testily, "you are very cool this morning and full of fine distinctions. But do you know that we are the target of some very sharp criticism already? Do you know that we are called 'fervent fanatics' by some, 'spiritually deluded' by others, and 'irrational rigorists' by most?"

Alberic held him with a quizzical glance for a moment, then said, "I thought the English were unemotional. Can it be that you are imbibing some of our French fervor?" Then he sat back, smiled, and asked, "Stephen, didn't you ever hear the little ditty that runs, 'Sticks and stones may break my bones, but names will never hurt me?' Let all of them talk. I have a plan."

"To silence them?"

"No, to let them talk! But in such a way as not to affect us." The prior looked baffled. "You've been in Rome, haven't you, Stephen?" The prior nodded. "A very powerful man lives there, they tell me. I think they call him the Pope. Don't you think that he might be able to keep the sticks and stones from breaking our bones?" When Stephen did not immediately answer the abbot went on, "Names will never hurt us. I rather like being called a 'fool' for Christ."

"You mean that you are going to report Molesme, Cluny and the rest to the Holy Father?"

"Nothing of the sort. I am going to report Citeaux to him. I am going to tell him just exactly what is going on here. I'm going to tell him that a fool of an abbot worries the very life out of a really excellent prior by getting his community to live as they vowed to live. I'm going to tell him that a few fervent fanatics, some spiritually de-

luded and—what was the other name? Oh, yes—
some irrational rigorists have forgotten that 'the
letter killeth,' but are just filled with the spirit of
St. Benedict. I'm going to tell him that some mad
monks want to leave the world alone, and want
to be left alone by that world. Only I won't use
those exact words."

"And what do you expect to gain by all
that?" asked Stephen.

"Pontifical approbation and apostolic sanction to keep on doing what we have been doing,"
answered Alberic triumphantly.

"But we've already got that from his dele-
gate," came the quick objection.

"I'm looking for more," said Alberic. "I
haven't forgotten Molesme, Stephen. I know
what a noisy majority can do; and the majority
is certainly against us. I am expecting much more
trouble than you have outlined. I am going to see
if I can steal a march on all our friends. Rome has
a long arm. She can protect us. But that is not
exactly what fills my mind this morning. Criticism from Molesme and Cluny bothers me little
at the moment. Two Cardinals were here yesterday Stephen. You saw them?"

"I did. What did they want?"

"Oh, they came to satisfy a legitimate curiosity. They had heard about us—good things and
bad. They came to see for themselves. Believe
me, they saw! I really think we gave them plenty
of matter for meditation. I know they gave me

plenty. They painted a picture, Stephen, that pains even as it inspires." The abbot paused, then suddenly turning he asked, "Stephen, what is your concept of life here at Citeaux?"

"Penitents for an unrepenting world," came the unhesitating reply.

"Good!" exclaimed the abbot. "That sounds like Robert. Anything else?"

"Yes, if it is not too presumptuous—angels of consolation for the agonizing Christ."

"That's even better than Robert's. That's your own. But tomorrow I'm going to give you one that I consider best of all. Tomorrow I am going to talk about being shields for the Sacred Heart. Tomorrow I am going to do something I very seldom do. I am going to tell the community much about the world out there beyond our woods. I am going to tell them what it is doing to the Christ we serve. Cardinal John and Cardinal Benedict gave me a lot of bad news, Stephen. I'm going to see if we can't change it into good."

"How?"

The abbot looked down at his desk as if he were marshalling his thoughts. Presently he sat back and asked, "Stephen, why did you go to Molesme instead of to Cluny?"

The prior was puzzled for a moment. His brow contracted. But he answered readily, "That is the question I have often asked myself, Reverend Father. I think the real answer is that Molesme was a challenge. You see, most men want to do the daring, difficult, different thing. Young men love adventure and romance; and I was young. There is adventure and romance in doing what is different. There is zest in facing what furnishes a challenge."

"Fine!" exulted the abbot. It was just the lead he wanted. "Those are the very elements I thought fascinated men—challenge, adventure, romance. You spoke about being a penitent for an unrepentant world and an angel of consolation to the agonizing Christ. There's real romance and stirring adventure in that. That's being different. But now I have something new. You believe that our life of prayer and penance helps the world and comforts Christ, don't you, Stephen?"

The prior was used to his abbot's approach now. He wondered what the old warrior knew of Socrates and his method. But the fire in the abbot's eyes kindled warmth in his own heart. He drew his chair closer as he answered, "I know it does."

"You believe that hidden away here in this swamp-land, singing psalms and chopping wood, tilling the soil and caring for cattle, you are fulfilling the sublime end for which God created you?"

"I'm positive of it."

"You believe that though you do nothing, as the world says, yet you help save that world?"

Stephen's eyes lighted. "I'm thoroughly convinced that we help save the world; and I know that the world is thoroughly convinced that we do nothing. Therefore, it is a case of those who do nothing saving the world."

"Good. Well, Stephen, now I want to convince you and all the community that we can also save Christ."

"Save Christ?" repeated Stephen wonderingly. "From what?"

"From being pierced again by a lance! We must be shields for the Sacred Heart, Stephen, for the Sacred Heart needs shields. From all sides spears are being pointed at that sacred breast." With a sudden angry flash of his eyes Alberic asked, "Do you know why those two Cardinals are in France?"

"No."

"Because Philip, our king, is aping Longinus. He has put away his own wife and taken Bertrada, wife of the Count of Anjou. He is living in open adultery. Oh, what a world of damage such example from those in high places does! Christ must be sad this day, Stephen, very sad. For from his beloved France comes a long, pointed lance of impurity. It is headed straight for his Sacred Heart. We must be his buckler."

"But how?" asked Stephen earnestly.

The abbot's clenched fist struck the desk as he said, "By living our life of no compromise! The Cardinals excommunicated Philip. We must win him back to God by our prayer and penance. We can do it. Yes, we can by living our Rule to the hilt."

"That's a challenge," said Stephen and his eyes were brilliant. "It's a challenge the community will gladly accept."

"Ah, but I have just started," said the abbot as he again shifted in his chair. "Henry IV of Germany is another Centurion. He has a long and very dangerous lance—his anti-pope! Think of it—a Catholic sovereign setting up a puppet of his own in opposition to the representative of Christ upon earth. It makes me want to don a suit of mail. Yes, it makes me long for a swift, stout horse and a brutal battle-axe." Then throwing out his hands in a gesture of exasperation he said, "And he still wages war for the right of lay investiture!"

"Still?" There was incredulity and chagrin in the word.

"Yes, and his attitude has affected your own England." Stephen sat up as if he had been struck. "Your Henry started well enough; but it was all policy Stephen, all policy. That man hasn't got a bit of principle to him. He has exiled Anselm, Archbishop of Canterbury, confiscated all his property, claims the right of investiture, and has even sent insulting legates to the Pope to tell him so."

"Insulting!" Stephen could not believe his ears.

"I call them such," replied Alberic warmly. "One of them had the effrontery to say to His Holiness, 'I assure you that the King will not brook the loss of the right of lay investiture, though it cost him his kingdom!'"

Stephen started and slowly asked, "What did the Pope say?"

Alberic's head came up. "He answered like the worthy successor to the fearless Peter that he is. He said, 'And I assure you that Pope Pascal will never allow him that abusive right, though it cost him his *life!*'"

"Good for him," cheered Stephen.

"Oh, Pascal is a fighter," said Alberic with a smile. "He used the same language to Henry that St. Ambrose used to Theodosius the Great. He said, 'The palace is the Emperor's; the Church the Bishops.'"

"That's pointed enough for anyone," said the prior.

But then Alberic's eyes lost their light of triumph, and the overtone of joy went from his voice as he said, "But, Stephen, don't you see the frightful picture our continent presents? From all sides lances are levelled at the Heart of Christ. I mean that literally; I am not using metaphor. The Church is the Body of Christ. St. Paul distinctly says so. Therefore, what strikes the Church, wounds Jesus."

Stephen paused before he said, "Those are

Paul's exact words. I never caught their full significance before."

Alberic went on, "Doesn't that fact spur you on to a fuller living of the Rule? Doesn't it fill you with the spirit of no compromise? Ah, Stephen, the truth's the thing! I'm telling the community that tremendous truth tomorrow. I'm also sending Ilbode and John to Rome. For, strange as it may seem, if we are to be shields for the Sacred Heart we must have papal protection."

"My abbot," said Stephen humbly, "may I say that your vision improves? You are looking into a very deep future."

The abbot smiled. "You're wrong, Stephen. I am only looking at a very shallow past."

As Alberic passed his hand lightly over his shoulder, Stephen remembered the scars that must still remain from the cruel imprisonment at Molesme.

Chapter Three
"White Is All Colors"

John and Ilbode, two sturdy sons of France, set out for Rome the next day. Alberic gave them a blessing, some influential letters, and good advice. That was all; for that was all he had. But it proved to be more than enough. The two Cardinals, who had come to excommunicate Philip, wrote powerful lines to the Pope, urging him to give his fullest support to this little band of monks. The Bishop of Châlons also wrote; while Hugh, Archbishop of Lyons and Legate of the Holy See, told a very intimate tale of the why and the wherefore of Citeaux. John and Ilbode did not have much for the journey; but they had more than enough for the journey's end.

Stephen thought he would not have disliked that journey. He had made it once, long ago and on foot. How vividly he could recall those rugged roads the Romans had built when France was Transalpine Gaul! Then the woods! They would just be breaking into bud now; trees would look thin, trim, and very shy with their myriad tips of green. Under foot, through the black of last year's leaves, crocuses would nod—yellow, white and lavender in a world of soft breeze and sunshine. Anemones would be there, too. Yes, the woods would be heavenly. How one would want to wander from the road!

Then the mountains! Their streams would be boisterous this early in the spring. What music they would be making—an accompaniment to the night breeze as it stole through pine and oak and ash!

Night in the mountains! Stephen sighed. Why was it that one seemed so alone and so perfectly at peace on a mountaintop? Why was it that God seemed so near? Why did one always fancy him leaning from out the Milky Way, viewing his wide creation and seeing that it was good—very, very good? Why…?

Stephen caught himself. He laughed softly. Let John and Ilbode make the journey. He would whisper a prayer every day that they would not miss the grandeur as they walked through God's wonderland of spring.

Stephen, the poet, once mentioned his reveries to Alberic. The latter listened attentively, but only remarked, "I wish they'd hurry back."

Stephen looked at his abbot closely, then broke into a laugh. "It's a waste of words," he said, "to talk to a man of one idea. But I understand your impatience. I, too, wish they'd hurry back."

And they did! For they had much more than Alberic had even hoped for. They handed him a letter and smiled as he tore it open. Pascal, Vice-regent for Jesus Christ, called Alberic and his monks "my most dear sons in Christ, whom I long after very much." They watched Alberic's eyes race down the page. It was too good to be true: "...We excommunicate any archbishop or bishop, emperor or king, count or viscount, judge or any other person, ecclesiastical or lay, who being aware of the protection granted by the Holy See, should dare to molest the abbot or the Abbey of Citeaux."

"God be praised!" Alberic exclaimed. "Get Father Prior. Get him quickly!" When Stephen came Alberic thrust the letter into his hands and said, "Read that! Read that and see if we need worry about Molesme, Cluny, or anyone else."

Stephen read. When he came to the excommunication he whistled softly, then read it aloud. When he finished he turned and said: "Why, Alberic, this is the *'Privilegium Romanum.'* We're independent of all archbishops and bishops. We're under the wing of the Pope. Why this is...this is...."

"This is marvelous," concluded Alberic.

"And do you note that it is granted to me and my successors in perpetuity? Let me read that date again. 'Given this eighteenth day of April, 1100, the second year of Our Pontificate, Pascal II.' That's one date I'll never forget. It's my birthday as a fearless radical. Now watch me grow!"

Stephen watched the lights dance in his abbot's eyes for a moment, then said, "We need not worry now what they say about our habits...."

Alberic carefully placed the papal document on the table. "What have they been saying about our habits?" he asked as he lifted the edge of his scapular and rubbed his fingers across the rough texture. "Not exactly silky, I admit. Not even smooth. But it is what the Rule called for."

"It is what our critics called for," said Stephen. "The monks of other monasteries are laughing aloud at what they call our inconsistency. We claim to be rigorists for the Rule, they say; and yet we do something no Benedictine has ever done in the five hundred and fifty years of the Order's existence."

"Just what are you talking about?"

"About our habits. Our critics are ridiculing us because we who claim to be penitents, instead of wearing sack-cloth and ashes, are garbed in the radiant white of the joyous. They are calling us fanatical innovators."

"I think it's our turn to laugh," said Alberic with a chuckle.

"At what?"

"At the forgetfulness of these monks. They have forgotten at least two things. First, they have forgotten that the fifty-fifth chapter of the Rule says, 'Let the monks not complain of the color or the coarseness of their clothes, but let them be obtained in the country where they live, or can be bought most cheaply.' So you see, my good prior, the rigorists are rigorous. The cheapest wool that I could buy in this part of the world is this coarse, undyed, greyish-white stuff. The color of our habits is not a departure from, but a return to, the Rule in its radical meaning. But what amuses me most is the second thing they have forgotten."

"What is that?"

"That white is all colors."

Stephen looked at his abbot. He had not caught the significance of the remark at all. After turning the phrases over in his mind a few moments he said, "I'm waiting. What's the point? I admit that white is all colors."

"Therefore, it is the *only* color that is perfectly suited to the state that embraces all sorts of people for all sorts of purposes; namely, the monastic state."

"Clever," remarked the prior with a smile, "but unconvincing."

"What?" snorted the abbot. "Unconvincing? Look here, man, black is the absence of color. How then can it be symbolic? How can it be suited to the monastic state? In every monastery you'll find ardent apostolic souls who live in the cloister that they may convert the world by burning out their lives in prayer. Red is the only color symbolic for them. They are martyrs. Then there are those of generous heart who must give their all to God in loving adoration. Gold is their color. Then for the fresh, unspoiled beauty of the young, who come in the springtime of life that they may bloom to God alone, you must have green. Black will do for none of these. Then for virginal souls you must have white. Flame-yellow will do for the sacrificial souls. But above all you must have true blue, or better, royal purple to symbolize the loyal grandeur of penitential love that absorbs those who, after having known sin, have come to know the Savior. What does black signify or symbolize? All I can think of is death, and men don't come to monasteries to die; at least, not to this monastery! No. They come here to live—to live to God alone."

"Yes, but a monk should be dead to the world and to his lower self."

"Right. But there's no sense in mourning over such a death. No, indeed. Put on the white of gladness and rejoice! Or if you want to insist on the idea of self being dead, then I say wrap it up in a shroud. And I've never yet seen or heard of a black shroud. So you see how convincing my cleverness can be." And with that Alberic eyed his prior challengingly.

"Yes, but how much thought did you give to

symbolism when you changed the color of our habits?" asked Stephen.

"None," laughed the abbot delightedly. "Absolutely none! Why, Stephen, if red wool were cheaper than white wool, I'd have you all clothed as Cardinals. The *Rule* is the only reason for the white. But the next time you hear a taunt about our habits just say to yourself, 'They ought to know better than that! They ought to know that white garments are the robes of fools!' And that is what makes them so suitable for the monks at Citeaux."

When the prior frowned, the abbot continued, "That's what we are—fools for Christ." Then he added, "But note that I advise you to say all this to yourself; for I have always held that it is better to keep your mouth shut and let people think you a fool than to open it and prove they are right!"

Chapter Four
"Don't Shear Too Close!"

When the news of Robert's recall (in 1099) spread about the monastic world, many a head shook knowingly, and many a monk spoke prophetically of the early death of the new monastery so auspiciously begun in the swampland. Few would have lamented its passing. The attempt was altogether too ambitious! Some scattered monks may have admired the daring that dreamed of transplanting men of the twelfth century back into the sixth. More pitied the delusion that led sincere men into such an extravaganza. But most had only contempt and condemnation for such fanaticism. So, the rejoicing was rather general when Robert returned to Molesme.

But 1100 was not two months old before it

was evident to all that Citeaux would not die. That she would not even grow sick! They saw that Alberic had injected new life into the little group in the swampland and that the rebellion against the common way of living was making swifter, surer headway. The white habits gleamed in those woods as brilliantly as fireflies in the black of night, and they told the world just as insistently of life.

One morning, however, Stephen found his usually smiling abbot looking glum. When he asked what was wrong he got the surprising reply, "Oh, just having a dried-apple day."

When he asked what kind of a day that was, he got an explanation that set them both smiling. Alberic asked if Stephen had ever put a small dried apple into his mouth and kept it there. The prior hadn't. "Well," explained the abbot, "the longer you leave it there, the bigger it grows. It soaks up saliva and swells. If you leave it there too long, you'll choke."

Stephen asked the point of application, and Alberic replied, "Most of our troubles, my good prior, are nothing but little dried apples; but we keep them in our mouths until we almost choke. Today is a dried-apple day for me, because I can't seem to get some of my tiny troubles from between my teeth."

"What troubles?"

"That's what exasperates me. They are not worthy of the name of troubles. It's just a little touchiness on my part, or perhaps curiosity. You see, reports of what the Cluniacs are saying seep through, and whether I'm hurt at being criticized, or humbled at being stupid, I don't know. But I do know I'd love to be able to answer the question: 'Why don't they let us alone?'"

After staring at the base of the distant wall for a moment he continued, "I can't understand it. Here we are, a mere handful, hidden away in this swampy wood; and there is Cluny with the whole of the continent under her jurisdiction and the whole world under her sway—for in very truth, she almost is the Church! And yet she becomes absorbed in what we are doing. Why should a colossus be disturbed by a mite? Stars don't shine when the sun comes up. What is she afraid of Alberic was both puzzled and peeved.

Stephen chuckled. "Your 'dried-apple' is almost choking you, Reverend Father," he said. "Just what have they criticized lately?"

"What haven't they? Our table, our bedding, our habits, our manual labor..."

"Didn't you expect it? You have criticized their table, their bedding, their manual labor...."

"I?...When?... Never!"

Stephen chuckled again. "Oh, no, Reverend Father, you never criticized them at all! But somehow or other most people take your every move as a criticism. You see, they have the peculiar habit of arguing logically. They say the one Rule demands the one observance. Therefore, if you are right, Cluny is wrong. But if Cluny is right, you are fanatical."

"Then they do not know the Rule," said Alberic as he reached across his desk for a text. Holding the little book before him he nodded to Stephen and said, "Father Prior, there is hardly a chapter in this book that the abbot may not temper if he thinks fit. St. Benedict did not mean to tyrannize; he meant to order. Now, that one truth makes this whole matter appear ridiculous. For Cluny can be Cluny; and Molesme Molesme; and Citeaux Citeaux—while all three remain Benedictine. Let them interpret the Rule as they see fit. That is none of my affair. But I would like to be allowed to interpret as I see fit."

Stephen only shook his head. "No, Reverend Father. That is not the way the human mind works. It says that if we can survive on the two cooked portions that St. Benedict prescribed, then other Benedictines do not need three or four; if we can thrive on the labor of our hands, then others do not need serfs…."

"Ah," cried the abbot enthusiastically, "that reminds me of a real problem. Never mind their mentality, and never mind the Cluniacs. But come and give me your full mind on this matter of labor and serfs." And Alberic energetically drew his chair up to his desk.

It was such a characteristic change that Stephen smiled and approached the abbot's chair. But the smile soon vanished as Alberic proposed his plan.

In 1101 the monasteries of France were being supported, and some even enriched, by revenues from ecclesiastical benifices, tithes, and the labor of serfs. Many an abbot was actually a feudal lord. His possessions were vast, his dependents many, his income great. This was a survival from the early centuries of the Middle Ages when monasteries had been the germ-cells of future cities and towns. Such sovereignty was good for the serf and good for civilization; but it was not so good for the spirit of poverty. Monasteries became wealthy.

At the time when Alberic bent to his planning with Stephen, there was not a monastery of any size on the continent that did not have its independent income. The monks did not have to work, for they were being supported by others. It is small wonder, then, that the monastic world gasped when it learned the outcome of Alberic's talk on his "dried-apple day."

He had taken the text of the Rule and pointed to the sentence, "They are truly monks when they live by the labor of their own hands." With that as a base he started to build. Before he finished, he had planned his most radical and rebellious of all moves. He would not only reinstate poverty; he would insure her lofty position. He had pointed out the dangers of wealth, and showed how the very beneficence of Odo,

Duke of Burgundy, might work them harm. To blot out all shadow of compromise he proposed that they maintain as much ground as could be cultivated by themselves and renounce every other source of income. "Let us live the Rule, Stephen. Let us be radical enough to be absolutely self-supporting. Let there be no semblance of compromise about Citeaux."

It was but a logical step in his program; but it was a step that only a hero would dare to take. Alberic took it. Stephen and the community followed. But their step amazed more than the monastic world.

Most of the nobility and many of the serfs had been marveling at the austerity of Citeaux and the generosity of her monks. They had been moved by the chivalry of men who dared be different enough to show gallantry to God. Of course, they heard the laughs and lampoons of the other monks. But simple men have a shrewdness that often enables them to hear the heart of the merely clever, despite the speech of his mouth. They may have joined in the laughs and enjoyed the cleverness of the lampoons, but they had admiration for the men in the swamp. When they heard of Alberic's determination to support himself, however, they shook their heads. Even the duke—loyal, admiring, ever-faithful Odo— did not unequivocally approve.

In 1099, after the church had been dedicated, the duke had obtained permission from

Robert to build himself a modest mansion close to the monastery. He was passionately attached to the place. He never allowed any great feast to pass without bringing a number of his companions to his mansion and having all attend the entire Office and the Solemn Mass. Citeaux completed the conversion St. Anselm began.

On the eve of Ascension Thursday, 1101, Odo, his son Hugh, and a goodly number of nobles stabled their horses in the monastery yard, retired to the private mansion, and prepared to celebrate the feast with the monks. The duke had been doing this for almost two full years now, but a far deeper seriousness marked his behavior as he made his preparation this particular evening. He went about the grounds slowly. He insisted on being alone. He lingered in such favorite spots as the little nook to the side of the church door. He had sat in the shade there with Robert often. But he lingered longest in the plot that had been selected as the cemetery. The gruff old warrior was like a lover revisiting the scene where he first found love.

No explanation of his strange behavior was given or even guessed at until after Mass on the morrow. He and his company had risen with the monks near midnight. They had spent those black hours from then till dawn in the dim church following the solemn chant of the Office and joining the monks in their prayers of praise. The duke then begged leave to serve a private

Mass. The remaining hour before the sunrise song he spent before the Blessed Sacrament. After the early morning prayers he took a turn in the garden, then returned to church for the Solemn Mass. It was noon when he met Alberic.

"It struck me this morning," he said, "that your men would make excellent robbers."

There was much in common between the abbot and the duke. Both were warriors. Both were outspoken. Both had keen humor. Alberic laughed and retorted, "Who could judge more excellently than Your Excellency? I have often heard it said that it takes a thief to catch a thief."

"That is precisely why I put it forth as a certainty and not as an opinion," replied the duke. "I know my old business and all through the night I watched your monks. I saw that they know their business! Father Abbot, the concentration of those men on the one work before them was inspiring. Indeed, they would make grand robbers, for a robber has to know how to concentrate."

"I think they are robbers," put in Hugh, the duke's eldest son, who showed more of his mother's features and fair complexion than he did those of his swarthy sire. When his father flashed a questioning glance at him the young noble went on, "They've stolen you from your old life and even from your old home. No wonder Mother taunts you with the question, 'When are you going to take the cowl?'"

By this time they were all seated around the special table Alberic always set for the duke and his escort. The Rule required that the abbot dine with the guests, and that he have one or two of the brethren with him when the guests were not too numerous. Usually he left Stephen with the community, for the Rule demanded that a senior be there for the sake of discipline. But today, for some unknown reason, Alberic asked the prior to eat with the duke. It was a jovial group that seated itself, for there was much mutual liking between Odo's followers and the monks of Citeaux.

After the duke had sipped his wine, he struck the board and said, "That settles it. We've got to have a new vineyard. What would you say to accepting that favorite of mine about a league to the north of us, Father Abbot?"

Alberic touched his lips with his napkin before he replied, "I would say it can't be done." The duke's eyes opened wide. The abbot chuckled, looked at Stephen Harding and said, "The truth is like murder—it always will out!" Then turning to the duke he said, "Excellency, did you ever know that wealth brings poverty?"

The duke frowned. "I could never make much of paradoxes, Father Abbot. The Gospel teems with them. Loss and gain; lose and find; life and death. But paradoxes only puzzle me. I'm just a simple soldier."

"Well, let me tell you a little story about Molesme," said Alberic. And then he recounted what had happened to Robert and his reform after the Bishop of Troyes had gone home hungry. It was cleverly told, convincingly told. The abbot ended with, "So you see, wealth can bring poverty."

"I was just thinking a good vineyard could bring good wine," said the duke with a laugh. "I'm not planning to endow you with my Duchy."

"It seems as if you've given us half of it already," put in Stephen. "When I returned from the last grange you donated, I told the abbot we'd all have to have ten-league boots if we are to harvest the crop in that field. I thought I had walked halfway to Paris."

"Let the serfs do your harvesting," grumbled the duke. "I left enough of them on that grange to care for it. You men are monks. Sing your Office; tend your garden; and let the serfs take care of the distant granges."

"Excellency," said Alberic, "my prior and I held a council of war a short while ago. We'll now continue it in your presence, for although you haven't got the cowl your son teases you about, you have been a member of our council ever since the day you rode through the woods and became horrified at what we were building."

The duke laughed heartily. "You needed counsel then. Perhaps you need it now. What have you planned?"

Alberic told him then of his determination to retain only as much farmland as his monks could cultivate, and only as much meadow, woodland, and vineyard as the monastery needed for its own support. The duke listened attentively. As the abbot proceeded with his outline, Odo began to drum on the table nervously. When Alberic finished he shook his head and said, "You're shearing too close, Father Abbot; you're going to cut the sheep."

Alberic pointed to the Rule itself and to his regime of "no compromise." The duke asked what he would do if the community suddenly enlarged. The abbot laughed and said, "Call on you!" That pleased the duke, but he still pleaded for prudence. Alberic shook his head and said, "Some people would preach prudence to the crucifix!"

The duke broke out into a rumbling, infectious laugh. "Tell me in all honesty, Father Abbot," he begged, "is your private motto: 'Though everyone else, not I'?"

"It can't be," put in young Hugh.

"Why not?" snapped his father. "Doesn't he differ from every other abbot in the land?"

"He does. But the motto you want to give him fell from the lips of Peter just before he fell. Father Abbot is not going to fall."

The duke laughed, then said, "'Look before you leap.' I have a solution for you, Reverend Father. You see, I don't take back gifts. So to satisfy both yourself and your humble servant, you'll have to make all the serfs on the various granges members of the community. Then you can keep your Rule, and I can keep my self-respect." It was meant as a pleasantry. At the moment Alberic and all at table took it as such, but it turned out to be the seed of Alberic's most revolutionary move. That, however, came later.

They sat long at dinner that day, discussing the abbot's plan. It had been a surprising announcement, and it had called forth much heated debate. But just as they arose from table the duke made an announcement that was even more startling: "This is my farewell to Citeaux."

Everyone looked at him in surprise. "My wife and son have had many a laugh about my taking the cowl. I can't do that. But I can take the cross! I can't be a Cistercian monk, but I can become a crusader. My fathers and friends, I go to the Orient soon. They tell me the new Christian kingdom set up there needs stout arms. I have two. I go to be gallant to God in a different way."

As usual after the meal, the duke retired with the abbot to the latter's room. This day, however, he brought his son with him, and asked the abbot to include Stephen Harding. The four then entered into a study of the monastery and its lands. The duke painstakingly pointed out all possible difficulties and their logical solutions. It seemed as if he was more concerned about the monastery than he was about his Duchy. Hugh paid close attention, and though Alberic again insisted that he was retaining only what was needed, the duke said, "I am just showing my son what may yet be needed. I mean to help, not to hinder, your reform, Father Abbot. But I am off to war. Men die in battle, you know. I'm looking ahead."

Late that afternoon as Alberic and the duke paced the paths of the garden that was just taking shape, the abbot said, "So you're off to the Holy Land. How I envy you, Excellency!" When he saw the duke turn sharply he smiled and said, "I suppose that does sound like a strange confession to come from a monk. But let me tell you, Excellency, there has not been a time that I have swung into a saddle that my blood did not leap. I've had many a stiff battle with myself in the years that are gone; but, thank God, I always defeated myself. I've proved that blood can be beaten."

The duke chuckled. "I'm glad you told me that, Reverend Father. I've often wondered about you and others like you. I've wondered if the lust for battle died the moment you donned the cowl, or did you have to kill it every time you heard the jingle of spurs or saw a suit of mail."

"We remain men when we become monks, Excellency."

"And men of war, I see. But now here is a puzzle for you. You envy me my crusading in the Holy Land, and I envy you your crusading in this swampland. Can you tell me why it is that the grass always looks greener in our neighbor's meadow?"

"I think it is a disease we caught when paradise was lost. You remember that Adam and Eve could have eaten of every fruit in the garden save one. That was the one their mouths watered for—and that was the one they ate! That is why I envy you, and you envy me. And so it will go on until paradise is again regained."

The duke's eyes were on the pebbly path before him. He was meditating aloud when he said, "Father Abbot, all through the Office of last night, all through the Masses of the morning, the one thought that kept throbbing in my brain was: 'How fortunate are these monks to be *locked up* with God alone!' That's a very exact description of your monastery here. You are really locked up with God. I was watching your monks during that long chant. It was evident that they had only one thought. It was God! It is clear that they have only one work, one life, one love. He is God! Yes, it is literally true, you men are locked up with God."

Alberic caught much of the duke's mood and something of his manner as he said, "That's a new concept, Excellency, and a true one. I have heard our life referred to as 'leisure to love God,' and believe me, it is that! You have your family, your Duchy, and a hundred and one other concerns. Even the serfs have worry about work and wages. But the monk in the ranks has only one thing to do—love God."

"It's a busy leisure, Father Abbot," chuckled the duke. "From shortly after midnight till shortly after sundown is a goodly stretch. Yet, your men have been occupied all day."

"Occupied with God. Their occupation is their leisure."

"Oh, I see what you mean. It is well named. This life of freedom from concerns is a life of leisure; and you occupy that leisure in loving God."

"But I like your idea even better, Excellency. Since we are cloistered, we are truly locked up. Yes, a monastery can be looked upon as a prison. We are all criminals. We were born such. And most of us added to our heritage. You did well to call us robbers. We have been thieving time."

"How so?"

"Well, we were given time to spend on the one work of life and we have spent it on others."

"One work?"

"Certainly. We all have but one work to accomplish before we die. Life has been given us that we may make an act of love."

"Well, I'm going to make my life an act of contrition. That's why I go to the Orient."

Alberic stopped. He looked long at the duke who had halted a step before him. Finally he said, "Excellency, you have seen deeper than I. I have always said an 'Act of Love'; but since the best of us is but a prodigal, that love should be burning, aye, blazing penitent love! Your term expresses more truth. We are on earth to make an act of perfect contrition, and that will be our act of love. You make yours by going to the Orient. We make ours in this penitentiary where sinners have locked themselves up with God in order to become saints."

They resumed their walk. When the duke told the abbot that he would carry Citeaux in his heart with him to the Holy Land, Alberic said, "And Citeaux will accompany you every step of the way with her prayers." As they parted, Odo expressed some concern for the abbey, but Alberic laughed it away with, "Hugh is a son to his father. We shall never want for a friend both powerful and generous."

Just as they were entering the house the duke turned to the abbot and asked, "Are you really going to shear as close as you have planned?"

"Excellency," said Alberic, and his eyes held fire, "I'm going to shear as close as the Rule demands. Citeaux is an abbey where there will be no compromise."

Chapter Five

"Can It Be Done?"

The duke went off to the Orient and Alberic's plan went into effect. It sounded through the monastic world like a thunderclap. The reverberations that came back to Citeaux caused Stephen Harding to say that it was a good thing that Ilbode and John had gone to Rome. Without that precious letter from Pascal, dated "this eighteenth day of April, 1100, the second year of Our Pontificate," Alberic most likely would have been in for a worse thrashing than he received at Molesme.

To say that Citeaux was a challenge to every other existing monastery is to understate fact. Wittingly or unwittingly, she was a condemnation. She was italicizing and underlining every word of St. Benedict's Rule with a stylus which wrote so vividly that it spoke. That stylus was the lives of her monks! Robert and his idealism had been strange. Molesme in her early days had caused quite a stir. But Alberic was of a different temper and Citeaux of a different cast. She was more rebellious because she was more radical; and he was more daring because she was more independent. No one could touch either her or him. Rome was protector of all that was hid in the swampland about Citeaux.

The monks of other monasteries had laughed at the white habits and lampooned the meager meals, but they could not even smile at the challenge contained in the outright refusal to be supported by others. The monastic world cried that it was beyond nature. Alberic retorted that it was according to Rule. Then, as years passed without shaking the fortress of Citeaux, the monastic world knew it was facing real rebellion. She resented it. But she had seen little as yet!

Some few months after Odo had set off for the Holy Land, Stephen came upon his abbot wrapped in thought. Before him lay a map of the abbey lands and to one side a text of the Rule. Stephen studied him a moment, then said, "You look serious."

"I am serious," came the speedy reply. "So serious that I'm positively unsociable. But a lamb like you doesn't mind lying down by a lion like me." He pushed the map to one side as he said,

"The duke made a remark at that farewell dinner that was meant as a joke but which has turned out to be the germ of a real idea. Do you remember his saying, 'The only solution is to make the serfs on the granges members of your community'?"

Stephen thought a moment, then brightened and said, "Ah, yes. It was after he told you he never took back gifts."

"Right," said the abbot. "Well, I've recalled that remark more than once since that day, and more than once this day." Then with a sudden change of front he asked, "What do you know about John Gualbert and Vallombrosa, Stephen?"

"Not a thing," said the puzzled prior. "Why?"

"Well, he founded an Order following St. Benedict's Rule, but he introduced a novelty into the world of religious. He had 'lay-assistants'—men who were exempted from silence and choir, but who were part of the community since their duty was to take care of all the external offices. Now, that historical fact, plus the duke's parting remark, has had me asking myself all day long: 'Can it be done?'"

"Can what be done?"

"Can I take both ideas, John Gualbert's and the duke's, fuse them and produce something unique—men who are real religious, but who are exempt from choir?"

"Well, how about the Rule? You're surely not

going to try an innovation after all these years of fighting for renovation, are you?"

"It's the Rule that gave me the idea," retorted Alberic. "The rigidity of the Rule, at that. Here's the situation, Stephen. Pull that chair over and study this thing with me." He drew down the map and pointed to a distant grange. "We can't do without that wheat field, can we?"

Stephen looked, recognized it, shook his head and said, "Indeed we can't. That means our bread."

"And yet, you can't harvest that wheat and attend choir, can you?"

"You mean it's too far away?"

"I mean that one or the other has to be neglected. Either you can't sing the Office or you can't harvest wheat."

"We sing the Office in the field."

"I know you do; and that's what I don't like. Now here," and the abbot pointed to a meadow that was even further away than the grange. "We need that meadow. Our cattle can't live on air. But how can a cowhand be there and here?"

"He can't."

"All right. Now, Stephen, look at this dilemma the Rule presents. I'm squarely on the two horns. I want to get off." And the abbot shook his head determinedly. "We're supposed to be self-supporting, aren't we?"

"We are."

"Therefore, we've got to keep these meadows, granges and vineyards, haven't we?" and he indicated them on the map. "I gave away all I could. But these we've got to have. Now, our great work is the Divine Office. We're choir monks. That's the heart of Benedictinism. Just look at the Rule," and the abbot turned the text toward Stephen, flipped over the chapters, counting aloud as he went. "Twelve whole chapters devoted to the details of the *'Opus Dei,'* as Benedict calls it. That tells a story, Stephen. The saint insisted that nothing be preferred to this 'Work of God.' Now see my dilemma. I want to be utterly self-supporting and yet I want a perfect choir; that is, all the members present for all the Hours and all the Hours chanted in church."

Stephen cupped his chin in his hand, put his elbow on the desk, and stared at the map and the Rule. Alberic watched him a moment. When no comment came he said, "Now, how are we to have a perfect choir when so many must be away at the granges or the meadows? And how are we to support ourselves if we have a perfect choir? That's my dilemma."

"You're on the horns all right."

"I know that. But what I want to know is whether I can get off."

"By combining the ideas of the duke and John Gualbert?"

"Exactly! But note that I insist on the duke's idea more than on Gualbert's. I want these lay-assistants to be lay *brothers.* I want them to be real religious—men who take the same vows as we do; live the same Rule we do; be brothers to everyone in the house and sons to the abbot; men who will be real members of the community and observe everything exactly as we do with the single exception of choir. That's my idea at the moment. Now, tell me. Can it be done? Can we make serfs monks?"

Stephen thought for a moment. The idea was so new to him that he dared not pronounce on it immediately. Objections leaped at him. Wasn't this seeking support from others by a subterfuge? Could men be religious who did not pray the Office? How could those who lived on the granges be under the abbot? Wouldn't this eventually lead to the elimination of manual labor for the choir-monks? He put these and other questions to Alberic in all sincerity. The speed and finality with which the abbot answered them showed that they were not new to him, that they had occurred to him long before he broached the subject to his prior.

When he had been satisfied on these points the prior said, "I shouldn't ask, 'Can we make serfs monks?' I should ask, 'Can we make serfs saints?' For that is what you're planning to do."

"Right! For all people are called to sanctity, Stephen. But I'll wager with you right now that many a man in the humble role of lay brother will scale loftier heights of holiness than their brothers in the choir. Their life will be simpler; and, believe it or not, there is an intimate connection between sanctity and simplicity. But at the moment I'm just looking at the demands of the Rule. I want to be self-supporting and I want to have a perfect choir. Can it be done?"

"You seem to have worked the whole thing out quite thoroughly, Reverend Father. I don't see why it can't be done. The Rule doesn't prescribe it explicitly; but your argument, your dilemma, comes directly from the Rule. What amuses me at the moment is to have the rigor— or, as you insist, the radicalism—that is so typical of us, leading us to what is actually an innovation."

Alberic pushed the map and the text of the Rule to the back of the desk, then turning to his prior he said, "The idea is not exactly new with me, Stephen. When we were at Molesme, old John, the widower, and his only boy impressed me as two very saintly souls. Do you remember them?" Stephen nodded. "They were religious in everything but name, profession and external garb. They prayed more than many of the monks. They worked for God rather than for the abbey; or rather they made their work at the abbey their tribute to God. I used to wonder then if some scheme couldn't be devised to incorporate them into the community. It is only now after listening to the duke and reflecting on what John Gualbert did that the scheme comes to me."

The idea was growing on Stephen. He recalled other serfs who were like old John and his son. He became enthusiastic. "Why, Father Abbot, there must be hundreds, yes thousands of men, not only among the serfs, but even among the lower nobility, and perhaps in the higher nobility who long for just such an institution. They want to give themselves and all they have to God, and yet feel no inclination toward the choir work. There must be hundreds of carpenters, smiths, masons, artisans of all sorts—stonecutters, wood-cutters, tillers of the soil—right here in Burgundy who would love to dedicate their talents to the service of God. Think what an opportunity you would be offering them."

"I've thought of them," said the abbot and his eyes kindled. "And I've thought of others. I'm sure there must be many a man who thinks himself unworthy to stand in choir and sing the praises of God, and yet is burning, body and soul, with a consuming desire to dedicate himself to God. Think what it will mean to such! Think what a thrill will be theirs to find themselves on a religious level with the choir-monks! I insist on that equality. They are going to be as much a part of the community as the abbot, the prior, or anybody else. You think it can be done?"

"I do. And I'm for doing it right away."

The abbot chuckled. "Ah, environment is telling. The fiery French are doing things to the conservative English. Well, I'll make a confession, Stephen. It's already been done! That is to say, practically done. I've approached Gilbert and his little group. They said they would talk it over and think it over. They did. They came to me a week ago begging to begin right away. I put them off for a week. It ends tomorrow."

"So, you've been keeping secrets from me?"

"Well, yes and no. I had to consult my Lady first. I had to offer her a week of prayer. She is my Good Counselor, you know, my Seat of Wisdom. The week ended this morning. So you see, I told you as soon as I could."

Stephen looked at his abbot with admiration and affection. Alberic always sounded like a little boy when he spoke of his "Lady." "Reverend Father," said Stephen, "your devotion to the Mother of God has done more for this community and for you than any other factor in the whole process of our foundation and growth. Your 'Lady' has become their 'Lady.' She sanctifies!"

"Children need a mother, Stephen; and the oldest of us is only a child of fuller growth. More, knights need a Lady—and we're knights of God. *Our Lady of Citeaux!* * What a beautiful title for us to give her, and how well she deserves it! She has led us by the hand all these years. She has inspired almost every move. She will yet bring us home. She has given me the courage to make

---

*This is the first time in history that the title "Our Lady"— *Notre Dame* was used.

this innovation. And here is a thought she inspired. We have been battling for manual labor, haven't we?"

"That has been the real crux of the whole situation," replied Stephen.

"Well, just think what this institution of a lay-brotherhood will do to manual labor. It will force the world to recognize it for what it really is—a sacramental! Too many nobles are looking down on manual labor, Stephen. They think it undignified. Great heavens! Don't they ever read the Gospel? Jesus Christ didn't merely dignify labor. He divinized it! Hands that traced the courses for the planets, and set the stars in the Milky Way grew calloused—*calloused*, Stephen—from hammer, saw and plane. Arms that upheld the universe grew weary from working on wood. The brow that hid divine intelligence grew wet with the sweat of labor! The world has never learned that lesson, Stephen. It has ever looked upon work as lowly. It is high time for the world to be re-taught. It is high time for us to re-teach what Christ taught so eloquently. The Redeemer of the world was a laborer, a common craftsman! Co-redeemers must be the same. Lay brothers, let us call them that—lay brothers can be other Christs. It can be done. We'll do it."

Alberic did it. He really gave a new principle to religious life by the institution of the lay brotherhood. Of course, John Gualbert was the first to introduce the idea. That was back in 1050. But

Alberic shaped his idea in so happy and original a fashion that it actually became a new principle. Before he died Stephen saw what a world of thanks heaven and earth owed to the Silver Lance and his "Lady" for that innovation. For he saw that heaven was being peopled by a veritable army of mighty saints—the lay brothers! Men who were great in their littleness, sublime in their simplicity and towering in their tremendously humble sanctity! As for earth—the lay brothers had preached as no one before them except the God-Man had preached! They told the world that labor is a sacramental—a means to sanctification.

Alberic got off the horns of his dilemma by making it possible for millions to win their crowns of glory. It gladdened everyone's heart—especially the heart of God.

Chapter Six
A Falling Leaf

As Stephen walked along the corridor that led to the abbot's room, he reflected that for almost ten years he had been making this visit daily. He had to report to Alberic, receive the instructions for the coming day, and tell him what had been accomplished the previous day. He marveled that he had never found its routine tedious or in any way monotonous. Then he reflected and saw why. Alberic opened his very heart to Stephen on these visits. It was during these that he had grown to know the mind and soul of the "Lance." "Perhaps I am his only confidant," thought the prior, as he knocked on the oaken door.

Stephen found Alberic seated at his rough desk fingering a leaf. It was a tiny thing, one that

October with her magic of frost and sunshine had colored a beautiful, brilliant crimson. It looked like a finger of scarlet flame as it lay in the abbot's calloused and work-worn hand.

Alberic's head came up slowly to greet Stephen. The light in his eyes told that he had been deep in musing. Carefully he placed the finger of scarlet beauty in the center of the unfinished board that served him as desk, then turned to Stephen and said, "This has been telling me much about the beauty of God, the grandeur of life and the loveliness of death. I was out to our latest grave today, Stephen. While there I saw the woods. Oh, God is magnificent in nature at this time of the year!"

"Don't you always find him so?"

"Well, yes," came the slow response, "but never more so than now at Autumn Compline."

"What a beautiful concept!" exclaimed Stephen. "Autumn Compline."

"And isn't it a true one?" asked the abbot. "Summer's day is done. Vespers have already been chanted. Now it is compline time. Soon the year will be dead. I was thinking much on death today, Stephen; and much more on life. As I knelt at Brother Christian's grave my prayers were short, but my thoughts were long."

"He was a good brother," said Stephen. "Earnest, simple, sincere."

"Yes, he was all that. But the thing that struck me today was the fact that this poor son of

Burgundy's soil, this peasant, is now out there lying side by side with Burgundy's duke. What a commingling of ashes that is! Indeed, death is a leveller! And yet there is perfect aptness in the nearness of their graves; for both were God's warriors! Both were battle-scarred penitents."

Stephen caught his abbot's mood and joined him by exclaiming, "Wasn't Odo magnificent in his conversion! It seems difficult to believe that Citeaux's greatest benefactor was once a high-handed, hard-hearted robber. He certainly loved this place, didn't he?"

"Indeed he did. And that last act of his crowned his life fittingly. Oh, the faith and the bravery of the man! To set out for Palestine at his age to become a Crusader—to make his Act of Contrition! Indeed, he was a nobleman. Do you remember how he enjoyed his last day here? He was enraptured by the Office and the Mass that day."

"Most likely that was the song that was ringing in his ears as he lay dying. You remember, they say he looked up, smiled and said, 'I hear the choir of Citeaux!'"

"He always had us in mind," said the abbot slowly. "And we must always have him in mind. Ah, that was a grand act of loyalty on the part of his men. They carried his body back over land and sea, just to fulfill his dying request that he be buried in our midst."

"He wanted our prayers."

"Oh, he would have had them, no matter where his body lay." Then in a quizzical tone he added, "Wouldn't you have expected him to prefer to lie near Godfrey de Bouillon, or at least to be buried somewhere in the Holy Land?"

"I would," answered Stephen honestly. "And it would have been fitting. The ashes of the great Godfrey and the heroic Odo. Two warriors. Two nobles. Two penitents. Two men who had turned to God after the mistakes of their youth. Doesn't it thrill you to think of Godfrey lying with those towering heroes of the old Testament—Joshua, David, and Judas Maccabeus? God has an exquisitely delicate sense of fitness, hasn't he?"

"That's exactly what struck me as I stood by the two graves in our cemetery today," said Alberic. "I thought of Odo and Christian—what a contrast in life externally, but what a parallel internally! And in death they sleep together."

"What was the internal parallel?"

"Penitence," answered the abbot. Then he turned and asked, "Brother Christian wasn't with us long, was he, Stephen?"

"Just under four years."

"What did he do in that time?"

"Nothing extraordinary," answered the prior with a shake of his head. "He was a good, sincere, simple brother. He did his duty. He was ordinary."

"Wrong, Stephen; very wrong," broke in the abbot. "He did a most extraordinary thing."

"He did?"

"Yes, indeed he did. He became completely God-centered, and wholly God-absorbed. Now, that may seem ordinary to some, but let me tell you it is one of the most extraordinary things a person does on this earth."

"Oh, that's true enough," admitted the prior. "What I meant was that he had done nothing extraordinary among us."

"Ah, what a compliment!" cried Alberic enthusiastically. "I hope we never have anyone who does the extraordinary among us. I don't trust it. But I ever hope and pray that we shall always have men who will do the ordinary extraordinary things that Christian did."

Stephen was not quite sure that he had caught all of Alberic's meaning. "Just what do you mean, Reverend Father?"

"I mean that he gave his all to God."

"But that's our vocation," objected Stephen.

"True," replied the abbot, "but it is good to stand off every now and then to get our vocation in perspective. Christian's grave and this falling leaf made me stand off today, and I saw the beauty of our lowly life as I haven't seen it in years."

Stephen rested an elbow on the abbot's desk. "Tell me about it," he begged.

Alberic began slowly, "Christian was a peasant, you know. He left the plough and a life of hard labor, came here, and found what? A

plough and a life of hard labor!" Stephen nodded.

"But," resumed the abbot, "there was a difference. You see, Stephen, even the peasant's
drab existence has its times of leisure, its true
pleasures and substantial joys. See them in the
summer after an evening meal, sitting relaxed in
the glory of a setting sun. Or watch them as they
gather round the glow of a winter's warm
hearth." When Stephen again nodded his head
in agreement, the abbot went on, "Listen to
them at vintage time, or watch them as they sing
and dance on a swept threshing floor, while
overhead a harvest moon rides high. Ah, indeed
they have their joys. Simple ones, I grant; but
they are most satisfying. What did Christian
have here?

"None of those. He had hardly a single moment all day that he could call his own! He was
up in time to see the stars to bed. Before the dew
was gone, he was at work. At hard work! When
the sun was high, he sweated and prayed. When
the day was weary and had turned to rest, Christian came home. And to what? To rest? Indeed
no! He came home to read and pray. Every
minute was spent according to regulations. Then
as the night grew lovely under the mellowness of
a magic moon and the silver grandeur of silent
stars, Christian went to a hard bed for a few
hours of well-earned slumber. Now, that was his
life, day after day, for four full years. Strictly

speaking, there was not a moment that he could call his very own; for everything was planned. What a life! Yes. What a glorious life! For every moment of it was given to God!"

The two men sat in silence. After a moment the abbot shifted in his chair and said, "Stephen, I see now why people call us mad; and I see, as I never saw before, how perfectly beautiful, aye, heavenly, is this mad life of ours. Our day and night is so planned that we cannot help becoming God-conscious, God-centered, totally God-absorbed. Christian was well prepared for heaven. He had spent four years in heaven's novitiate—our lowly, little monastery tucked away in this swampy wood." Then picking up the bit of crimson loveliness that lay on his desk, he continued, "When Christian fell, he fell like this tiny leaf. Oh, how like it!"

"You mean all changed, beautiful...?"

"Yes, I mean all changed," said the abbot emphatically. "As I was turning from his grave this morning, this little leaf fluttered down through the branches of a tiny tree. It looked like a frail, floating flower, a flower of flame. Beautiful beyond words. I stooped to pick it up, and as I did so, a lance of golden light shot down from the skies, pierced through the trees and splintered itself at the base of the oak where my little leaf lay. I linked all three: Christian, the leaf, the lance."

"Christian came here green," Alberic went

on. "In time he changed. He became more God-loving. At the end he was red; red with the rich redness of a true man's love. He caught the spirit of Citeaux quickly. He was in love with Jesus Crucified, Stephen. He told me so often."

The abbot sighed after that last sentence. Stephen wondered if it were a sigh of envy. But almost immediately Alberic resumed, "Stephen, our lowly life here is more magical than autumn's thrice-magic wand. She changes the woods to a wonderland of green, red, russet, crimson and gold, a wonderland of yellow, scarlet and burnished browns. Our lowly life here changes souls of all colors to a silver-white purity and to a red, and at times even a searing-white, love. Stephen, do you thank God enough for your vocation, for calling you so close to his Sacred Heart?"

The prior had been lifted out of himself by the musical rhythm of the abbot's voice and by the intensity of his description. He straightened and finally answered, "Who can thank him enough, Reverend Father? I do the best I can, but I know that is poor thanks. The magic of which you speak seems to be especially effective among our lay brothers. You did a marvelous thing for earth and heaven when you dared introduce the novelty you so stubbornly insist is but the radical Rule. Indeed, most of them change to the color of love before the autumn of their life is done."

"Yes," said Alberic slowly, "they are a choice group of men. But my point in all this has been to tell you that I now feel that the leaf of my life is turning. It will fall soon, Stephen. No, don't argue. I know. But pray, pray, pray, Stephen, that when it does fall, it falls as flame!"

The abbot rose. He looked at Stephen and realized that from long years of comradeship this man had become to him more than a son—he was brother, helper and friend.

"I'll leave this with you," he said, holding out the leaf. "I must talk to God."

Chapter Seven
The Flame Falls

Stephen went out to the little graveyard where Alberic had won his inspiration. But, instead of the dead, Stephen thought of the living. The abbot filled his mind. As he stared at the color spendthrift autumn had scattered in the woodlands, he understood Alberic's nostalgia for heaven and for the artist behind the masterpiece of the world. Citeaux in the glow of the sinking sun was breathtaking.

Stephen came back to the thought of his abbot. Was Alberic uttering prophecy, he wondered. He had spoken of the leaf of his life turning, and even of falling! Could it be that he had a premonition of his death? Stephen shook his head. Alberic was not an old man, as monks go. More, he was a healthy man. Stephen could not recall his ever being seriously ill. He looked well right now, thought the prior. Perhaps it was only a mood caused by the visit to the grave and the sight of the leaf.

"Pray that when I fall, I fall as flame...." What a request! As if Alberic needed such a prayer! Pray that *he* love God whose every word was about God, whose every breath was for God, whose every heartbeat was for God alone! Pray that he who had gone to Colan because it meant a fiercer living, to Molesme because it meant a more generous giving, and to Citeaux because it meant a wholesale abandonment, an unconditional surrender of his entire self to God.... Pray that *he* love God! Stephen almost laughed aloud at the memory of his request.

As he stood there, thinking of Alberic, a late afternoon breeze stirred the woodland of color that fringed the little cemetery, sending ripples of gold and green, of scarlet and yellow, running over the leaves. His eyes were caught by a shower of crimson flame petals that fluttered and fell a little to his right. No wonder Alberic wanted to be changed like them, he thought, as he gathered a few and gazed on their brilliant glory.

But then Stephen stopped in wonder at another thought. Hadn't his abbot already been changed, he queried. Only nine and a half years in office and look what he had accomplished! Every last vestige of custom that was contrary to the Rule had been cut away. With an intrepidity that astounded all, he had led men back through six hundred years, and fired them with zeal enough to live as Benedict had stipulated his monks should live.

Suddenly Stephen caught his breath in an audible gasp. The leaves fell from his hands unnoticed. He looked up to the sunset sky and exclaimed, "Good Lord, he has done it! He has laid the foundations for a new creation. We are unique in the world of monks. Yes, he has given us all the materials for a new Order!"

Up and down the gravel paths of the little cemetery the prior paced. This sudden recognition of what Alberic had actually accomplished startled him. As he walked, he began to marvel at the fearlessness and forcefulness of the man. Where did he ever get the courage to be so defiant of all other men, he wondered. Where? He knew he was a warrior. But this was not ordinary daring. This was the bold, adventurous courage of the hero. Where did he get it? Then Stephen muttered a single word. It was the solution. "Love," he said. "Love that casts out fear!" That was Alberic's secret. His courage was not seated in high-hearted bravery. No, it was in great-hearted love. Alberic was the lance of which he so often spoke—the lance which sought only one point. The abbot was a spear levelled at the very heart of Christ—not to pierce, but to be buried therein and absorbed.

Somewhat more slowly, Stephen now

walked the paths. "He has done it!" he said aloud. "Yes, he has conceived something entirely new." He stopped a moment and counted off the main points on the tips of his fingers: simplicity, poverty, self-support, liturgical prayer. "Benedictine it certainly is; but not the Benedictine of the present day. His stark simplicity has created a new Order. I wonder if he realizes it. His lance has found its mark. His ideal is so nakedly bright it can be expressed in two words: God alone!"

Stephen halted after those two words. "And that is the man," he exclaimed, "the Christ-centered soul, who asks me—me of all people— to pray for him. Oh, dear God, bless his humility, and grant me a touch of the same."

The vesper bell was ringing. Stephen started in, but at the door he turned for one last look at autumn's wonderland. As he did so a breath of wind again stirred the woodland and sent another shower of flame petals fluttering to the ground. Stephen recalled the words of his abbot. "Dear God," he murmured, "when I fall, let me also fall as flame...."

Autumn sang her compline till the snows. Advent gave way to Christmastide, and the year 1109 was ushered in with chill whiteness. All things moved along with their usual well ordered quietness in the little monastery sunk in the swampland. Then, just as January neared its cold close, the flame fell! Alberic, brave man of

God, went to God on the twenty-sixth day of the first month of 1109.

Citeaux was cold that day, bitterly cold. So was the whole wide world for Stephen Harding. He felt as if all the warmth in the universe had suddenly been taken away. The sun shone, but its brightness only accentuated the chill. The distant, cloudless blue of the sky made one's blood run slow. And when the day was done, cold stars came out in a frozen heaven, glittering like crystals of silvery ice in a world that had suddenly gone frigid. Indeed, the flame had fallen. Stephen felt alone, terribly alone, and cold to his very marrow.

The next day they buried Alberic. Out to the little cemetery they went, and in the white snow lay-brothers and monks knelt and prayed. Stephen sprinkled the body, prayed the liturgical prayers, swung the censer that was ice to the touch. Last of all, with a great lump in his throat, he let fall a spadeful of frozen dirt on the cold body of him who had prayed, and asked others to pray, that he fall as flame.

Back to the chapter room they filed. It was not a large group, but it was a loving one. When all were seated, Stephen cleared his throat and, brushing the mists from his eyes, said, "My brothers, in the midst of this universal loss I am poor comforter indeed, for I myself need comfort. You have lost a father, it is true, and the guide of your souls. But I have lost more. I mourn my *comrade!* He was my companion-in-arms, my fellow soldier in every mighty battle for the Lord. He is gone from us. But yet," he said, "he...is not gone from us; for he carried us all away with him in his mind. And now that he has been led into the presence of God and been joined to him in individual love, he has joined us too, who are in his mind, to God. Why then should we mourn? Why grieve for him who is in joy? Why mourn the soldier who is at rest? ...Come, my brothers. Let us turn our mournful words into prayers. Let us beg our abbot, who is in triumph, not to allow our savage enemy to keep us from one day joining him, and rejoicing with him in heaven."

With those words, devotion to Alberic began. From that time on it grew. When he had been hidden away from the eyes of men by heaped up clods of frozen dirt, people began to see him in his true perspective. Gradually they came to realize that the silver lance was a perfect symbol for his sterling soul.

As they talked among themselves, they slowly came to the realization that a hero had been their abbot. In all his years he had never once given voice to a pious platitude. He had stirred their emotions often; but they were emotions—deep, lasting, manly things; not superficial, ephemeral feelings or mere surface sentiments. Food, bedding, clothing had changed at Citeaux because of the virility in the soul of this man. Poverty and simplicity shone there, because, like a lance, Alberic was ever seeking the heart of the target.

As is so often the case, appreciation came too late. They could not tell their thanks to ears that had gone deaf. Nor could they smile their appreciation into eyes that had lost all sight. So they beat their breasts sorrowfully, and accused themselves of having been stupidly blind. But they prayed for the old warrior, and they prayed to him. They told him that they longed to hear his virile, challenging rallying cries of "to the hilt" and "no compromise."

Some weeks after, when one of the community asked Stephen if Alberic had intended to found an Order, the Englishman replied, "Alberic did not really intend to wage a rebellion. He only wanted Citeaux to live the Rule to the hilt." When asked why, Stephen gave a very solemn answer. He said, "Because he thought it the right way to heal a heart that had been pierced and broken; the right way to lift a crown from a thorn-encircled head; the right way to draw steel from hands and feet that had been cruelly spiked. That was his only aim. He wanted Citeaux to live the Rule to the hilt because that was the only way he knew to repay a tremendous debt contracted one Friday afternoon on Calvary. In short, *love had found a way to repay Love.*"

Epitome and Epitaph

Alberic had no pre-natal; we shall give him no post-mortem. But for all those who claim that men become Trappists because they were disappointed in love, we underline and italicize the last line of Alberic's life.

It was six hundred years before the Church gave any official pronouncement on this radical who had so successfully carried on the rebellion. But Citeaux's sons and daughters had ever been mindful. Like the community he left after him, they prayed *to* him; and in 1701 the Holy Father sanctioned their prayers by granting them a Mass and an Office in his honor. This is what is known as "equivalent canonization." You can be sure it greatly rejoiced the heart of every white robed monk and nun who called the Silver Lance "Father."

The pen picture given by those who knew

him best is small, but it is very clearly drawn. They say: "He was a lover of the Rule and of the brethren." What could be a better picture of the model monk—a great-souled lover of God? For the Rule is the will of God, and the brethren are his image. Therefore, the epitome that the Radical deserves is this:

Alberic—a manly lover of Jesus Christ!

Let that serve not only as an epitome but also as an epitaph. The lance had found its target. The flame had fallen. But the rebellion still went on! Stephen, the other half of Alberic's soul, completed it....

Part III

St. Stephen Harding
the Rationalist

Chapter One
Stephen Furnishes the World with Amusement

It had rained steadily all morning. Stephen had been dimly conscious of the tinkle of the water as it trickled from an end gable and struck the pebbles of the path beneath. When it gradually quieted and finally stopped, he became distracted. The silence was much more disturbing than the noise had been. He turned and looked out the window On the far fringe of the black heavens he found a silver-gray band which widened as he watched, for the somber clouds were scudding to the east. Stephen was caught by the strength and symmetry of the trees, as they stood silhouetted against a dark sky. Immediately below him he saw that the yellow fleurs-de-lis shone more brilliantly than they ever did under a summer sun.

"Strange," he mused aloud, "I never noted that before—darkness brings out beauty."

After the cleansing rain, and in the shade of the hurrying black storm clouds, the garden was showing tints and tones that it hid when the sky was brilliant. The green of grass and leaf seemed softer, livelier, more glowing; the reds were warmer; even the purple that fringed the curved petals of the fleurs-de-lis was richer and more royal.

As he turned back to his writing, Stephen wondered if souls too were not seen best in shadow. Picking up his stylus he poised it in mid-air and focused his eyes on it. He thought of Robert, the old giant of Molesme—unquestionably, the statement was true of him. The shadowy background of trouble silhouetted his gigantic character and edged the mighty virtues of his soul.

Stephen again bent over his desk and was about to continue his writing when the squishy clop-clop of a slow-footed horse came to him from the road beyond his window. He looked and saw a black-cowled rider whose clothes sagged clammily, and told of long hours in the rain. Stephen could only see the man's swaying back; but as the horse and rider rounded the curve of the yard, he thought, "Whoever he is, he is a tired man."

Not very long after, there came a tap on the abbot's door. Who could this be at such an hour, he wondered. He opened the door in puzzlement; but recognition and pleasure immediately took its place. Before the lay brother who stood there could say a word, Stephen strode past him, threw his arms around the black-robed stranger, kissed him on both cheeks, and cried delightedly, "Peter! Peter! Peter!"

"Be careful, Reverend Father," protested the enfolded monk. "I'm wet."

"You're Peter!" cried the abbot laughingly, as he drew him into his room and closed the door. The good lay brother who was left on the other side of that door, shook his head in puzzlement over the strange ways of this Englishman who was his abbot. Usually dignified and calm, he was now more excited and demonstrative than a Frenchman. And toward a "black Benedictine," at that! No, there was no accounting for the ways of these foreigners, he thought, as he made his way back to the stables.

Twenty minutes later the robes of the "black Benedictine" were hanging by a fire to dry, while the "black Benedictine" himself stood before Stephen, tugging at the folds of the white cowl they had lent him, and laughing at the thought of what the Grand Abbot would say if he could see his brave Cluniac at the moment.

"Now you look right," said Stephen. "White suits you admirably. You should wear it always."

As Peter smiled, the abbot went on, "While you were changing, Peter, I did some counting. I'm sure my figures are correct, and yet I can't believe the result. Can it be thirty-two years since we parted?"

"Almost to the day!" agreed Peter, as he took the chair Stephen had drawn up for him. "Over three decades of years have passed since you went your way and I went mine. And a rain storm had to bring us together again. Had the heavens not burst asunder the way they did, I would have had to continue on to Cluny, and missed the opportunity of seeing whether my quondam fellow pilgrim is as bad as people say he is. You look human. In fact, you don't look so very different from the merry young Englishman I parted from after that blessed journey to Rome."

Stephen had been studying his friend as he talked. He saw what time had done to the face of the boy he had met in Burgundy that far off day thirty-two years ago. Stephen had been troubled that day and lonely. Paris and its years of study lay behind him. They had been the culmination of a life devoted to learning. As a boy he had been sent to the Benedictines at Sherborne, England. When he finished their course of studies he had crossed the seas to the Isle of Saints and Scholars and frequented its celebrated schools, only to end where most scholars of the day ended—at Paris. But there he had grown restless. His life seemed empty. This quest for knowledge seemed vain. He suddenly decided to quest after truth. He began by donning the pilgrim's cloak and setting his face toward Rome.

He had been on the road just long enough to be desperately lonely when, passing through Burgundy, he met an attractive youth of his own age, of good education, and almost his own temperament. He, too, was on his way to Rome, a pilgrim. Together they made the journey.

That it had not been an easy one was evident from their laughing recollections of the difficult snow covered passes of the Alps; the night they got lost and frozen in the depths of a forest; the dangerous looking strangers who had joined them, but had not robbed them; the hunger they had known before they met the warm-hearted, open-handed, ever-smiling Italians of Lombardy.

"And we separated in the woods of Molesme," said Peter in conclusion. That had been their parting. For on the way back, when they came to Burgundy, Peter had pushed on to Cluny, while Stephen, attracted by what he had heard of the holiness of Robert and his rebels turned aside to join the aging giant and his handful of ex-hermits.

"They tell me that old men sigh for 'what might have been.'" said Stephen. "And while we are not exactly old, we are not too young to take a quick glance at what could have been. Tell me, have you ever regretted not having taken the turn I took that day in the woods?"

Peter looked at his old friend. He decided he could be as open as ever. "You're the man who should sigh for what might have been," he said. "I can't tell you the number of times I've thought how perfectly Cluny would have suited you, and how perfectly you would have suited Cluny. How often, when I'd be among the manuscripts, did I literally ache for you down among the carrots and turnips at Molesme! In all those thirty odd years, Stephen, the only moment that was not filled with regret for you was the moment I heard of your Recension of the Bible. Up to that time I could only see the burial of your talents; and I used to wonder just what the Master of the house would say when he made his reckoning."

Stephen smiled. "You sound just like a little imp who used to visit me daily during my first few years at Molesme. He used to say just what you've been saying, Peter. Believe me, he could quote Scripture most exactly. He used to frighten me with that parable of the talents. Do you know that little imp's name?"

"No."

"Satan," said Stephen with a laugh. "Let me tell you, Peter, he tried me often with that temptation, couched almost in the identical words you just used."

"Was it a temptation?" asked Peter with a meaningful look.

Stephen studied his friend for a moment. He found him most serious and even anxious. "I take it that you do not approve of Citeaux," he said.

"Not for you, Stephen; even though you are its abbot. You won't mind my speaking honestly. I think it was our mutual honesty that linked us so closely the year we journeyed to Rome. Stephen, Stephen," said Peter sadly, "how is God glorified by this entombing of your brilliance? Not ten men on the continent had your native intellectual endowment. I told you thirty years ago that you belonged in Cluny. That conviction has been deepened with the years, both by what I know of that monastery and what I have heard of this."

"What do you know of this, Peter?" asked Stephen. He was sorry the conversation had taken this turn so early. He feared that it would ultimately reach this pass, but he hoped to forestall it. However, he would face the issue now. If Peter was the Peter of old, it was the only way to act.

"What do I know of this place?" repeated Peter. "What everybody knows. That it is beyond nature, that it is asking for more than man can give and more than God demands; in short, that it is fanaticism. You want me to be honest, don't you, Reverend Father?"

"I do," replied Stephen, "and I don't want you to call me 'Reverend Father.' You know my name; and you know my nature. You called me 'The Rationalist' once because I insisted on reasoning everything out so thoroughly. You meant it as a condemnation. I took it as a compliment. Whichever it was, it was an excellent analysis. I do like to reason things out, and to reason them out thoroughly. So now let us see just what there is in what everybody knows about this place."

"Ah, Stephen, the world is laughing at you."

"I'm glad to furnish the world with amusement," said the abbot lightly. "I know another man who was laughed to scorn once. It was just after he had worked a miracle. Perhaps you remember?"

"Come, Stephen, you spoke only a moment ago of the devil quoting Scripture. You know better than I that no heresiarch of the centuries, no deluded fanatic from the days before Christ down to the present day, has failed to do the same. Come, face the facts. Haven't you gone too far?"

"I hope not, Peter; for I haven't yet gone as far as I intend to go. There are a few things that Robert and Alberic left for me to complete."

"Robert!" snorted Peter. But then catching the fire that leaped in Stephen's eyes, he grew calmer. "A holy man in his own way, I suppose; but as steady as a weathercock. As for Alberic...."

"Still speaking from 'what everybody knows,' I notice," interrupted Stephen quickly. He would not trust himself to listen to anything against the Silver Lance he had loved so well. "Let us just face the facts, as you say, Peter; and let persons and personalities alone."

Peter sat back in his chair and chuckled. This sudden change surprised Stephen. "What's so funny?" asked the abbot.

"I am," answered Peter. "I haven't seen you in over thirty years, and yet we are not together thirty minutes when I have renewed the very argument we settled by going our separate ways thirty long years ago. Worse! I'm arguing on hearsay, as you so deftly pointed out. Forgive me, Stephen. But now do rationalize the situation for me. I have been sorely puzzled for all of thirty years. Tell me truthfully: aren't you asking too much of human nature?"

Stephen was pleased with the new tone the conversation had taken on. He loved to think, to reason, to argue, to discuss, to debate; but he detested wrangling. For a moment it had seemed that he must wrangle; but now that his friend had laughed at himself, the abbot could be freer. "I use your own criterion to answer that, Peter. Look at the facts. We've been here twelve years. Nobody has starved to death. Nobody has died from overwork or under-nourishment. At least, not to my knowledge." And the abbot smiled.

"I have heard it said that Alberic practically starved to death."

Stephen laughed aloud. "Did you ever see the man, Peter?" The monk shook his head. "Well, even the year he died he looked like a warrior! And not like one who was weary after a long, hard campaign, but like one in the finest fighting trim, fresh for the battle. Ah, Dame Rumor has a long, long tongue; and a twisted one! No, no, Peter, that's absurd. Do I look starved?"

"Not at all."

"And neither do any of the brethren," went on Stephen. "Benedict's allotment of two cooked portions, one pound of bread and three quarters of a pint of wine, will not only keep body and soul together; they will keep body and soul apart! The flesh won't lust so much against the spirit if it is not overfed."

"But, Stephen, this is surely more than God demands."

"It all depends on what you mean, Peter," said Stephen quietly. "It is true that God does not demand that we do all that is being done here at Citeaux in order that we get to heaven. But, for that matter, he doesn't demand all that you are doing at Cluny, either. A command is one thing; a counsel another. But if you think that we are doing more than will please God, how do you translate this?" And Stephen held up a crucifix.

When Peter did not answer immediately, Stephen nodded meaningfully and said, "He was laughed at, too." The Cluniac only stirred uneasily, and Stephen went on, "There's our ultimate answer to every charge, Peter. I have heard most of them. I know we are considered fools. I know that some are saying that we have debased the meaning of the Rule, the nature of man, and the dignity of the priesthood. I have heard the world laughing at what it terms our 'Pharisaism.' But after the first sting to my natural sensitivity it does not bother me. Nor should it bother anyone who has read the Gospel."

"Oh, Stephen!"

The abbot leaned forward as if to emphasize his point. "Peter, the Gospel contains the biography of a man who went about doing good. You know the reward he received for it. He was called 'wine bibber,' 'friend of publican and sinner.' He was taunted with having a devil, decried as a violator of the law, and looked upon as mad by his own relatives. That is the man who said: 'Come, follow me.' And that is the man we are trying to follow."

"And whom are we at Cluny following?"

The question had come with so much fire that Stephen could not restrain his chuckle. "Let me explain," he said and sat back.

Peter stirred as if he would object but Stephen hurried on, "The monastic world was getting soft, Peter; and it still is complacent. That is always a danger sign. History is a great teacher, and she shows that time always brings a very congenial smoothening and softening of what has come to seem harsh. Robert called these softeners 'mitigations.' Alberic always insisted they were 'compromises.' But whatever their name the facts are there. With the years there always comes a toning down of ideals, a dilution of the uncompromising dicta of the law. They are all the more deadly because they are so perfectly prudent and utterly reasonable. Course through the history of the Church or even through the history of a single Order of the Church, and you will find this thing which I have called the 'weathering process.' The years round off the rough edges and soften the hard spots.

"Then there comes a check. It is offered by a man who is labeled a rebel because he revolts against prevailing custom. But, Peter, actually he is the only non-rebel of his age; for he accepts uncompromisingly the naked wording of the law without so much as a sneer for contemporary opinion. Such were your early abbots—Odo, Aymard, Mayeul. Such was Hildebrand. Such was Benedict of Nursia, Benedict of Aniane, and every other great reformer. Such, unconsciously, was Robert of Molesme. I'm becoming more and more convinced that this is not so much the work of man, or of men, as it is of God. It is becoming my confirmed belief that Citeaux is not only a challenge to such places as Cluny, but it is actually a *check* to the weathering process that has softened the entire monastic world."

"I haven't found it soft, Stephen, and I've lived it thirty years. It is not as hard as what you are doing here, I admit; but I don't see where it is soft."

"I'm talking general principles, now, Peter, with only a very few specific facts. I do not mean to censure anyone. But I must tell you that the effect of the life of any reform or reformer on contemporaries is that of a dash of ice-cold water on a nicely warmed back. It shocks. It shakes complacency. It stirs them to anger."

"That almost sounds complacent," said Peter bluntly.

"Sorry," said Stephen with a smile. "I only mean to read a little history to you and present some present day facts. If you mean that being an instrument of God sounds complacent, I'll tell you a truth. It makes me as complacent as the power to consecrate bread and wine makes me complacent. I don't know how you feel, but I can tell you that I never feel so small, so utterly unworthy, so crushingly humiliated as I do when I, Stephen Harding, a sinful man, hold God in my hands. Why, Peter, every time I reflect on the power God has given me, I blush as deep as my soul. No, my friend, to be conscious of being God's instrument does not make a rational man complacent; it makes him confused and deeply, deeply humble."

Before another word was said a bell tolled vigorously. The abbot arose, smiled and said, "Come, that's for Vespers. Stand beside me in the choir, and for once sing the praises of the Lord while robed in the white of Citeaux."

It was almost an hour later that they returned to the abbot's room. Peter's face was hard. In it there was a trace of sadness. As soon as

Stephen had opened the door, the visiting monk said, "It is all too true what people have been saying about you and your church, Stephen. I'm hurt, deeply hurt. I had heard that you had denuded the house of God, stripped it naked. I couldn't believe it of one of your culture, refinement, aesthetic and spiritual sense. But it is too true. That's not a church. It's a bare barn!" There was an angry light in Peter's eyes.

The abbot noticed it, and wisely refrained from comment for a space. He arranged the chairs and seated himself after gesturing to his friend. "Christ had a stable," said Stephen.

"That was once too often. Why do you repeat Bethlehem? Give him the best of the earth. Nothing is too good for God. Make your church magnificent, just to show him you regret the stable cave and the coldness of the Bethlehemites. Oh, I'm hurt. No wonder the world is laughing at you, or rather sneering!"

Stephen scratched a piece of parchment with his stylus. It was the thoughtless action of a deeply thinking man. He realized that the world had summed up his action in a neat and very expressive phrase. He had stripped his church, and stripped it naked. The windows were of unstained glass; there were no statues; there was but one candlestick in the sanctuary, and that was of iron. He knew that the contrast between Cluny and Citeaux must have shocked Peter.

Cluny was magnificence itself. Gold, silver and precious stones glittered in her floor, ceiling and walls! The sanctuary was sumptuously rich and strikingly beautiful. Even its exterior was such a work of art that Stephen predicted it would be the admiration and desperation of all succeeding ages. But what he was especially thinking of now was the shock Peter would receive in the morning!

Stephen had commanded that the sacred vessels of Citeaux should be of silver-gilt, that the censer be of brass, and the vestments of wool or linen. He knew the vestments and vessels to which Peter was accustomed at Cluny. They were creations of supreme art, marvels of skill and delicate workmanship. Peter had been among them for over thirty years. On the morrow he would vest in linen or wool, and carry a chalice of silver-gilt to the altar. Stephen thought he had better prepare him for the shock; but before he could speak the visiting monk had leaned forward, touched him on the knee, and said, "That horror of a crucifix! Oh, Stephen, I'm hurt."

"I understood your reaction, Peter," said the Abbot quietly without lifting his eyes from the parchment he was scratching. "The bareness of our little church must shock one who has been used to the opposite all his life."

"But why did you do it? Why not give God all the grandeur possible?"

"There's a difference between grandeur and

the grandiose, Peter."

"I know there is. It's the same that exists between poverty and penury; between unadorned simplicity and crude nakedness; between good taste and gaudiness. But if I have to choose, I'll prefer the overdressed to the denuded."

"Did you ever look closely at a Grecian column, Peter?"

"No," he answered shortly.

"You'll not find it bare, though you will find it utterly unadorned. If you look closely, you'll find it chaste, simple, sublimely beautiful. And what is more, Peter, you'll find it solid enough to support substantial weight."

"What has a Grecian column to do with your bare church?"

"Nothing, and everything," replied Stephen slowly. "You see, Peter, I was brought up with men who were somewhat given to symbolism. Robert found his in the lone star you see in the sky just after sunset or just before sunrise. There's a simplicity, a chasteness, a splendid beauty about that star, isn't there?" Peter nodded, not knowing what else to do. "Alberic was a warrior. It is not unaccountable then, that he should take a naked saber and a long silver lance as his symbols. For myself I have taken the Grecian column."

When Stephen paused and looked as if he would say no more, Peter again blurted, "Well, what's the point? What has all this symbolism to do with your church? And, above all, what has all this talk about chaste beauty to do with that horror of a painted crucifix? I had heard that you removed the corpus and painted a garish figure on the wood, but even my imagination fell far short of what you have accomplished. That's a horror!"

Stephen sat up. He looked at Peter a long time before he asked, "Have you ever tried to picture to yourself just how Christ must have looked as he hung on the cross that awful Friday afternoon? Calvary was hideous, Peter! Christ writhed in torture. His body had to be roped lest it tear itself from the wood as it twisted and turned in agony. And, after watching men die, I know that when Jesus Christ breathed his last he was not beautiful to look upon. I have our wooden crosses painted vividly, for I want our men to realize vividly that Jesus Christ was *crucified!* "

Peter was silent. Stephen saw that the argument had struck home, and so changed his tack. "What did you think of the choir?"

"Not exactly musical," said Peter with his usual honesty, "but truly fervent. Your men do not sing too well, but they pray better than any choir I have ever heard. Their voices are not the best in France by any means, but there was heart and mind behind the words. They really prayed! They truly praised God. I was edified and inspired."

"So, the barn-like appearance of the church did not detract from their fervor, did it? Doesn't that say anything to you, Peter? We are creatures of sense. We need externals. But we are not only sense creatures! I believe in ornament, but not in ornamentation and certainly never in ostentation. Our church may be under-decorated, but such overbalance is necessary to bring the scales back even."

"Is that your prime purpose?"

Stephen thought a moment. Then very slowly he said, "No, Peter, that is not my prime purpose. In all truth, that is not my purpose at all. I was not thinking of other churches when I 'stripped mine naked,' as you say. I was thinking only of the Rule."

"The Rule?" exploded Peter.

"That's all, Peter—the Rule. The *spirit* of the Rule. The very first sentence on 'The Oratory of the Monastery' is a veritable volume. It says: 'Let the oratory be what its name signifies! And let nothing else be done and nothing else be kept there.' To me that says two things very vigorously. It shouts: 'Be simple! Be poor!' That's why you find no ornamentation in our church. Simplicity and poverty demand that it be as unadorned as a Grecian column. Poverty will not allow for silver, gold, or precious stones. Simplicity will not allow for storied stained glass, nor for vessels or vestments that delight the connoisseur of art. It was the Rule that moved me."

Peter smiled. "It strikes me as strange to hear anyone at Citeaux speak of the 'spirit' of the Rule. For over ten years now the world has been laughing at this place and calling you Pharisees, because you have been so taken up with the letter of the Rule that you seemed to ignore its spirit."

Stephen joined him in a smile. "I know it," he said. "But the world has not yet caught the spirit of Citeaux." Then, leaning toward his friend, he continued, "Peter, long before Citeaux was founded—long before Molesme was founded, yes, even before Robert had been sent to Colan—the ideal you now see nearing realization had been conceived. From the day the chaste evening star appealed to Robert as his symbol, poverty and simplicity have been the ideal toward which he and all his followers have worked. I am but doing what Robert or Alberic would have done had God given them time. There is nothing in the church now but what is chaste, simple, necessary—and poor. I know that Robert jolted the monastic world with his rigor for the Rule. I know that Alberic with his spirit of 'no compromise' shook the world. But despite what that world says or thinks, as long as the Rule calls for simplicity and poverty, everything about Citeaux is going to be both simple and poor. We've gone back to the letter to catch the spirit. We are now almost all the way back."

"Almost?" questioned Peter with a laugh. "It

seems to me you're already further than 'back'; you're quite a good way beyond. But, Stephen, I must admit that this visit and this talk have opened my eyes. I see your ideal. You certainly are realizing it. I can't say that I sympathize with the ideal as yet, but I do say that the world has laughed too loud and too long. You're the same old rationalist, and you have very sound reasons for what appeared most irrational. Forgive me for my seeming censoriousness. But believe me when I tell you this is like being in another world. You can't imagine how bare and cold this place seems after Cluny."

"When I make my next move it will seem even barer and colder."

Peter looked at his friend quizzically. "Are you deliberately setting out to stagger the world, Stephen? What's your next move?"

"If I read Benedict's Rule aright, he wanted his monks to be cenobites, but at the same time he wanted his monasteries to be solitudes. Again I am aiming at the *spirit*."

"Yes, and you are hinting at something I don't quite catch."

"Well," began Stephen, "when Benedict expressly states that 'a monastery should contain within itself water, a mill, a bake-house, a garden, and the various workshops...' and then immediately adds: 'thus eliminating the necessity for the monks to go abroad,' I hear him crying more than: 'Monks, stay in!' I very distinctly hear him commanding: 'World, stay out!' In other words, Peter, the third star in the Cistercian firmament is *solitude*. Now you have the complete ideal of Citeaux: simplicity...poverty...solitude."

"Go on, elucidate," commanded Peter, who was all attention.

"You've visited monasteries, Peter. Didn't you find them little different from feudal castles? Weren't they noisy with the horses of knights, the carriages of nobles, and the bickerings of serfs?"

"Some are," admitted Peter. "But I fail to see even a remote danger of this swampland becoming feudal territory or this little monastery a castle."

"No, as long as poverty and simplicity hold forth. But its solitude can be destroyed. The Duke of Burgundy has been very good to us."

"Much to the chagrin of many a monk," laughed Peter. "They say Hugh is just as friendly and as generous as his father."

"And just as pious," admitted Stephen in a tone of voice that brought Peter's eyebrows up. Stephen smiled. "You saw that mansion down the lane?" The monk nodded. "Odo built that for himself and his suite. He never missed a feast day. He'd come on the vigil and leave after vespers. His son has done the same. I'm going to put a ban on such visits."

"What?" shouted Peter as he rose partly out

of his chair. "Great heavens, man, where's your gratitude, your prudence, your respect for nobility, your zest for the honor of God, your...."

"That's enough," cried Stephen laughingly as he held up a restraining hand. "And that is mild to what the world will say."

"But, Stephen, you're mad! What do you mean by such a thing?"

"Without solitude there is no real recollection; without real recollection there is no true prayer; without true prayer we are eggshells— empty eggshells."

"But the nobility come only on feast days, Stephen. Surely your community can stand that little distraction."

"You never met the Silver Lance, Peter, or you'd never talk that way. He had one cry: 'No compromise!'"

"But how dare you take the gifts and ban the giver? Odo built this monastery and maintained it for years. He was the real founder; Robert was only the monastic head. And now you ban his heir from the house his father built."

"You don't know all that Odo did for us, Peter," agreed Stephen. "We were putting up a fight when he came along. He sent men and materials and the monastery went up. That was only the beginning. He donated pasture lands and set herds grazing over them. He set up granges and staffed them with serfs. He presented us with choice vineyards and gave us the most skilled of his workmen to care for them. Why, over half of our lay brothers were the duke's vassals. He loved this place as a mother loved an afflicted child. He lies out there buried among the brethren, for he really was their father. His son, Duke Hugh, has followed in his father's footsteps. He is our powerful protector and our very generous friend. And yet, before the week is out, I'm going to tell him that he can no longer come with his retinue to celebrate feasts here."

"But why?" cried the excited Peter. "This is the maddest thing I've ever heard. You're abolishing a privilege that is centuries old. You're insulting nobility. You're biting the hand that has fed you, Stephen. Stephen, what means this madness?"

The abbot's smile was a little grim as he answered, "It means I'm completing the rebellion Robert began. It means I'm being rational enough to be as radical as was Alberic. It means that the purity of the Rule, letter and spirit, will be the boast of Citeaux."

Peter shook his head sadly. "It means that you're going to bring the whole monastic world and the whole world of Burgundian nobility swarming around your head like angry hornets. No, no, Stephen, the Rule does not call for this mad measure."

"Peter," said the abbot very seriously, "you have outlined what I have already foreseen. The only one who will not be offended is the man you'd expect to be offended most. I'm expecting Duke Hugh to understand. I could tell you a long story about the tiny germs of worldliness that creep into a monastic heart and gnaw away silently till its very substance is gone; but I won't. I could tell you the effect atmosphere, environment, weathering have on everything in creation, even the monastic heart; but I won't. I could tell you of the veritable army of distractions that come from a mere glimpse at the pomp, the parade, the color and show inseparable from a duke and his escort; but I won't. I'm simply going to ask you to read that passage of the Rule I quoted a while ago, then ask yourself if St. Benedict is not shouting: 'Let there be complete separation from the world. Let there be strict cloister!'"

"But no women come...."

"Ah, Peter, that's what I call being literal-minded. That's the purest of pure Pharisaism. Cloister does not mean: 'Women, stay out!' It means: 'World, stay out!' And let me tell you, Citeaux is going to be cloistered."

"It's unnecessary, Stephen," was Peter's final comment, "totally unnecessary. You're going beyond the rigor of the Rule. You're going against moderation, gratitude, reverence...."

"Don't you really think many overstress moderation, Peter? Look!" he said and held up the crucifix. "Not much moderation there, is there? Although Christ could have redeemed the world with a drop of his precious blood, he drained himself! And yet there are Christians who will cry, 'Moderation!' It has always struck me that they are most immoderate in their insistence on moderation."

"All your arguments end with Christ and the crucifix, I notice."

"Your eyesight is poor, Peter. They all begin there! Benedict said: 'Let nothing be preferred to the love of Christ!'"

The monk was not impressed. He sat there shaking his head. Finally he looked up and asked, "Have you counted the full cost, Stephen?"

"To the last sou!" cried the abbot. "And I'm going to pay it."

"This move will cap the climax," interjected Peter. "White habits, sparse diet, labor like serfs, letter of the Rule, denuded church, and now the banning of nobility. You're certainly furnishing the world with a lot of surprise."

"You're complimenting the wrong man, Peter," smiled the abbot. "Pay your tribute to Benedict of Nursia. I'm only following his Rule."

"And what am I following?"

The abbot arose. "That last bell we heard was a summons to the reading before night prayer. Sit beside me in your flowing white robes and during your meditation tomorrow morning answer your own question."

Chapter Two

Stephen Furnishes
Heaven with a Problem

Peter put on his black habit the next morning. He felt better. As he stood with one foot in the stirrup, ready to vault into the saddle, he turned to Stephen. "I'm glad it rained, Stephen. I'm glad I got soaked. This visit has been a blessing in more ways than one. I understand Citeaux a bit." As he swung up into the saddle, his horse pranced a little. Peter reined him in, looked down on the abbot, and laughed, "But I'm glad I'm heading for home."

"You don't like Citeaux?" asked Stephen.

"I didn't say that," replied Peter as his horse side-stepped a pace, "but I do say that I love Cluny. My parting shot, Stephen, is this: you've justified everything about the place, even that denuded church. You're still the rationalist. But don't be irrational enough to ban the duke."

Stephen laughed, raised his hand in blessing and said, "I hope the clouds burst soon again. You're old enough now to know that you should come in out of the rain. Give the Grand Abbot my sincerest sentiments of esteem and my warmest affection. Tell him we are not condemning Cluny; for just as 'in my Father's house there are many mansions,' so on earth there must be many monasteries. Then beg him not to be too shocked when I ban the duke."

"You're going to do it?"

"I'm going to do it," answered Stephen with a resolute nod of the head.

"For good or ill, you're a man that knows his own mind," Peter answered with a smile. As he looked down on the abbot, he continued, "Our pilgrimage to the Eternal City was made together, Stephen; our pilgrimage to the City of Eternity is being made...."

"Together in spirit," broke in Stephen. "It's the same God we worship. It's the same home for which we are heading. Peter, I'm very grateful to God for allowing you to spend the night with us. Pray for me when I ban the duke; then spend the night that follows with me in spirit, for I'm quite sure it will be very black. But simplicity, poverty, and solitude must shine at Citeaux like stars in the midnight heaven."

"You're stubborn, Stephen," chuckled Peter, "but I'll be with you." Then as he put spurs to his horse he traced the sign of the cross over the head of the abbot of Citeaux.

Before the week was out, Stephen had talked to the duke. The duke listened as sympathetically as he could. He tried hard to understand the abbot. His only fear was that he or his men had given some offense. Reassured on this point again and again, he gave fuller mind to what Stephen had to say. When told of the high aim of the contemplative—intimate union with God—he understood Stephen's zeal for solitude. Before the conference ended it was made clear to Hugh that he would be welcome always as a visitor; that the Rule provided explicitly for guests; but what the Rule did not provide for was the noise and bustle of a large gathering and the distraction inseparable from the colorful retinue of a duke.

Hugh admitted the principle and accepted its application. He warned Stephen, however, of two things: first, that he was inviting sharp criticism even from those who had heretofore been sympathetic; and second, that he would alienate the nobility. He went further and pointed out that Citeaux had retained just as much land as she could cultivate herself. She had refused all other sources of revenues. She had cut herself off from what all others considered legitimate sources of income. She insisted on being self-supporting. What now, if there should come a rainy day? Just as a person needs friends, so does a monastery, he warned.

The abbot replied that he had weighed all that but he was ready to hazard everything so long as the duke was not offended. He even admitted that it was not prudent policy to attack long-standing custom as he was attacking it; but he insisted that principle would allow of no other course.

Hugh bowed before the abbot's decision. Before the next feast he told his intimates that they could no longer celebrate the solemnities at the abbey. When he gave the reason, angry fires of indignation were kindled which soon burned away all friendship for the little monastery in the swampland.

Peter had predicted that Stephen would bring a swarm of hornets buzzing around his head; but Peter proved a false prophet. There was much buzzing, and it was done by nobles and monks who were as mad as hornets but they did not buzz about Citeaux. No, that little monastery was left severely alone. The nobles shunned it as resolutely as a burnt child shuns the fire.

But this isolation did not immediately produce anything save joy for those in the swampland. When the duke had so royally accepted the situation, Stephen felt that the rebellion was at last complete. Mitigations were gone; all com-

promise had been cut away; Citeaux was sup-
porting herself by the labor of her hands;
simplicity shone in her Office, her Mass, and in
her entire monastery; poverty reigned supreme,
and solitude was at last assured. If ever a man
had perfect surroundings in which to live with
and to God alone, that man, thought Stephen,
was the monk of Citeaux. The place now, with
the world locked out and the monk locked in,
was a veritable paradise for prayer; while the
nature of the terrain, with its woods and swamps
and soggy undergrowth, made it a real purgatory
for penance—a monk *had* to labor if he would
live.

Before July had burned herself into August,
however, Stephen was frowning. His monks
may have been free from distraction; he had
provided for that by banning the duke. But he
himself was far from free; and day by day he
grew more and more distracted. For July was really *burning* into August, and even clammy,
swampy, ever-wet Citeaux was dry. Vegetables
do not grow in dust. The abbot began to fear for
his harvest. By the end of September his worst
fears were realized. There was no harvest. Soon
it was evident that even the sparse diet prescribed by St. Benedict could not be provided for
the little band lost in the woods. So before the
leaves had fallen and November grown grey,
Stephen, who had locked out the world, had to
go out into that world and beg. From castle to

castle he went, and while he was received with
reverence he was not welcomed with warmth.
Nobility had been outraged by his act. Most gave
him something, but they very persuasively
pointed out that the summer's drought had been
universal. Stephen accepted the little with gratitude and went away as he had come—with a
smile!

There was much derisive laughter over the
abbot and his smile. Nobles and monks who had
long predicted Citeaux's demise, were having
their hour of triumph. It was only a matter of
time now until their prophecy would be exactly
fulfilled. The twelfth century was the twelfth,
and not the sixth! In it, St. Benedict's Rule had to
be interpreted, not read literally. Citeaux would
soon be a swamp again! So they talked. But ex-
ult as they would, they could never free themselves from an element of puzzlement and doubt
that was produced by that unfailing smile on the
thin and worn face of the abbot.

But a greater puzzle existed for those simple
souls who had watched the growth of the abbey
and marveled at the zeal of her monks. Here
were men who had done all that it was humanly
possible for a person to do in order to glorify God
in the most generous way. Here were men who
had risen above the mediocrity of the world
around them and the sluggishness that lies deep
in every human soul. Here were men who had
battled their way up to the very heights of heroic

Christian living; men who had brought chivalry and gallantry within cloister walls; men who had flung themselves down before God—a holocaust. And their immediate reward was—*affliction!* These sincere, simple souls were more than puzzled by Stephen's smile; they were shocked by it. How dare a man smile in the face of such trouble?

But they never knew the secret source of that tranquillity; for they never knew the abbot's deep devotion to the Mother of God. From her he had learned her whole story; how, after answering the angel's salutation with a whole-souled, generous "Fiat," she immediately became the Mother of Sorrows! That had been a life-lesson for Stephen. He used to go over and over the facts he had learned at his "Lady's" knee: how, when her Child was ready to be brought forth, she was hurried from her home to a town of crowded inns and closed doors; how she had scarcely given birth to the world's Savior when she was driven across desert sands and forced to dwell among the swarming gods by the teeming Nile; how she lost him at the age of twelve; at thirty he left her; and at thirty-three she held him—blood-clotted and cold—outside the temple-crowned city and the home of his Chosen People. It was at Mary's knee that Stephen had learned how to say "Fiat!"—how to suffer, and how to smile.

But there was another lesson he had also

learned from Mary. He had watched her at a wedding feast, and saw how she presented facts to her Son, and demanded the miraculous. Stephen would be like her in this also. He would present heaven with a problem! If water could be changed to wine just to save a young couple from embarrassment, surely three sous could be changed to something worthwhile for a starving community. So just before the snows of winter, when he heard that there was to be a fair at Vézelay, he called an obedient monk to his side and said, "I have scoured the house. This is all the ready cash I could find." The monk held out his hand. Into it Stephen placed three little sous. When the monk looked up, Stephen said, "Go into Vézelay. There is a fair there. Buy three wagons. For each wagon buy three horses. Then load those wagons with clothes, food, and all the things we need. Come back to us then, in prosperity and joy."

The monk gazed down at his hand. The three sous looked unbelievably small. Then he looked up at his abbot. Stephen was smiling. The monk did not answer that smile. He looked down at his hand again. Then Stephen laughed aloud, took the monk by the arm, walked him to the gate and with the tiniest shove said, "Go, God will provide."

The monk went. Naturally he was puzzled, very puzzled. As he walked along, the suspicion grew that perhaps hunger had addled his abbot's brain. But he kept on his way, for obedience becomes instinctive with a thorough religious. But often along the road he took out those three little sous, stared at them, shook his head, looked to the skies and sighed, "Lord, you'll have to provide a lot! Three wagons. Nine horses. All the clothes and food we need. And all for three sous! Oh!"

When he arrived at Vézelay he put his hand into his pocket to be sure that the three little sous were there. He found them. They seemed to reassure him. Then he did the natural thing. He sought out a friend to tell the whole sad story and to get his sympathy. He found the house, entered, took out the three sous and said, "Look at what I've got to get all that Citeaux needs." Then with a meaningful nod of the head toward the little sous in the outstretched palm of his hand, he told his friend the whole story.

Just as he finished, his friend slapped his thigh, rose with a sudden spring, grasped the forlorn monk by the arm and excitedly cried, "Come! I know the man who must see your sous and hear your story. Come!"

Out of the house they went, the friend dragging the monk along behind him. Down the street, across a wide lawn, and into a great mansion. Here, with very little ceremony, the friend hurried the monk to the bedside of a very sick man.

The story was briefly told. The sick man

heard it, raised himself on his elbow, and in a weak, cracked voice called to his wife, "Give this monk every sou he needs. Citeaux shall have her wagons, horses, and all she needs." Then as he sank back on the pillow he gasped, "Tell them to pray for me."

Next day Stephen and the community were out in procession to meet the man who had still the three sous, but who was leading back three wagons, each with its three horses, and each piled high with the things Citeaux needed. As he handed the sous to the abbot, he said, "God provided but I certainly was scared." Stephen only smiled. He saw that Mary had not forgotten how to get favors from her Son.

But those three wagonloads only took the community through the winter. As March winds began to blow, sickness struck. Plague was stalking the land in the wake of famine. Citeaux was not passed by! Then for the first time in thirty-odd years Stephen's smile vanished. Hunger and real want never shook his confidence; but death did! Into those usually clear eyes clouding uneasiness came, and on that usually placid brow there appeared a frown as the Grim Specter, with merciless regularity, walked into the church and emptied stall after stall.

Recruits had never been plentiful. Not all who came had stayed. After the banning of the duke they stopped coming altogether. In church Stephen had to look at the ever shortening line of the choir, and listen to the ever thinning volume of song. He grew deeply troubled. Week after week he had to kneel at newer graves. The crosses kept thickening in the graveyard, and the troubled abbot began to suspect that soon Cîteaux would be but a haunted house with a crowded cemetery.

Were the critics right? Had he and Alberic and Robert gone too far— demanded too much? Was he entirely mistaken in the newly born belief that they had been raised up to shock the complacency of the monastic world of the day? Had six centuries so changed men that Benedict's Rule could not be observed? Was God himself displeased with the presumption of Cîteaux? If not, what meant these thirteen years of comparative barrenness and this devastating mortality now? The furrows deepened and the clouds of doubt grew thicker.

He remembered what Robert had said about the evening star—his evening star, so solitary and alone. "Others come out after it," he had said. "But before they do, we will have to see the dark."

"Oh, God," cried Stephen, "it is dark now— pitch dark!" And even while he cried there came the hollow, chilling sound of that loud wooden tablet that told of death striking again. "Oh, dear God!" groaned Stephen, "it's growing darker! It's time to do the daring, it's time to do the desperate thing."

With that resolution firmly fixed, Stephen

went to the deathbed. Then, in a silence that was nerve-shattering, he gave a command that struck fear in the heart of the boldest. "Brother Felix," he said, "by virtue of your obedience I *command* you to return to us after your death with information concerning our state of life, telling whether it be pleasing to God or no."

The monk died. A few days passed and nothing happened. Then Stephen began to grow frightened. Had he been too daring? Had he been presumptuous in thus presenting heaven with his problem? But what could he do? It had grown so dark! He had to do it. His horizons had all gone black. He had to send someone to the Source of all light. Then one day when all were working in the fields and Stephen was at their head, he gave the signal for their usual short rest in the middle of the work period. Walking to one side where he could be alone, he suddenly found himself in a blaze of light. Startled, he lifted his head and looked directly into the eyes of Felix, the brother he had commanded to come back from the dead. Stephen gasped and fell on his knees. But Felix only smiled and said, "Lay aside all doubt, Reverend Father, and hold for certain that your manner of life is holy, and very, very pleasing to God. Furthermore, your grief at your want of children will soon disappear, for many will come to you, men of noble birth and learning. Yes, and like bees swarming in haste and overflowing the hive, they shall fly away and spread themselves through many lands."

Stephen smiled his old radiant smile! Furrows faded from his brow and clouds disappeared from his eyes. He looked like the young, eager Stephen who had listened to Alberic talking about Crusaders' sons with the Crusaders' spirit. He looked even younger! He looked like the mere boy who had stared at the evening star and heard Robert's prediction about other stars coming out after dark. Then his hand came up, and striking his breast he breathed, " 'Oh, you of little faith! Why did you doubt?' Forgive me, Lord."

That same evening he stood at his window and watched the sky. When the west was white he saw the brilliant silver radiance of vesper—all beautiful, but all alone. He stood at that window and kept staring into that sky. The dark came slowly that evening; it came subtly, imperceptibly. In the more distant and deeper blue, Stephen saw tiny silver anemones break through and flower in five-petalled loveliness. It was long years since he had watched the blooming of the sapphire skies. He felt that he was seeing it now for the first time, and he found himself softly singing, "It is the glory of God that the heavens tell!" Mists rose before him and through his tears he saw shimmering silver grandeur.

"Robert was right. Stars do come out after dark. Many stars," he thought. Then with lifted face he prayed, "But, dear Lord, it has been so dark, so pitch-dark and I have been so alone! Robert went. Alberic died. We lost our benefactors. Poverty came. Then want. Beggary. Hunger. Suffering was followed by sickness, then death. Yes, it was pitch-black, dear Lord. There were no stars! But I should not have faltered. Forgive me my weak faith. I know now that it is only after dark that stars come out."

Next day Stephen was in a far corner of the little cemetery standing by Alberic's grave. "The leaf of his life fell," he thought, "and when it fell it was flaming red. Many, very many, have fallen since. The ground around me is covered. Thank God, they too were scarlet when they fell. All changed. All beautiful. But the tree whence they fell became more bare and I grew frightened. Winter had come. Alberic spoke of the Crusaders' spirit. They had it, these few; but most had fallen. The shields for the Sacred Heart lay battered and broken, and there were no strong arms to snatch them up. But spring is here now. The ground grows softer around his grave. The tree whence fell his scarlet leaf is shooting with tiny green tips. The woodland breeze grows warmer. And hope, the hope of younger years, comes warm again to my heart. I miss him, that old Silver Lance; but when I stand here he seems close to us, and he brings me strength. I must complete his work. God has said that men will come. I have no doubt that they will be what Alberic promised and prophesied—Crusaders' sons with the Crusaders' spirit." Then he knelt and prayed from the innermost core of his being, "Dear God, grant that those who do come grow as this man grew—strong, straight and true. And when it comes time for them to fall, let them fall as he fell! Let them fall as *flame*."

Naturally, the message Felix had given him that day in the fields filled Stephen's mind. He went over it again and again. "Men of noble birth and learning," he had said. Stephen loved that first word, "Men." Yes, he wanted men, real men; for only real men would stay and live the life of Citeaux. It was a rugged world, this little monastery in the swampland and in it there was no room for the effeminate or the weak. It was a world that demanded passion, but had no time for sentimentality. It was a world that challenged the depths of man and called forth his highest vigor and bravery. That was why Stephen loved the first word of the message; for he well knew that the virile can be brought to high virtue, and the strong to towering sanctity. He thanked God for the first word with its latent promise of strong, virile, vigorous men.

The qualifications Felix had added set Stephen dreaming. "Men of noble birth," he had said. Stephen recalled a remark he had made to Robert years before. They had been discussing Alberic and the secrecy about his lineage. Stephen had laughed at his abbot and said, "Even if Alberic is sprung from the lowliest of serfs, he is still a nobleman!" Stephen did not care so much whence men came; he cared a great deal about what they were. Then he reflected that his often-used illustration worked all ways. Good atmosphere and environment "weather" a soul and shape a character, just as an atmosphere that is tainted and an environment that is evil can soil the purest and warp the stoutest. Gradually that first qualification made some appeal to Stephen. *"Noblesse oblige"* spurred knights to magnificent daring and immortal doings in the world. Why then could it not send souls of nobles scaling sanctity's topmost heights from within the lowly cloister? The argument seemed sound, and slowly Stephen grew fond of this first qualification.

But the second held no immediate appeal— "men of learning." Of what use was learning in a world such as Citeaux, where from foundation stone to cornice the substance was simplicity? Of what use was learning to men whose one work was to praise God in the Psalms of David, and to humble themselves as serfs, sweating in the soil? Of what use was learning in a world where the only science was the science of the saints? Stephen frowned over the qualification. What did it mean? He himself was accounted a "man of learning." He had spent all the years of his youth in school—first those of England, then those of Ireland, and finally those of France. And yet he felt that he had never been to a real school until he entered the Abbey at Molesme, and endeavored to forget the learning he had acquired, as he bent all his attention to learning how to walk in the footsteps of the Nazarene. Of what use was learning to a lowly monk?

But then Stephen stopped frowning and opened his eyes in wide surprise—at himself! What was coming over him? Was the "weathering process" taking effect on himself? Was he being conquered by environment and made subject to suggestion? Was the oft-repeated but untrue cliché that "learning is no aid to sanctity" working its way into his subconsciousness?

He sat down at his desk to reason out the problem. It was true that God is charity; but the God-Man did not so characterize Himself. His words were: "I am the *Truth!* " Christ said he was Truth. That is also true of the Godhead. God is substantial *Truth*. It must follow then, argued Stephen, that every tiny truth firmly grasped, no matter in what order, is really getting a firmer, fuller grasp on God. And that is why a monk lives! He wants to grasp God. His life is nothing but groping, a continual groping, after God. Eternity will be the everlasting embrace of him he longed to hold. Everything, then, from the abstract mathematical truth that two and two make four, up to and including the subtlest, purest and most refined of metaphysical notions contained in the concept of God's essence, must be interrelated! Hence, they are manifestations of the Being we love and adore. Therefore, the sharper the intellect, the keener the ultimate sanctity!

"That would be a truer saying than 'learning is no aid to sanctity,'" said Stephen aloud.

But true rationalist that he was, Stephen paused and asked, "True in the speculative, how about the practical order? How has my education helped me in my strivings after sanctity?" He had not reflected long when a wide smile lit his countenance. For he saw that it had helped and helped immensely. Further, he saw that it always would help; for the more vivid the fancy, the more lively the imagination, the keener and quicker the perception, the firmer and fuller would be the grasp on truth. Stephen was really thinking now. God is not grasped by hands, he argued. He is not folded to one's breast and hugged by arms of flesh. No. He is spirit and can only be held by the spirit. That is why the intellect is of such paramount importance in the spiritual life! Sanctity is a product of the head and heart, not of the heart alone.

Stephen drew his chair in to his desk. This subject deserved attention. He had never realized how important the intellect was. But now he saw that the will was a blind man who was led along by the one faculty of the soul that could see. Love is the result of knowledge, he reflected. Then he thought of faith and grew enthusiastic as he defined it as an *intellectual* assent, not a palpitation of the heart or a surge of the feelings!

It is the mind that matters, he almost cried. For it is the mind that acts as helmsman for the monk, steering him between the whirlpool and the rock, keeping him from the Scylla of mere pietistic mouthings and sentimental effusions of feelings as well as from the Charybdis of callous, cold, mechanical performance of duty. A monk must not be a stoic nor a gushing geyser; he must be a rational being. Mind must be his mentor. Indeed it must, for faith, hope and charity depend on the faculty that *knows!*

Stephen sat back and shook his head in hearty agreement. He saw now why some souls were abashed as they entered the religious life and began their quest for intimacy with God. Their wills were right. They longed after the Divinity. They wanted to grasp him and hold him to their hearts. But their minds were wrong. They were not men of learning! They thought that some infinite abyss yawned between them and the One who made them and saved them. They had never grasped the relation of all things to the Absolute. They had never known that the way to God is the wide-open way of the universe, and that no matter where they stood, and no matter how they turned, their first step could be a step toward God.

"That's the truth," mused Stephen. "They were not men of learning; hence, they did not know how to read the signposts that a provident God has set up all along the way. They had never learned that every creature, from a tiny violet nodding in the breeze to those mighty silver spheres whirling through the stretches of the skies, is an index pointing directly to God.

"What a subtle heresy is abroad in the world of religious!" exclaimed Stephen. "Too many are confusing simplicity with stupidity. They are looking on science as an enemy to sanctity. They firmly believe that an intellectual person cannot be humble." Then the abbot smiled. "If it weren't so tragic, it would be amusing. I wonder what they think Christ's intellect was like. They cannot deny he was humble!"

From that day on the entire message of Felix pleased Stephen greatly; but it also stirred his impatience. He smiled and prayed much those days, and his greatest prayer was for patience. For after reasoning long on each phrase in the message, he had concluded that every qualification had place at Citeaux. And since he had the assurance that his manner of life was pleasing to God, his only remaining problem was how to hold himself in calmness until heaven would fulfill the promise it had made. That problem he also presented to heaven.

Chapter Three

Heaven Furnishes
Stephen with a Problem

The lenten fast was over. Stephen and his handful had sung the first glorious "Alleluias" of Easter and were exulting with the triumphantly risen Christ. Their band was small now, smaller than it had ever been; but the air of glad expectancy that had filled Citeaux the day Stephen had his visit from Felix still lifted every heart in the monastery. They, too, prayed for patience even as had their abbot. But each succeeding day, full of bright hope though it was, wore their patience thinner and thinner. The austerities of the season of special penance had not robbed their expectancy of its edge, but with the dawn of Easter a new calm seemed to settle on all, even on the abbot.

One afternoon not long after that first glad "Alleluia" had burst from their joyous throats, Stephen was at his desk studying the recension he had made of the Bible. He was deep in his work when there came a sharp, nervous knock on his door and the breathless porter burst in with the shout, "They have come!"

The abbot looked up. He had been far away in his thoughts. "Who?" he asked calmly.

"The men of noble birth and learning!"

The book fell from Stephen's hands. He felt his pulse quicken. "How many?" he asked.

"Thirty-two!" cried the excited porter.

Stephen walked to the gate as calmly as he could, but the effort was noticeable. Color glowed in his usually pale cheeks while his eyes were unnaturally bright and sparkling. The porter swung the door open and thirty-two noblemen saw a stately abbot step into the frame and smile.

It was all that Stephen could do at the moment. Before him stood nobles ranging from the tender age of thirteen to that of over fifty years. Stephen saw them through a tremulous mist. Tears of joy refused to be stemmed. With wonder he learned that these men were all knitted by the ties of blood and intimate friendship. Their spokesman was a handsome, light-haired, large-eyed, trimly-built lad of twenty-two. His name was Bernard. He had come from Fontaines. He was scion of one of Burgundy's best families. Behind him stood four of his brothers, one of his uncles, some of his cousins, and many of his life-long friends. The one question he asked was, "May we come in?"

Stephen blinked. "Could they come in?" Ah, if only he were French he could answer that with an effusion! "Could they come in?" For years he had been waiting and praying. For weeks he had been watching. And today! "Could they come in?" Stephen was sorry he was not French. He wanted to be voluble. He wanted to make expressive gestures and have a flood of warm words flow from his lips. They were all there in his heart! But all he could do was smile and say, "Yes, come in. But this one? No— I fear he is too young." He touched Bernard's young cousin, Robert. The lad was only thirteen.

Many things happened to Stephen Harding's heart that afternoon in Eastertide when he stood framed in the doorway greeting Bernard and his band. It responded to the freshness and warm appeal of youth, the dignity of sober, steadfast middle-age, and the grey hairs of warrior Gauldry, Bernard's maternal uncle. Most of all it was overwhelmed with the fidelity and goodness of God.

That night he tried to appreciate what had happened. It was difficult. What a band of novices had come! Knights had laid aside sword and spear; nobles had left wives and children; youth had left life, adventure, romance in the world; and all had come to little Citeaux to seek God alone!

From that day Citeaux changed. New life pulsed in her veins, a more vibrant tempo beat in her choral song, and a younger heart throbbed at her manual labor. And from that day Citeaux's abbot changed. He grew young again. A happier light came into his eyes, a more musical ring to his voice, and a greater spring to his step. It was then that Stephen began his greatest work—the molding of the greatest man of the twelfth century and the greatest glory of Citeaux, young Bernard of Fontaines. He had sensed that fact the moment his porter had opened the door and he had heard the light voice of the young Burgundian noble. He had sensed it with a touch of fright, but it was a challenge to his manhood, a stimulus that made him seek out God the Father for strength, God the Son for wisdom, and God the Holy Spirit for light.

Springtime filled the woodlands and the heart of Stephen of Citeaux. He walked to the cemetery morning after morning to bring Alberic news of the hoped-for men of nobility and learning who had come to them. He told the Silver Lance that some of them were Crusaders' sons and that all of them had the Crusaders' spirit; told him how he must now set to work teaching them to make God the focal point of their thoughts and affections. With a smile he used the phrase so dear to Robert and Alberic—"God-orientated." With God's help, he would do that—he would God-orientate these men!

It was not the difficult task he expected. For he soon saw that their environment and education had worked on their souls. Before the month was out, Stephen had learned how much a mother can do to the mind and heart of children. Secretly, the abbot admitted that Alice of Montbar, wife to Tescelin of Fontaines, and mother of Bernard and his brothers, had been "Master of Novices" for this select group.

But Stephen was wise enough to realize that heaven had furnished him with a problem. He knew that these men would be tempted. He knew that the lowly life at Citeaux would not be easy for Gauldry, the knight and noble who had left castle, vassals and wealth. No, it would not be easy for him to take orders and work like a serf. Nor would it be easy for Guy, Bernard's eldest brother, who had left wife and two charming baby girls. It would not be easy for him to live alone in silence. Nor would it be easy for Bernard's other brothers, Gerard and Andrew. They had been knighted and had already tasted the heady wine of triumph in battle. Indeed, it would be difficult for such men to rest satisfied with the dull, prosaic life of following a plough. And so for the rest of the thirty it would not be easy. But Stephen *must* find a way to make it less hard.

He did! He found the only way. He found him who said of himself, "I am the way!" How Stephen's solution worked is the fascinating story of *The Family That Overtook Christ*, a continuation of this Saga of Citeaux. Here, it is enough to say that Stephen presented his solution clearly. What he especially impressed on them was the fact that Christ was a *man*. Hence, they were to take for their motto, "Act manfully!" Do everything for God in a virile way. That would be the Christ-way. For practical purposes he brought it down to "do well what you're doing." Be intent on the task of the moment. Bend heart and mind and all your energies on that one thing to the utter exclusion of everything else.

It was a simple lesson, and one that was easily learned, for it was thoroughly taught. And these men, most of whom had spent their lives in the saddle with a mettlesome charger between their knees and a spear or mace in their hands, took the lesson Stephen taught them and twisted it into a battle-cry. They used it the rest of their lives. It steadied them when they were wavering; it spurred them on when their energies flagged; it blew the fire in their souls to brilliant flame when they needed flame. It was: "All for God!"

When Stephen saw how quickly they grasped the lesson and caught the spirit of Citeaux, when he saw how in one lightning sword thrust they had pierced to the very heart of St. Benedict's Rule, he knelt down humbly, and from a grateful heart poured out fervent thanks to God for having sent men, real men—men of nobility and learning.

But that was only the beginning of the problem heaven had presented, for Bernard of Fontaines had started something! When Burgundy learned that the Lord of Fontaines was alone in his castle with his only daughter and his youngest son, there was a mighty stirring. Tournaments still went on, and young nobles were knighted, but the attention of the Duchy was not on these things alone. The air became alive with talk of the abbey lost in the swampland. The leading topic of conversation was neither the latest champion of the tourneys nor the fairest lady; it was Bernard, his band, and little Citeaux! Day after day knighthood grew more and more conscious of a higher chivalry and courtiers learned that there was a place for them behind cloister walls.

At the moment, the soldiers of the Duchy were laying siege to Grancey; but even this was no deterrent to nobles who had caught the spark from Bernard, to knights who had been stirred by young Andrew, nor to older warriors who knew Guy and Gauldry. There were many heated arguments. Charges of desertion and fanaticism were levelled against those who would imitate the men of Fontaines, but despite the sting of taunts, and the ridicule of the unheeding, old and young kept going to Citeaux.

Week after week the iron knocker on the abbey gate was lifted and resolutely banged by men who were used to battle and who were ready to fight. Week after week Stephen Harding welcomed new novices, and found among them Crusaders' sons ablaze with the Crusaders' spirit. Week after week he welcomed not only men of nobility and learning but also ignorant men, men of the soil and serfdom. Both he welcomed equally!

Abbot Stephen could hardly believe it. He saw his problem grow, but he was not afraid. He would find a solution in time. At the moment he was satisfied to be humbled, and more than once he walked to the cemetery to tell Alberic and the others of the wonder that was taking place, and to beat his breast as he said, "And to think I actually doubted!"

But beating the breast was not enough when the influx continued and little Citeaux became overcrowded. What should he do? Was this sudden flow after the long years of drought a mere spring freshet? Would it stop with the summer? Should he enlarge the abbey? Would the postulants stay? These were some of the questions that turned in Stephen's mind as he paced the cemetery paths. He remembered that it was here, on these very paths, that he had first been startled by the realization that Robert and Alberic had really created something distinct. And it was here, on these very paths, that Stephen decided to complete that creation.

He would not enlarge the abbey; he would enlarge the Order! "Yes," he said, pacing more rapidly, "Order it is going to be!" He had seen it coming before Alberic died. It is true that he had doubted when death had emptied stall after stall with chilling regularity, and the iron knocker on the abbey gate was silent. But that was his sin. He was making reparation for it now. He talked earnestly to the dead as he paced the paths, and he heard the dead talking to him. He talked to the lay brothers who had so edified him and en- couraged him; he talked to the men who had died under him as abbot; finally he talked long with Brother Felix, the man he had commanded to come back from the dead, and who had come back! He said: "The applicants are 'like bees swarming,' Felix. It is time for some to 'fly away and spread themselves to other parts.'"

With Stephen, to think had ever been to act. He had reasoned the situation out thoroughly; he had arrived at his conclusion. So one morning in the early May of 1113, when the grass was thick and very green in the mounded cemetery, the abbot knelt at the grave of the Silver Lance. His face was rigid. After kneeling like stone for a moment, he said slowly, "Tomorrow, Alberic, they go...Crusaders' sons with the Crusaders' spirit...."

With eyes fixed on the turf as if he were looking into the face of his friend, he went on, "You remember Bertrand. He came with us from Molesme. I am giving him a cross, tomorrow, and twelve men. They go south. They are to take up their abode by the Grosne. Walter, Bishop of Chalons, and two noblemen gave us the land. It is a goodly stretch. This will be our first foundation. Let us call it *La Ferté* or *Firmitas;* and let us pray that it be strong, that it be true to all we have worked for."

"Alberic," he continued, "your silver lance must lead the way so that my Grecian column may arise. These men know the cause and the commander. See to it that the secret spot, which you say lies deep in every man, be touched. See to it that La Ferté be a home for shields for the Sacred Heart. See to it that poverty, simplicity, and solitude be the guiding principles and the leading stars. Tell Robert that stars are beginning to come out after the dark."

The next day they left. Bertrand was at the head bearing a large cross; behind him trailed twelve silent monks. Many who saw them were struck by the number and spoke of Christ and his twelve. That was the very idea behind the number and that was the spirit that animated the group. That was the day on which Citeaux became a "Mother"; her "daughter," her first daughter, was living in the south. Stephen Harding rejoiced in the solution he had found for heaven's problem.

But as the months mounted he soon saw that the problem was far from being fully solved. Postulants kept lifting that heavy iron knocker on the abbey's front gate; and the church, the refectory and the dormitory kept being overcrowded. The "bees" were still "swarming," as Felix had foretold. But the problem became more intricate for the abbot. The veterans of early Molesme and even of early Citeaux were few, and not all of them were leaders. Whom did he have to place at the head of a band? And where should they go? Stephen grew worried. One day he called Gauldry to him and very bluntly said, "You know something of men. Is Hugh of Macon a leader?"

The old warrior chuckled. "Men are difficult animals to lead, Reverend Father. In fact, they don't like to be led." Then rather musingly he went on, "The real leader of men is the man who can make others believe they are accompanying him, not following. He is the man who is wise enough to recognize, respect, and show due deference to the manhood in other men. He is the man who wins their confidence by showing his confidence in them." Then with a quick lift of his eyes to his abbot he said, "Not many men are that wise. But I think young Hugh of Macon is."

Stephen smiled. "Don't you demand real superiority in your leaders?"

"Oh, it's got to be there," said Gauldry quickly. "But it must not be paraded. Men demand superiority in their leaders, but, at the same time, they resent being made inferior. So the true superior is the man who makes inferiors feel equal; even though they know in their heart of hearts that they are not. This honest duplicity is one of human nature's queerest quirks. But why do you ask about Hugh?"

The abbot drew out a map of France and placed beside it a list of the community. "We've got to make sense out of these two confusing things." Placing his stylus on an inked "x" he said, "This is Citeaux. South here we have La Ferté. As a soldier, where would you say our next daughter house should be placed?"

Gauldry glanced from his abbot to the map, then back to his abbot again. "It depends on what you want to do, Reverend Father. If you want to defend Citeaux you should surround her on all sides, and keep your daughters close to home. If you want Citeaux to expand, you've got to do two seemingly contradictory things. You've got to radiate even as you attract."

The abbot smiled. It was good to be plotting with one who knew how to plot. "You've outlined my principles, even before I've presented them, Gauldry. I want union. That's fundamental. But obviously, as you look at this list, I've got to have expansion."

"That's phrasing it more exactly than I did,

Reverend Father. Here then is our center. This will be the hub of the wheel," and the old soldier placed his finger on Citeaux. "You've already got one spoke down here in the south," and he indicated La Ferté. "Now you need three others; one here, one here and one right here," and his finger touched spots to the north, east and west of Citeaux. "That will give you the union and expansion you desire. I speak of a wheel, for I think of the two forces in a revolving wheel. You see the application of the hub. We've got to hold our daughters to Citeaux even as we send them out to the circumference of the circle," and his finger traced an arc through the points he had indicated.

"But you spoke of radiating and attracting. What did you mean?"

"Practically the same thing. You see, Reverend Father, I've watched the steady stream of postulants come here. Citeaux is attracting them. And now Citeaux can radiate because of them. She has started already with La Ferté in the south. But now if she is to continue to grow, La Ferté and every other daughter house must attract even as does Citeaux. In that way only they will be able to radiate. Therefore, you've got to place your houses as near as you can to the intersections of different dioceses, on the border of different provinces, and fairly near to populous centers. That's what a soldier would do."

Stephen bent over the map. He studied the

position of La Ferté. She stood close to the intersections of the dioceses of Mâcon and Châlons.
Her position then was fairly satisfying. The abbot
now placed his stylus on a spot where three
provinces met—Auxerre, Tonnerre, and Champagne. "Look at this, Gauldry. This spot is not
only tangent of three provinces, but also to three
dioceses. I could set a table there and seat the
Bishops of Sens, Langres, and Auxerre to dinner
without having any one of them leave his own
diocese. Do you think that would be a favorable
spot for a foundation?"

Gauldry squinted at the point, smiled, and
said, "Excellent!"

"All right," said Stephen as he pushed the
map aside and drew over the community list.
"Now for the men. How does one train com-
manders, Gauldry?"

"One doesn't," replied the old soldier. "We
learn to walk by walking. We learn to command
by commanding." Then he chuckled as he said,
"We learn everything by making mistakes. The
stumbles, falls and bumps of babyhood were our
most expert instructors in the art of walking,
Reverend Father. And I more than suspect that
our errors of judgment, our too hasty orders,
and our humiliating defeats best teach us how to
command. But something is worrying you, Reverend Father. What is it?"

"Time," said Stephen. "Are they sufficiently
trained? Are they grounded in the simplicity, the

poverty, and the solitude that are the bases of our spirit? Do they love prayer and penance?"

"Halt!" commanded Gauldry as he smiled at his superior. At Stephen's look of surprise the old warrior said, "Your last question was wrongly phrased, Reverend Father. Nobody loves penance. Nobody can love penance. And I'd almost dare say the same thing for certain forms of prayer. They love the God to whom they pray, and the God to whom they pay reparation. But they do not and cannot love penance."

"Becoming a philosopher in your old age, eh?"

"No, no, Reverend Father. Becoming God-conscious, that's all."

"Well, what do you think Gauldry? Do you think Hugh of Macon could lead twelve men to the spot I pointed out and have them live there as we are living here?"

The old warrior thought a long time before his gray head nodded in assent. "As well as any man you've got on that list," he finally said. "But I must tell you that if you send him away, you'll be sending away half of young Bernard's heart. They have been the fastest of friends since childhood."

"I've thought of that," said Stephen slowly. "But Bernard must get used to having his heart broken. It seems part of God's technique in the sculpturing of his saints, Gauldry. He breaks the human heart again and again; but only to refashion it closer to his own. Who knows but that is the secret of the seven swords that were scabbarded in Mary's immaculate breast?"

"Sanctity costs, doesn't it?" came the slow question from the warrior whose eyes were looking far, far away.

"Yes," said Stephen quickly. "It costs much. But, Gauldry, the price is always in our purses. We fail to purchase it, not because we are poor, but because we are miserly. We won't pay the price! Here is a perfect example of how easy it is to purchase sanctity if we will. This separation between Bernard and Hugh is going to hurt. Now they can react naturally or supernaturally. They can take that hurt and nurse it, pout over it, groan and lament over the loneliness and lovelessness in the religious life or they can smile outwardly even as inwardly they smart; they can cheer one another on as they part, even as they secretly tell Christ to take the pain that is in their soul and use it as incense to be burned in the brazier of his Sacred Heart and offered to the Godhead in praise and reparation. To do this latter thing does not take away the sting. No, indeed. It often increases it because of the very denial of the relief that would come from an outward expression of human grief. But you know which of the two ways is the virtuous way. You know which will make the man of God and which the maudlin monk. Yes, Gauldry, sanctity costs; but we always have the price. The only question is, will we pay it?"

Gauldry rose on that question. "Thank you, Reverend Father," he said. "You have shown me a valuable truth. Sanctity has always appeared some distant, practically unattainable thing to me. Because it is supernatural, I suppose I believed that it had little relation to the natural me. I see now how dull I have been. I see now that my sanctity must be bought with the coin I make from the metal of my everyday actions and reactions. I also see that Bernard and Hugh must mint their sorrow." Then slowly he added, "Perhaps that is the easiest of all metals to work on, Reverend Father. My difficulty is coining the pleasure God sends me."

The abbot looked long at the old warrior who had gray at his temples and sincerity burning as bright as silver in his eyes, then he smiled warmly. "Gauldry," he said, "if the youngsters have learned as well as you, I can put aside all my worries. They will be gallant to God."

"That's a very choice compliment, Reverend Father," said the nobleman with a bow. "I thank you for your kindness, but must refuse to accept the praise. Those youngsters have learned faster and more fully than I."

"We must wait and see," said Stephen as the old warrior left.

A week later Hugh of Macon shouldered a five foot wooden cross, and, with twelve men marching behind him, walked west to Pontigny.

Citeaux had her second daughter, and there was a little more room at the motherhouse.

That was in 1114. But 1115 gave Stephen little rest. The influx of novices had been greater than ever. Busy as he was with their training he did not forget his own plan for the Order. He talked the situation over with Gauldry a few times, but nothing new came out of the discussions; the plan of a wheel with Citeaux as its hub was Gauldry's fixed plan. Whenever Stephen spoke of leaders, the old warrior always pointed to younger men. They had the daring, he said; and daring was needed for such an enterprise as this. Old men were too cautious.

That his abbot took his advice was evidenced the day Arnold of Cologne was selected to lead a group of twelve to the east. He founded the Abbey of Morimond which lay close to the dioceses of Toul, Langres and Besanç on. Gauldry's plan was being very closely followed.

Then before the year was out, Stephen did one of the most human things of his saintly career. Over the protests of some of the elders, he called Bernard of Fontaines to him, and despite his youth, his delicate health, and his exaggerated zeal, he made him the leader of the group that was to go north. In that group were his uncle Gauldry, his four brothers, Guy, Gerard, Andrew and Bartholomew, and seven of his cousins and intimate friends. It was a very select group. Had Bernard been allowed his own choosing, he would have named the very twelve the abbot had designated.

Just before the group gathered for departure, Gauldry went to the abbot's room and said, "Some of God's saints can be very human persons, can't they, Reverend Father?" The abbot smiled. "That's a very considerate thing you are doing for Bernard and his brothers."

"And how about his uncle?" asked Stephen with a broader smile.

"His uncle has a puzzle, Reverend Father. You see he wants to become a saint; and one time you said that to make his saints God breaks their human hearts so that he can remodel them on his own divine one. Now Gauldry's heart is not broken by this appointment."

Stephen arose, and as they made their way to the door he said, "When I was a boy, I heard an old farmer say, 'Never count your chickens before they are hatched.' When I was a young man I heard an old sailor say, 'There is always a calm before a storm.' Now that I am an aging monk, I know that he is a very wise man who, in time of consolation, prepares his soul for desolation. Watch your heart action the next few years, Gauldry."

The old warrior smiled. A few minutes later his smile was forgotten in surprise as he watched the usually undemonstrative Stephen Harding break down in tears as he bade the little group farewell. When he heard the humble abbot begging young Bartholomew to pray for him, Gauldry said to himself, "I had forgotten that someone else's heart was engaged in this affair. It looks as if God is still at his sculpturing."

Chapter Four

The Problem Becomes More Complicated

Stephen Harding's heart had been wrenched that day, just as it had been wrenched those other days on which he had said farewell to little groups of men he had trained to be gallant to God. But a few weeks later, when he took down the map and placed an inked "x" to the north and printed in "Clairvaux," he breathed more easily. The four spokes of Gauldry's wheel were now complete. Citeaux was circled by daughter houses. Stephen could look north, south, east and west, and no matter which way he turned he would be facing some of his men. But then, just as he began to breathe more easily, he was forced to catch his breath!

An unexpected, but very welcome visitor came one day in the person of his quondam fellow-pilgrim, Peter. It was not raining, but the monk from Cluny claimed to be drenched. He said it was his only excuse for stopping. When the abbot felt of his clothes, Peter smiled and said, "Sun-drenched, Reverend Father. I need the shade of Citeaux for a few hours."

Stephen tried to persuade him that he needed it for a few days, but Peter's only reply was, "Get behind me, Satan!" The monk from Cluny warmly congratulated Stephen on the success he was having at Citeaux. He told him that the world had stopped laughing and had begun to marvel. Nothing like it had happened in the history of the Province. Burgundy was dazed. Only five short years ago she had predicted the death and the burial of the fanatics in the woods. Now she had to witness the growth and diffusion of the very group she had expected to dwindle and die. Citeaux was still the talk of the Duchy; but the tone of the conversation had greatly changed.

When Stephen showed him the map, Peter nodded approvingly and said, "You will grow. Yes, you will grow."

The friends were having a delightful visit until Peter said, "I suppose you will be grand abbot of all these houses."

It was then that Stephen Harding caught his breath. He had not thought of this. "You've given me something to think about, Peter," he said slowly. "I do not want to be grand abbot."

"Why? Because it would make you like Cluny?"

"No, because it would make me unlike St. Benedict."

"He legislated for a single monastery; not for an Order. And you're growing into an Order."

"I know it. But it's going to be a Benedictine Order. The saint legislated for a single monastery, as you say, but his plan of absolute self-government is clear."

"Don't be foolish, Stephen," retorted Peter. "You can't reconcile the irreconcilables! Either your daughter houses are going to be dependent, or they are not going to be daughter houses. And Citeaux is either going to be supreme, or she is not going to be Mother. Cluny has solved the problem that faces you. Her ruler is grand abbot; the superiors of all daughter houses are priors, subject to him. Therefore, we have extended the patriarchal form that St. Benedict planned for a single monastery to a whole host of family houses."

"You have destroyed Benedict's patriarchal form, you mean, and set up an absolute monarchy."

Peter made an attempt to protest but the abbot continued, 'You know you must admit that, Peter. Cluny is a monarchy. She always has been, and always will be. There is great advantage in that form of government. With a capable, saintly man as Abbot of Cluny, the Order will function perfectly. You have a union and a unity impossible under any other form of government. But I don't like it."

"You're hard to please."

"Very," admitted Stephen, smiling but insistent. "I have two big objections to a monarchy. It places too much power in the hands of one man, and it is not Benedictine."

"Well, if you don't adopt it, your reform is going to fail. 'Divide and conquer,' is more than an axiom; it is a whole plan of campaign. Diffusion is always dangerous, Stephen. Wise mothers always tie young children to their apron strings. Let your daughters go their way, and away will go your reform."

"I know it," said Stephen with a frown. "Concentration is one secret of power and success. Diffusion always lessens fervor, and ultimately leads to failure. Cluny survives and survives well. And yet I can't adopt her system."

"Then how in the world are you going to keep the next generation of Cistercians from being merely 'white Benedictines'—or, if you prefer it, 'Cluniacs not in black'? You've got something unique here. You've done what no one but yourself thought possible."

"You admit it?" asked Stephen with the trace of a smile.

"Oh, all of us who are honest must admit it.

But that's not my point. My point is that you should hold on to what you have; you should perpetuate it. And the only way you can do that is by tying your daughters to your apron strings. Everything has a tendency to go down! Man is no exception. I don't mean the physical man; I mean the spiritual one. Now, how are you going to keep your daughter houses and your granddaughter houses from forgetting the poverty, the simplicity, the silence, the solitude, the rigid regularity of Citeaux? You simply can't do it unless you become a monarch."

"Well, Peter, I'll not become a monarch, and I will find a way to keep my daughters and their daughters from being wayward."

"How can you…?" But there Peter stopped and laughed. "You've been doing such amazing things already that I guess I had better hold my tongue."

"I'm glad you loosened it, Peter. You've helped me see how complicated my problem really is. A wise general learns the strength of his enemy. Yes, you've opened my eyes by loosening your tongue. You've presented me with a seeming impossibility. I want every daughter house of Citeaux to be absolutely self-governing—for that is what St. Benedict demands. And yet, I want them to be daughters to Citeaux. How can I wed dependence and independence?"

"I'm glad it's not my problem," said Peter. "But don't despair. You've made black white already," and he touched his own and the abbot's habit. "You've made the ancient modern and the modern ancient. You've made the letter of the law its spirit, and the spirit of the law its letter. I'm beginning to suspect you're a magician."

"And I'm beginning to suspect that I'm a bewildered and very befuddled monk. You've given me enough matter for wrinkles as deep as the bone. How can I keep my daughters from running away, and yet not behave as a domineering, tyrannical mother?"

"You're not going to give me wrinkles, Stephen. I was never good at riddles, and I've shied from the impossible all my life. I hate to leave you to your problem, but I know I couldn't help you, no matter how much I worried over it. I'm not the planner you are. But I'll remember you in some of those Rosaries I say every day."

For weeks after Peter left, Stephen's brow was wrinkled. He became the rationalist again, the man who looked through facts to get at principles. Other reforms had flourished, then faded. He was determined to discover why. Peter had given one reason when he spoke of the innate tendency downwards that is in every man. What is true of individual men would be true of individual monasteries, he argued. How could he keep his new houses on the level of old Citeaux? How could he check that innate tendency downwards, and yet not disturb the individual's independence? He took his problem to

Alberic, but for once his old friend was silent. He took it to the church, but neither the tabernacle nor the crucifix spoke to him as yet.

For months and months he thought and prayed, prayed and thought. Then it came! When it came, it seemed so simple that he feared it would not work. It seemed so obvious that he marveled that he had not thought of it before. He wrote his ideas in longhand and read his plan. It seemed so easy a solution that he wondered if it was really the answer. He took down his map and studied it. Lines were drawn from house to house to show their relations. It seemed the most natural thing in the world. Why hadn't someone thought of it before? Could there be something he was missing? "I wish I had Peter here to argue it out," he thought. And close on this came the realization, "If I can't have Peter—I can find as good, if not better!"

He did. In 1116 he summoned the four abbots of Citeaux's four daughter houses. If two heads are better than one, then four heads should be better than two, thought Stephen. But he did not get four. Only three came, for Bernard of Clairvaux was too ill to attend. Before Bertrand, Hugh and Arnold, Stephen laid his plan. They understood his antipathy toward monarchy and his desire for the patriarchy of St. Benedict, and also his hope to bind the houses together in some sort of union. Then he outlined the idea—which appealed to him as highly practicable. It was this: *each house was to be autonomous.* Morimond was to be Morimond and not a subject to Citeaux. Pontigny was to be independent Pontigny, and not an appendage; so also for Clairvaux and La Ferté. That was what St. Benedict prescribed. But to keep Pontigny from being different from Citeaux, to keep La Ferté from having customs at variance with those at Citeaux, to keep Morimond from introducing "compromises" and Clairvaux from countenancing "mitigations," all four houses must be bound to Citeaux. Let the bond be that of *charity*, a *mutual charity*, manifested in mutual supervision.

He then explained what he meant by this. The Abbot of Citeaux would visit his daughters once every year—not to interfere in purely temporal affairs, not to administer the estate, not to dispose in any way of the personnel of the community, not to do anything but to see that *the daughter was staying true to the family traditions.*

Hugh asked, "Suppose a difference of opinion should arise, what then? Charity is the bond, I know; and charity covers a multitude of sins. But suppose La Ferté should deny that she was sinning and Pontigny should insist she was? Or suppose Clairvaux disagrees with Morimond, is Citeaux to be the final court of appeal? And what if all the daughters disagree with the mother? In other words, Reverend Father, where is authority vested? The natural place would seem to be Citeaux. But if you do that, then, despite your bond of charity, expressed in mutual supervision, you have another monarchy—a Cluny with a Cistercian frill."

Stephen shook his head and drummed on his desk. "I thought my plan was too simple. Pontigny has seen deeper than Citeaux. You're right, Hugh; authority must be vested in somebody, and that somebody must not be Citeaux. How are we going to get around that?" There was silence for a while. "There must be a final court of appeal," mused Stephen.

"Why can't it be Citeaux?" asked Arnold.

"Because, as Pontigny has pointed out we would then be Cluny with a false face."

There followed a few other suggestions, but none of them satisfied. Either they ultimately came down to a monarchy, or they did not represent a court of final appeal. At length Bertrand said, "Your ground plan is sound, Reverend Father. Mutual charity can be the bond, and utter independence can be had by each individual house. Your idea of mutual supervision is sound too. That will keep us all like Citeaux This difficulty, presented by Hugh, is a difficulty but it does not destroy your ground plan. It is merely a final detail that needs elaboration."

Nodding heads told Bertrand that he had pleased both Arnold and Hugh; but Stephen was frowning. "I wish I could see it as a mere detail, but there is little more that we can do about it today. I know you men are anxious to get back to your monasteries. Let us all pray over it and think over it. If any suggestion comes to you, send it on. If I elaborate this mere detail of Bertrand's, I'll send for you. In the meantime be true to your traditions."

They left then, and it was a full three years before they met again. But when they did meet, it was not three abbots and Stephen that entered into consultation, but nine abbots and Stephen! From 1116 to 1119 Citeaux had sent out no fewer than five new colonies. How exactly Felix's words were being fulfilled! Citeaux was "swarming," and her abbot was busier than any bee. He trained novices, chose groups for new foundations, selected superiors, arranged locations, and ruled Citeaux. In the midst of all these activities, he found time, somehow or other, to "elaborate the mere detail," as Bertrand called it. And it was this elaboration that gave the world that masterpiece of monastic legislation, Stephen Harding's justly famed "Charter of Charity."

This he laid before the assembled abbots. The veterans from La Ferté, Morimond, and Pontigny enjoyed the expressions of warm enthusiasm of the younger members of the assembly for the first part of the document. This described the plan as they had heard it at their last meeting: each monastery was an individual family under its father, and yet each house was in a certain sense under the abbot of the "motherhouse" whence she sprang. He was the "Father Immediate," who was to visit his daughter annually to see that she was manifesting every family trait.

But what the veterans were anxious about was the second part. Could it really solve Hugh's problem—provide for both unity and freedom?

When they read it, they were silent. It seemed unbelievable. Stephen had done it again! He had united dependence and independence. Hugh of Macon chuckled as he pointed out the passage to Bernard of Fontaines. "I am responsible for this," he said. "Three years ago I proposed what looked like an insurmountable difficulty. I wanted authority vested in someone, and I said if that someone was Citeaux, then we were a monarchy. Look at the solution! It seems so obvious and simple that one is tempted to say, 'If it was a dog it would bite you.'"

Bernard smiled. "Don't you know, Hugh, that every discovery of genius has appeared obvious and simple—*after* it has been discovered! Let me look at the solution again." Taking the paper he read the passage. "Yes," he said, "that's the solution. Stephen places supreme authority in the hands of a body, not of an individual. He wants all the abbots assembled in General Chapter to be the final court of appeal. That certainly is avoiding a monarchy, isn't it?"

"Now why couldn't I have thought of that

three years ago!" exclaimed Hugh. "The three of us were sitting here, Arnold, Bertrand and myself. There was Stephen. I proposed the problem. I said, 'If we place all the authority in your hands, we have a monarchy; which we don't want.' Now why couldn't I have gone on and said, 'Let us place it all in our hands, and we'll have an aristocracy; which we do want'?"

"Simply because you're not a genius, Hugh."

"Then you admit that this is a stroke of genius?"

"Who would dare deny it?"

"Stephen."

Bernard's large eyes danced with merriment. "You sound 'put out' that he should deny it. Don't you know the man's humility? He'll most likely beg our pardons for having been so stupidly slow."

Just then Stephen came in. The ten abbots sat around a long table. With care and precision Stephen explained every line of his "Charter." It was to create a new Order in which the legislative, judicial and coercive powers were to be placed not in any one individual but in the moral person constituted by all the abbots assembled in General Chapter. It was to be an Order in which every house was to be absolutely autonomous, yet under the supervision of one whose duty it would be to see that the customs of Citeaux were observed. It was to be an Order whose members were bound to their local abbot by the bonds of filial love; to their fellow members by the bonds of brotherly love; and to the motherhouse and all other houses by the bonds of mutual love.

Then Stephen defined very clearly the duties of the "Fathers Immediate." Again and again he insisted that they were not to rule the house they visited; they were merely to make a paternal call to see that the Rule was being observed in the manner of Citeaux.

Finally he read the stipulations governing the General Chapter. They were few, but stringent. It was to be held once a year. All were to be present. Only the gravest of grave excuses would exempt any abbot. Its work was to correct abuses, maintain regular discipline, and strengthen the bonds of peace and charity.

At the close of the session, Hugh, still rejoicing over the new Charter, exclaimed to Bernard, "His purpose reads like a lyric. Listen! '…that we live united in the observance of the same Rule, according to the same Customs, and in a common charity.'"

"Those aren't the lines of a lyric," replied Bernard. "They are the prologue to an epic!"

Chapter Five

The World Provides Stephen with Amusement

Stephen was amused to hear his spiritual sons so enthused over his *"Carta Caritatis."* But he felt very much as Hugh had felt. He wanted to know why he hadn't thought of all these simple solutions before. Nevertheless, when the abbots unanimously accepted it, he made a move very reminiscent of Alberic. He took his *"Carta,"* bound it with the *"Instituta"* drawn up by the old Silver Lance, joined to these the *"Parvum Exordium"* (a short history of the founding of Citeaux) and sent this threefold volume to the Pope!

The Rationalist had argued thus, "My abbots have approved the Charter and accepted it as the fundamental institute of the Order but in the last analysis that is only a private agreement, entered into by independent individuals. What is to prevent an abbot in later years from saying, 'I was not party to such an agreement'? There is nothing. But if I can get papal approval of the charter, and ecclesiastical sanction of the Order, my worries are over."

Callixtus II was at Saulieu at the moment. He was the son of a Burgundian count, and Stephen felt sure that the lines in the *Exordium* would awaken echoes of Citeaux's woods in the mind of the Pontiff. He waited and prayed. Then for a Christmas present he received a Bull dated "this twenty-third day of December, 1119, the first year of Our Pontificate." It gave unconditional approbation to all three works that were in the volume. But more! It gave papal recognition and ecclesiastical sanction to the greatest work—the Order of Citeaux. The Christ-child, through his visible representative on earth, had presented Stephen with the one present he longed for; in turn, Stephen offered to the Infant the gold frankincense and myrrh that was the Order of Citeaux. It was perhaps the happiest Christmas Stephen had ever spent.

March, which had come in like a lion, had not yet shed his mane for the fleece of the lamb before the abbot began to laugh at the world and chuckle at himself. The world was puzzled and somewhat bewildered. It could not understand what was taking place. Not only Burgundy, but all France seemed to be drifting toward Citeaux or one of her daughter houses. Stephen laughed at the world's perplexity. He could have solved it by telling the world that an old soldier had planned a wheel with Citeaux as its hub; that he had insisted that the wheel's spokes be placed in such a position that they drew even as they radiated. The world would have understood; for Citeaux was now a grandmother! Her daughters had so grown that they had children of their own. Indeed, Gauldry's tactics were telling.

Stephen's laugh at himself, however, was not so filled with amusement. For he saw that he had not yet solved all of the problems heaven had presented him. Just as Hugh had pointed out one deficiency in his original plan, he himself now saw one in the plan he had thought completed.

Stephen knew something of the convolutions of the human brain. He felt sure that some day, somewhere, someone would come along and begin to distinguish and subdistinguish the various lines and even the various phrases and words, in his Charter of Charity. It had been done with St. Benedict's Rule. And look at the confusion that resulted! He must plan a preventive. He must devise some method to keep future generations from saying: "That is not the way Citeaux interpreted it! That is not the way it was done in the old days! That is not what our Fathers meant!"

He went to his desk, bent over it, and stayed at the task until he could say, "It is finished."

The idea had come to him that the only remedy, the only preventive, would be a *"Book of Usages"* in which, with extreme exactness, every custom of Citeaux would be stated. It was a trying work for there were many customs. It was a time-consuming work; for it demanded great precision. But Stephen did not scruple about the time; for he knew he was preserving an Order. The years went by, until one day he sat back from his desk with an emphatic and expressive, "There! It is done. It will take real mental magic to deny or distinguish any of those lines. At last I think the problem is solved."

It was! With the final punctuation point to his *"Book of Usages"* Stephen actually completed the rebellion that had been begun almost a century before. In 1033, Robert, a boy of fifteen, fresh from Troyes, heard an aging abbot ask: "What would Benedict say?" That sentence had served as a flint from which to strike the spark that would one day light all Europe. But it was a very slow mounting fire. For it was only now, almost one hundred years later, that Stephen could ask the same question and answer it with: "Benedict would say it is perfect!"

Year after year a steady and ever-swelling stream of knights and nobles, vassals and serfs, went to Citeaux and her daughter houses. Burgundy soon ceased to be the only province in the land with her "white monks." Before long France was not the only country in the world that could boast of her silent Cistercians; for Italy had her foundations and Hugh of Mâcon at Pontigny became "Father Immediate" to many German "daughters." The entire continent was becoming conscious of Citeaux. With something like a touch of nostalgia, Stephen saw his sons cross the seas and settle in his native England. Finally in 1132 the Pyrenees were crossed and Spanish hidalgos were set seeking heaven the Cistercian way—of being gallant to God.

The world was not only puzzled, she was somewhat angry. Only a short twenty years had passed since she predicted the slow death of the abbey in the swamp. Now she found Citeaux overshadowing congregations that were centuries old. The Citeaux that Stephen had feared might be a haunted house with a crowded cemetery, had suddenly sprung to life, burst its swaddling bands, and spread out to seventy-five different places!

In 1132 Stephen surprised the world again. He founded the first Cistercian monastery of nuns! People had said the Cistercian regime was too strenuous for men. Stephen showed what he thought of the world's opinion by giving the identical regime to women. It was at Tart, near Dijon, that he opened the first house. And the women outdid the men! Their houses multiplied faster and they went further. Small wonder the world was shocked and bewildered.

Ladies and lords, knights and highborn maids, servant girls, and serfs flocked to this austere mode of living. Europe could not believe its eyes. Stephen thought again and again of how right Alberic had been: there is a secret spot in the soul of every man and woman which, once touched, makes each one more than man or woman. He himself, too, had been right in thinking that men and women love a challenge; that they love to do the daring, difficult, different thing. And old, brave Robert had been right: stars *do* come out after dark. He thanked God again and again. But in his deepest prayer he saw that Christ had been most right: "And I, if I be lifted up, will draw all things to myself." That was the real explanation for this extraordinary drift toward Citeaux and the Cistercians. Christ was calling. His voice was irresistible. Citeaux had found her place in the Mystical Body.

In late August, just as summer began to droop, an aged monk made his way to Citeaux and asked to see Stephen Harding. When asked his name the old man smiled and said, "Tell him it's his fellow pilgrim. He'll understand."

And Stephen did understand. With more energy than he had shown in months he groped his way to the door—his eyes had gone dim. As he took his friend's arm and slowly led him to a chair, he said, "We have almost reached our journey's end. Come in, Peter, and tell me how goes the road."

"I have come to learn the road," replied the smiling Cluniac. "There's something magical about Citeaux. I must learn it. Tell me what it is, Stephen."

The two friends sat then and looked at each other. Stephen was the first to smile and say, "We're withered, Peter. We're two yellowed leaves, slowly shriveling in the sun of life's late autumn."

"I know it," replied Peter. "And I marvel at the fact; for spring seemed only yesterday. What happened to our summer?"

"Mine went draining swamps," laughed Stephen. "Yours went singing the praises of God."

"Yours went digging deep foundations for a structure whose height no one yet dares guess. What has happened, Stephen? And what is yet to happen?"

"Don't ask me riddles, Peter," said the old abbot as he shook his head. "My weary old brain won't work on them. Years and years ago I told you that I felt that Citeaux's mission was to shock the world. I told you then that I felt it was the work of God more than the work of man. I think that you will now admit that she *has* shocked the world."

Peter's old face wrinkled and his eyes danced as he shook with laughter. "Ah, the old fire still flames. Good for you, Stephen. But come now, let me in on the secret. How do you do it? Show me the mold in which you cast your men...."

Hours then went by in wide-ranging conversation. Bernard, who was now recognized as the voice of Christendom, was a fertile source for comment. He had made kings tremble, sustained Popes, swayed whole nations, and was now dominating Europe. His Abbey of Clairvaux was outdoing Citeaux in the number of new foundations. Such a topic was dear to the heart of old Stephen. And there were other topics, just as dear, but not so comforting.

Peter talked of the papacy—an ache to the aged abbot's heart. At the moment, Christendom was almost split in schism because of the rival claims of two men for the Chair of Peter. Anacletus and Innocent both called themselves "Pope." Bernard had declared for Innocent, and had won France, Germany, England, and parts of Italy to his side. But Peter de Leone was stubborn; and the battle still went on. Stephen ached for his boy Bernard who was in the thick of the fight, but he ached even more for the Church of Christ.

But Peter was ever coming back to the same topic—the wonder of Citeaux. When for the sixth or seventh time Peter asked, "What's the secret?" Stephen said, "I'll tell you if you'll tell me what's wrong with the world."

"Greed," replied Peter with conviction.

Stephen shook his head. "Not deep enough, Peter. You're explaining much, but not all. Nobles are greedy. That explains quarrels with the Church, quarrels with other states, quarrels with themselves."

"It explains everything," said Peter with warmth. "We wouldn't have near schism if Peter de Leone and his faction were not greedy for power. We wouldn't have this constant struggle between princes and prelates if kings and emperors and all under them weren't greedy for the wealth they say lies in the estates of the Church. We wouldn't have scandals if lords, knights, and ladies weren't greedy for pleasure. We wouldn't have a lot of things if greed was not right in the very makeup of man. Indeed, Stephen, you can bring most of our troubles right down to greediness."

The abbot nodded. "True Peter. But when a tower topples, don't look to the walls; look to the foundations. When a flower is puny, don't examine the leaves; examine the roots. When the fruit of a tree is bad, don't blame the blossoms or the bark; look under the soil."

"What's deeper than greed?" asked Peter. "It's in the very marrow of the bone."

"Perhaps it is. But there is something that produces that marrow. For instance, Peter, we have heard much about feudal lords and feudal barons, about feudal kings and feudal emperors, haven't we? We have been told that lay investiture has been the result of the greed of these men. That's not the ultimate cause. No. The ultimate cause is not the feudal sovereigns; it is the feudal system!"

"How?" questioned Peter.

"If bishops and abbots were not themselves temporal lords with vast estates and many vassals, the temporal sovereigns would never bother them. You can't imagine the Duke of Burgundy or the King of France becoming interested in little Citeaux or Citeaux's abbot, can you? No! Why? We're poor. Our estate is small. We have no vassals. So neither men nor money is to be had from the swamplands. Therefore, we are left alone."

"But if you keep on growing..."

"If we keep to our ideal of simplicity, poverty, solitude, we'll never be bothered. The houses may multiply and the Order become powerful, but no individual abbey will ever be the envy of any temporal lord. But the point I make is that there is always something deeper than what appears. It would seem that lay investiture were the result of feudal sovereigns; it is not; it is the result of the feudal system. So, too, with the world. It would seem that her troubles come from greed, from lust, from selfishness, from sin. But the root of all her troubles is lack of faith!"

"But, Stephen, they are calling this the Age of Faith...."

"I know they are; and it amuses me. One look at the history of the papacy for the past century will tell you how well the age is named. If the Italian counts and the Italian people had faith, do you think they could riot and revolt the way they have at every papal election for the past hundred years? If the German emperors had faith, do you think they could set up anti-popes the way they have, and handle the Chair of Peter as if it were a prince's bauble? If our French kings had faith, do you think we would have had the matrimonial scandals that have shamed us and our rulers for years and years? The truth is, Peter, that the people do not believe what they profess to believe!"

Peter realized that Stephen was right. The trouble with the age was not what so many had been decrying. It was not avarice, not ambition, not mad hunger for glory. The trouble lay deeper. Stephen had touched bottom when he touched lack of faith. Thoughts were tumbling through Peter's mind in frightening fashion. The abbot's last phrase—"people do not believe what they profess to believe" had him examining his own conscience. Did he believe with a telling, throbbing, productive belief that he was in the service of *God*? When he sang his Office, did he really believe that he was singing as the angels sang— directly into the face of *God*? When he received Holy Communion!

But before the questions became too disturbing, Stephen interrupted, "People do not believe the first commandment, Peter; and that is why Citeaux is shocking the world. She does!"

"What do you mean?"

"I mean that we are *living* the tremendous truth that people treat so triflingly. God made us to *adore*, Peter. That is humanity's prime function. Adoration is in our blood, our bone, our deepest being. Just as flame naturally leaps up, so do our souls surge to adore." The abbot grew intense. "Why did God make me, Peter? Or you? Or those thousands and hundreds of thousands out there beyond our woods? Why? To adore! To adore him! Oh, Peter, believe me, that first commandment is *first*. We must *adore* God! The prime purpose of creation is to give glory to God, and what an opportunity is given to monks to fulfill that prime purpose! The world does not yet know just what it is about Citeaux that amazes her."

"It's the austerity, the penance, the utter other-worldliness," put in Peter.

"It is not! What amazes her is Citeaux's burning sincerity! Here men are living the belief they profess. They are keeping the first commandment first. Penance, austerity, other-worldliness? Look deeper, man."

"But your labor, your fasts, your extreme poverty...."

"The rind," said Stephen. "Only the rind. The pulp, the edible part of the fruit, is beneath all that. You want the secret of Citeaux? Well, I'll give it to you. The bleeding hearts of the two broken-hearted lovers of the world are our secret. The hearts of Jesus and Mary! That is the whole secret of Citeaux, Peter. Cistercians are lovers."

"We all know Jesus and Mary. We all know their love. But...how is it that you take world-lings—nobles, knights, lords, and serfs—and make them lovers of Christ? That's the puzzle. You make those truths true. Now, that is magic. What wand do you use?"

"Come," said Stephen as he laboriously lifted himself from his chair. "Come with me. I'll show you."

Slowly the two old men went along the corridors. When they reached the church Stephen pointed up to the life-sized crucifix. It was plain wood with a bloody, bruised, horribly beaten Christ painted on it. "There," said the old abbot breathlessly, "there is my magic wand. If the wood of the cross won't change men, nothing will. Christ took all that—all those blows, all that blood, those nails, those thorns, the spittle— all, all for me! He loved me!"

Stephen sank to his knees. Peter knelt down beside him. The abbot was weeping. For quite some time the two old men knelt in prayer. Stephen was the first to move. By grasping the cross he was able to raise himself, and when he looked up at the bleeding figure so realistically painted on the wood, Peter saw a light in his eyes that he had never seen on earth before. It was ecstasy!

Silently then the abbot led him to the sacristy and drawing forth the brass censer he stretched it out on the vesting table. Pointing to it he quietly said, "There is my mold."

Peter frowned. "Mold?" he repeated. "I...don't...understand...."

"Think, Peter, think! The first commandment. We Cistercians are adorers. We take our lives as so much aromatic incense and fling them with reckless hands into love's brazier. We want to burn out in the presence of the two I told you about—the broken hearts. We want perfumed clouds of white adoration to ascend unceasingly before the throne of God. That's why we have locked ourselves behind monastery walls. That is why we came to this swampland. We want to *adore!* You asked to see my mold. There it is. Into it I try to cast every soul that comes under my care for I am convinced that the first things should be first." Then he looked at Peter intently and said more slowly, "Peter, I am convinced that a monk is one who should lie prostrate endlessly before the majesty of God, worshipping him with all his might."

The two old friends groped their way back to the abbot's room. When they were seated, Stephen smiled and said, "You asked for the secret of Citeaux...."

"I think you have shown it to me," said Peter slowly.

"No," replied Stephen with a shake of his head, "I have not. For the secret of Citeaux is that she has no secret."

"And I say hers is an open secret. It is there for all the world to read. It is evident even in the position of your church. Stephen, you used a barbarous word with me once. You spoke of being 'God-orientated.' Well, that's the secret of Citeaux. Even your church is facing due east! You've got your face to the sun. And if you'll allow me to play on words, you've got your face to the Son of God. I see now why Cistercians are so little self-conscious and so utterly unconscious of the world. They are entirely Christ-conscious, totally God-conscious; that's the reason. I'll now allow you your barbarous word, and congratulate you on your achievement of all that the word connotes: Citeaux is completely 'God-orientated.'"

Stephen nodded gratefully. "Thank you," he said softly. "Tell that secret to everyone you meet, won't you, Peter? God wants to look on faces that are lifted to his Son."

The friends parted next day. It was their last meeting on earth.

Chapter Six
Side by Side

A month after Peter's departure the trees around the abbey were heavy with luscious, mellow fruit. Stephen's eyes had gone dim, but he scented golden maturity in every warm wind that climbed to his window from orchards and vineyards. The rich fragrance in these winds made him recall what he had said to Peter about being in the yellow leaf of life's late autumn. This in turn made him think of Alberic. He saw now why the Silver Lance had meditated so long on the scarlet leaf that year in the distant past. Stephen shook his head. He knew what this sensitivity to nature meant. Night was near. He must prepare for it.

On the fourteenth of September, 1133, seventy-five abbots had assembled at Citeaux for their annual General Chapter. Stephen had waited for this gathering anxiously. When all had taken their places in the meeting hall, the old abbot entered. It was a pathetic sight. His hands were trembling. He was groping his way, feeling for his chair. He sank into it weakly. With a prayer the Chapter was formally opened.

When all were seated Stephen arose and, looking at the assembly from his almost-blinded eyes, said, "My Fathers, had I laid down the burden of office when still young, you might have accused me of faintheartedness. But now, as you see, I am old. I am burdened with many infirmities. So if I beg to resign, tax me not with being presumptuous, but rather say that I am modest. As long as I was able, I put my shoulder to the wheel, I shrank not from any obligation. Thanks be to God I saw to it that this tender plant strike deep root. Thanks be to God the one little monastery I received has multiplied to almost a hundred." He stretched out his hands pleadingly, "My Fathers, it is not the will to serve that is wanting. No. It is the strength to do so...."

There was a long pause. Abbots of all ages, some nearing eighty, some not yet forty, were silent. Their eyes surreptitiously traveled from the old, old man who stood at the head of the table, to the little place card that stood before them. It seemed that they did not trust themselves to look at one another, lest they see reflected in the eyes of others the grief they felt was mirrored in their

own. It was heartbreaking. The voice was pleading, and yet in it there was a note of regret. "My
Fathers, allow an old man...." There was a noticeable lingering on that word "old." "...Allow an
old man to take his rest...."

Stephen Harding...Stephen Harding...ask-
ing for a rest! Was it possible? But no. The question faded from every eye as the old man went
on. It was in a clearer tone and a more vibrant
voice with a ring of determination in it. "Allow an
old man to take a rest that he may provide for all
his own needs." No, indeed, Stephen was not
asking for a rest; he was asking for freedom to
begin more intensive work.

With reluctance, reverence, and regret the
abbots yielded. Tears were seen in many an eye
as they voted acceptance. They knew that the
request was reasonable. Age and infirmity were
on him. But so, too, were sanctity and love.
However, they yielded and proceeded to elect his
successor.

Then a strange thing happened. Guy, the
abbot of Three Fountains, was elected. But Guy,
the abbot of Three Fountains was not a holy man.
Stephen knew that. He was the only one in the
Chapter who did know it. Guy was not the man
to head the young Order of Citeaux. But what
could Stephen do? His resignation had just been
accepted. If he interfered now, what sort of a
resignation would it appear? He must remain silent. It was an effort. But he preserved his silence

before men that he might become more and more conversant with God.

Day after day the old man groped his way to the life-sized crucifix and bent himself like Magdalene at its foot. Day after day he prostrated himself before the tabernacle asking Christ to protect little Citeaux. A month went by. It was a worry-filled month and a prayer- filled one. Then the others saw what Stephen had known. Guy was immediately deposed. Rainard was elected. He had been a monk at Clairvaux. He had been trained by St. Bernard. Stephen rejoiced. He knew his young Order was in capable hands. Then he went to work on his last great work—his immediate preparation for death.

Winter was melting into spring. Daffodils nodded above the cracked and softening earth. Fresh green was showing above the graves in the little cemetery as the abbots gathered again at Citeaux. But no General Chapter summoned them this time. They had come to crowd around the death-bed of their founder, to receive a blessing, to catch a last word, and to assist him if they could. Stephen was dying.

The old man lingered. One would have thought that he was loathe to leave without a word from his boy, Bernard. But Bernard could not come. He was away in the cause of Innocent, still fighting for Christ's true Vicar on earth. The old heart pulsed slowly. Stephen was fighting his last fight.

The kneeling abbots began to whisper to one another. They were soft sentences, sentences full of reverence and love.

"He has had a long life," said one. "Yes, and one filled with good works," replied another. "He won't be empty-handed when he meets his Maker."

"His was a generous life," whispered a young abbot.

"Indeed it was," came the answer, "and God will reward him for it."

Then a little louder than the others one voice was heard saying, "Indeed we can call him blessed...."

Stephen stirred. Light came back into the old, old eyes. Turning a weary head, he raised a thin, vibrant voice and said, "I hear you speak, my Fathers. What is this you say?... I tell you truly, I go to God trembling.... As anxious as if I had never done a single good deed...." He paused. The old eyes closed a moment. The breathing was labored. But again that thin, vibrant voice was raised, "If there has been any good in my actions...or if any good has come from my poor labors...it is all due to the grace of God."

In the hush the labored breathing of the dying man was greatly accentuated. Then came the last sentence: "I...fear and tremble much...that I have not fully corresponded with...that grace

...and that I have not received it...with the proper-...humility."

Stephen Harding's last sentence had been spoken. He had strained to get out that last word. He had lingered on it. The kneeling abbots knew that in it he had summed up his life and given the key to his sanctity. More. They knew that he had indicated the predominant virtue of his Order when with his dying gasp he had said, "...*humility.*"

It was the twenty-eighth of March, 1134. Spring had just arrived. It was a glad spring and life was bursting in flower and tree. Citeaux herself was quietly happy in the midst of this resurgence. She was lonely as she stood by the corpse of her father but she was not sad, for she knew that he had gone to God. No longer would the venerable abbot grope after him; no longer would he strain those dim eyes in an effort to pierce the veils; no longer would he gaze on God through the twilight of faith; he now saw him "face to face." And little Citeaux quietly rejoiced.

Next day they carried the worn frame to the graveyard. They sang as they did it. And their music was not somber nor sad. It was song that was reverent and holy. It was brightened by overtones of joy. And why not? Were they not doing honor to a warrior? Were they not paying homage to God? They begged that all be forgiven, it is true; but what they really meant by their song was, "Welcome him home!"

They laid him beside Alberic. It was most fitting, for their lives and their loves had been the same. And the rebels would ever lie side by side, so that they might rise shoulder to shoulder for the last grand General Chapter of the whole human race....

Chapter Seven

A Crooked Staff

When all was over, the abbots, monks and lay brothers returned to the monastery. Many were looking for remembrances; some openly called them "relics." Their search was almost vain; for Stephen lived his poverty, and poverty in life meant poverty in death. Citeaux, however, found a remembrance and she made of it a relic. It was not much to look at; it was a perfect emblem of his life. To those who could read, it told the whole secret of the sanctity of Citeaux. It was Stephen's crozier—just an old crooked staff.

For centuries Citeaux venerated that relic; and during those centuries future Cistercians learned the story of the Rationalist who completed the rebellion by his sustained drive for poverty...simplicity...and solitude. The staff told them even more. It told the virtue which should shine brightest in their lives. A virtue greater than their poverty—the virtue that Christ and St. Stephen loved—the virtue of *humility!*

Yes, he is St. Stephen Harding, for Benedict XIV recognized his sanctity and in 1584 approved his cult. His Cistercian children observe his feast with more pomp and ceremony than they show on the feasts of his two friends, Robert and Alberic; for Stephen was the rebel who completed the rebellion. He was the founder of the Order. More! They remember that he was father in religion to the boy from Fontaines, the boy who became the man of Europe—Bernard, who aimed to overtake Christ.

The crooked staff was the only material remembrance that Citeaux kept of this lovable Englishman. But Citeaux always kept his spirit—the spirit of being so thoroughly rational as to live poverty, simplicity and solitude in all their grandeur; the spirit of being reckless enough to take life and fling it into love's brazier, there to burn and send up fragrant clouds of adoration to the One who made us all.

The *three religious rebels* taught Citeaux how to be gallant to God. She has never forgotten!

Afterword

Give God His Due

And in that we have the answer to the question, "Why do men of the twentieth century become Trappists?" We can say, "Because men of the twelfth became Cistercians." But that is not being as rational as was St. Stephen, as radical as was St. Alberic, nor as rebellious as was St. Robert. That does not fully answer, for one must logically ask, "Why did men of the twelfth become Cistercians?" A partial answer to that is, "Because Benedict became a monk in the sixth." But the full and deeper answer is, "Because God became Man in the first!"

That is the final answer. There are Trappists now, not precisely because there was a boy from Troyes in 1033 who decided there was "a higher chivalry," but because there was a Man in 33 who said, "Not my will but thine be done." Christ is the whole answer. There must be men who give themselves to God, because there is a God who gave himself to man. There must be cloister because there is a Creator. There must be adorers because there is the Maker to be adored. There must be Trappist monasteries because there must be trysting places where lovers can meet! God must receive his due.

Yes, the Trappists have been "disappointed in love"—so disappointed in the love of all things finite that they have fallen in love with the infinite. There is a Gethsemani in Kentucky because there was a Gethsemani in Palestine; there are Cistercians because there is a Christ; there is a burnished brazier wherein lives burn on until they burn out—for God must be given his due!

Now, if all that sounds like a boast, just pray that we Trappists make good that boast. For if we do, it will be good for us, good for the world and a glory for God.

Let us give God his due in the way these *three religious rebels* did by giving love for love, life for life, and all for all!

END OF FIRST EPOCH, THE SAGA OF CITEAUX

Bibliography

(A partial list of sources)

Analecta Bollandiana, Brussels, 1882-1836.

d'Arbois de Jubainville: *Etudes sur l'état intérieur des Abbayes cisterciennes au XIIe et XIIIe siècles, 1858*.

Bollandists: *Acta Sanctorum*, 1643-1925.

Brunner: *Ein Cistercienser Buch, 1881*.

Caesar of Heisterbach, *Dialogus Miraculorum*, Ed. Strange, 1850; Ed. Coulton, 1921.

Chartres de Molesme, Ed. Laurent, 1907.

Chronique de Clairvaux; Migne, P. L., 185, 1247.

Cistercienser Chronik, 1889-1936.

Collins, Henry: *Spirit and Mission of the Cistercian Order*, London, 1866; *Cistercian Fathers* (2 volumes), Dublin and Derby, 1872.

Cram, Ralph Adams: *The Gothic Quest, 1905; Substance of Gothic, 1917.*

Cuignard: *Les Monuments Primitifs de la Règle Cistercienne, Dijon, 1878.*

Dictionnaire d'Archêologie chrétienne et de Liturgie, 1907-1936.

Exordium Magnum Cisterciensis Cenobii, Grande Trappe, 1884.

Exordium Parvum, Grande Trappe, 1884.

Gallia Christiana, Paris, 1876.

Germain: *Monasticon Gallicanum,* Paris, 1882.

Hannay: *Spirit and Origin of Christian Monasticism,* London, 1903.

Hélyot: *Dictionnaire des Ordres Religieux,* re-edition, Paris, 1858.

Henriquez: *Fasciculus Sanctorum Ord. Cist.,* 1631.

Janauschek: *Originum Cisterciensium,* tom. 1, (Vienna) 1877.

Luddy, O.C.S.O., Rev. Ailbe: *The Order of Citeaux,* Dublin, 1932; *Life and Teaching of St. Bernard,* Dublin, 1927.

Mabillon: *Acta SS. Ordinis S. Benedicti,* Paris; 1707; *Annales Ord. S. Benendicti,* (1753-59).

Manrique: *Annales Cisterciennes,* I, Lyons, 1642.

Martène: *Thesaurus Anecdotorum,* III, Paris, 1717.

Newman: *Historical Sketches*, London, 1873; *Lives of the English Saints, 1898*.

Othon: *Les Origines Cisterciennes*, Rev. Mabillon, 1932-33.

Sharpe: *The Architecture of the Cistercians; Architectural Parallels*, London, 1848.

Symphorien, Dom., O.C.S.O.: *La Règle de Saint Benoit Meditee.* Nevers, 1909; *La Règle de Saint Benoit Traduite et Commentie*, Montlegeon, 1908.

Vacandard: *Life of St. Bernard*, Paris, 1875.

Vie de St. Alberic, Ed. Lerins, 1897.

Vita S. Roberti, Abbatis Molismensis, auctore monacho molismensi sub Adone Abbate Saec. XII.

Vayage Littéraire de deux Religieux Bênêdictins, Paris, 1717.

William of Malmesbury: *De Rebus Gestis Anglorum*, P. L., 1259, 1286.

Zimmermann: *Kalendarium Benedictinum*, I and II, 1932-1936.